SHALLOW
WATERS

SHALLOW WATERS

A Port Stirling Mystery

KAY JENNINGS

PARIS
Communications

ISBN (e-book edition): 978-1-7339626-2-9
ISBN (Paperback edition):978-1-7339626-12
ISBN (Hardcover edition): 978-1-7339626-05

This is a work of fiction. Names, characters, places, and incidents are the product of the author's imagination or are used fictitiously to give the fiction a sense of authenticity. Any resemblance to real people, living or dead, government organizations, establishments, businesses, or historical events, is entirely coincidental.

Although, Jerry Jones could have used a good cornerback about then.

Cover image: istockphoto.com
Cover and Interior design: Jessica Reed

Printed and bound in the USA
First printing 2019
Published by *Paris Communications*
Portland, Oregon, USA

kayjenningsauthor.com

To Steve, because.

PROLOGUE

Friday, 7:45 p.m.

"What fool would be walking on the beach now, Mr. Darcy?" Lydia Campbell said to her border collie, who looked up at her from his bed near the fireplace, cocking his head in recognition of his name. She peered out her floor-to-ceiling window, focusing on the shoreline through the murky January gloom.

Lydia thought she saw a light down below on the beach through the soupy fog. It flickered once or twice, and then it disappeared.

There it was again. Definitely someone walking, closer to the cliff than the water, probably carrying a flashlight. The unsteady beam seemed to be moving in spurts from the base of the cliff toward the water. She hoped it wasn't crazy old Ted Frolick from up the road.

Turning her back on the window, Lydia pulled her cream cashmere cardigan closer to her slender body, shoved her bifocals up into her thinning silver hair, and went to the kitchen. She liked to have a glass of wine while the *PBS News Hour* was on, followed by dinner before the hour was out. Lydia liked proper order. She would check on Ted later to make sure he hadn't wandered off again and gotten himself into a jam.

While she poured herself a glass of her favorite pinot noir, the fog continued to roll in off the Pacific Ocean, drippy and menacing. It swirled in and around the gigantic sea stacks just off the southern

Oregon coastline at Port Stirling, and continued its assault on the 300 foot cliffs rimming the deserted beach. Rarely a crowded seashore even in daylight hours, it was more isolated than ever on this damp, chilly Friday night.

Lydia, a Port Stirling resident for the last fifteen of her seventy-six years, returned to the jigsaw puzzle on the card table in front of her window. She sipped her wine and listened to Shields and Brooks argue about the chaos at the White House, as the occasional star twinkled through the murky fog billowing in and out. Even with the TV on, she could hear the roar of the mighty Pacific meeting the headland. Her wood fire crackled and filled the house with cozy warmth, and a beef stew, smelling of the root vegetables in her pot, wafted from the kitchen. Lydia did not notice the light on the beach again.

CHAPTER 1

Saturday, 8:40 a.m.

Matt Horning, Port Stirling's first new police chief in 24 years, brushed aside an intricate spider web and ducked as he entered the tunnel. Three huge rocks huddled together on this stretch of the wild Pacific Ocean, and the one housing a tunnel carved out by centuries of the sea making its rush to the land, was as tall as a three-story building. Matt noted that the big-ass rock would be classified as a mountain in his native Texas.

Foam left over from the 3:00 a.m. high tide churned around the entrance to the mouth of the tunnel. Matt was unaccustomed to the ocean's fury, and he hesitated as he approached the opening in the passageway, his heart beating fast, and his mouth dry. He knew the eyes of the others were on his back, expecting their new police chief to be unwavering and resolute, but still he hesitated. *Are you a good cop? Did you choose this place at the end of the world to prove it? Then fucking toughen up and prove it.*

He stepped gingerly into the shady opening, feeling the inside walls of the rock, pock-marked by centuries of unrelenting weather and monster seawater. Remnants of dead crab legs framed the shaft's entrance, sending up a pungent stench.

The space was claustrophobic to him, darker inside here than it had been on the open beach. Matt could see a slender shaft of light at the far end where the tunnel opened up again, and he kept a wary eye on the approaching waves. The smell of rotting vegetation and stagnant seawater was strong, with the barnacles and mussels clinging high up on the walls adding to the briny fragrance. As the wind ruffled Matt's uncovered hair, he stepped over a small puddle left by the outgoing tide.

"Oh, shit," Matt said in a hushed voice, bending over with his hands on his knees.

Over his shoulder, Officer Jay Finley, who had first alerted Matt to the grisly discovery and followed his new boss into the tunnel, croaked "Yeah".

The child was washed against the tunnel wall, her long blonde hair swimming out away from her fair face. Matt stared hard at her body, recognizing, of course, that the girl was dead, but wishing with all his strength that he could turn into a wizard and give her new life. Little Emily felt like his first friend in his new hometown, and, without wanting to, Matt loved that slight girl. But saving her now was beyond his powers. A sad, lifeless little body. All Matt Horning could do for her now was find her killer. This little girl's death was a gross wrong that must be somehow righted.

Emily was laying half in and half out of a shallow pool of water. She was wearing blue jeans, a white tee shirt, pink pullover sweater, white anklet socks, and one pink Nike—her right foot was missing a shoe. A barrette clung to her long blonde hair, in danger of falling off.

"Mrs. Campbell and her dog found the body at about 7:30 a.m.," said Jay. "She said there was no one else on this part of the beach, and she didn't see anyone else until I arrived about 7:50 a.m. I was starting my shift and was up at City Hall when she called in to the dispatcher."

Matt moved in a slow, careful circle around Emily's body while Officer Finley continued.

"I can't believe it. I just saw her a couple weeks ago at the Port Stirling holiday party. Mayor Fred and his wife, Marjorie, brought the whole family—Gary, Susan, Jack, and little Emily here. I was talking to Gary at one point, he's the oldest, home for the winter semester break from his first year at the University of Oregon. Emily came up to her big brother. Offered him a cookie. All smiles and happy. Gary introduced me to her, and she stuck out her hand to me and said 'It's nice to meet you, Mr. Policeman'. She's a cutie. Was." Pure anguish swamped his voice. "Who the hell could do a thing like this?"

Nothing Matt could say right now would help his young officer, so he concentrated on the task at hand. He leaned over closer to the body, not disturbing the sand and rocks around her. A lot of blood was visible on the front of Emily's sweater, and he could see what looked like blood residue in splotches on the tunnel walls. The scattered dregs indicated that the previous high tide had likely washed away most of the residual blood. He could make out multiple stab wounds in the girl's abdomen, but couldn't, at first glance around, see any kind of weapon in the area. The girl's skin was grayish white and waxy-looking, and she looked stiff.

"I don't suppose you found a weapon?"

"No, I did not," Jay answered. "When I first arrived, I took photographs of the body and every square foot of the immediate area because the tide is coming in. There's no weapon. I suppose, if the killer had dropped a knife before he left the scene, last night's high tide would have taken it."

"What time was the high tide, and how much higher does it get?"

"I won't know for sure about the exact timing until I look at the tidal charts, but I would guess the high tide would have been between 2:00–3:00 a.m.," Jay said. He explained to the native Texan how the ocean's high and low tides varied depending on the moon's cycle, the weather, and other factors.

"I guess tides never mattered in your cases in Dallas, huh?" Jay asked in all seriousness. He was not a man of the world.

As they surveyed the incident area, Jay continued to fill in his new chief. When he finished communicating everything he knew, and he and Matt had one last look around the scene, Matt turned to face the young officer.

"Ever worked a murder before, Jay?" The greenish tint to Jay's young face foretold the answer.

"No, sir, I haven't."

Matt motioned for Jay to follow him out of the tunnel. When Matt left Dallas for this tiny town on the edge of the ocean, he hoped he would never see another dead body. And, now, he wished he could protect his young officer from this gruesome part of their business. What would Jay think if he saw the darkness that hid inside people? What would he think if he knew the truth about Matt?

They exited the tunnel, and approached the two people and one dog waiting for them higher up on the dry sand, away from the sea's noisy, angry edge.

"The first murder investigation is always tough. Don't feel badly if it gets to you," Matt said walking in step with Jay.

"Officer Finley may not have worked on a case like this one previously," piped in City Manager Bill Abbott, who had just picked up his new police chief at the airport and driven him directly to the crime scene. "But he's one of your vets on the force . . . what's it now, Jay, about five years?"

"Almost six now, Mr. Abbott," Jay replied.

"He's also got more local experience than almost anyone else at City Hall," Abbott added.

"I grew up here," Jay told Matt. "But I've never seen anything like this," he said, his chin pointed at the tunnel and Emily's body.

"You've done good work here, officer," said Matt, acknowledging Jay's efforts. He ignored Abbott and moved to Lydia Campbell and her dog, Mr. Darcy.

"I'm Matt Horning," he said, reaching to shake Lydia's gloved hand. He put his other hand lightly on her shoulder and said, "You must be Mrs. Campbell. I understand you had the unpleasantness of finding the body."

His kindness made her tear up, and with her voice gone suddenly mute, she just nodded at him.

"Thank you, ma'am, for having the presence of mind to call us right away. Please bear with us a few more minutes, and then we'll escort you home."

Bill Abbott blew his nose loudly, then stepped forward and said, "Jay, may I borrow your badge for a minute? We were supposed to be at City Hall this morning to make it all official, but then . . ." Bill gestured back toward the tunnel as his voice trailed off. "Well, we do what we have to do. I don't have a bible or the Port Stirling city charter, so I'm going to swear in our new police chief by asking him to hold your badge. –That okay with you?"

Without saying a word, Jay unpinned his badge from his uniform and handed it to Matt. When Abbott finished the swearing in, all present, including Lydia, shook hands with Port Stirling Chief of Police Matt Horning.

"Time to get to work," Matt said, handing Jay's badge back to him. He clapped his officer on the back, and wondered if, years later, the two of them would remember this moment. "Hell of a way to meet, huh?" Matt's jaw had a grim set even though he directed a brief smile at Jay. "I thought I'd be sworn in at a quick little ceremony, and then we'd all go have a burger."

The gangly 28-year-old officer tried to smile back at his new chief, but the past hour had made that impossible. "Yeah. That might have worked better than this."

"You've done everything by the book, Jay," said Matt gently.

"Thanks, that means a lot, man. I don't mind telling you that I'm scared."

"If you weren't, I wouldn't want you on my team," Matt said. "I feel fear, too, but I don't follow it. Don't worry, son. This is a bad deal, but we'll unravel it piece by piece, and we'll break it. You with me?"

Jay still looked like he could throw up at any minute, but stared his new boss in the eye and gamely said, "I'm with you."

Good thing, thought Matt, as he allowed himself a moment to gaze out to the craggy sculptures and beyond to the ocean's horizon. Because someone in this beautiful place is a murderer.

CHAPTER 2

Saturday, 9:00 a.m.

Lydia had taken several steps further away from the mouth of the tunnel, and was looking south down the beach now, watching a nearby seagull swooping in for a nimble, careful landing at the water's edge. Now that the new chief had arrived and Jay's and her watch over the child's body had ended, it was as if she had permission to relax her vigil. Her ramrod back and shoulders slumped, and she stuffed her hands in the pockets of her blue Columbia Sportswear jacket. While the sea roared behind her, Lydia tried to focus on the lilt of the waves as they gently lapped near her feet, at the end of their long journey. Mr. Darcy heeled quietly at her side, and had perhaps inched a bit closer to his owner, one eye never leaving the seagull.

Turning his attention to Lydia, Matt said, "Sorry to keep you, ma'am, but I have just a few questions for you. Are you doing OK?"

"Why do people keep asking me if I'm OK?" Lydia said, rather more strongly than she intended. "Having just discovered a dead child, I'm doing as well as can be expected. And I've already answered many questions from Officer Finley; he was most thorough. But I want to help you if I can, so proceed, Mr. Horning."

She took her first real look at Matt since his arrival, and, noticing her eyes looking over his jeans, black sweater, black leather jacket with its burnt orange Texas Longhorns logo, and ridiculously out of place cowboy boots, Matt realized he didn't look like much of a police chief to her. He fought the urge to smooth the dark hair curling around his collar; he had planned to get a haircut in his new hometown before starting his job.

"Matt and Jay are just doing their jobs, Lydia," Abbott inserted. "You've been very helpful, and we won't keep you out here in the cold much longer." He looked pointedly at Matt.

"I understand you live near here, correct?" Matt said to Lydia, as if Abbott hadn't said anything.

Lydia pointed to one of the houses on the bluff above them. "That's my home, there."

"Did you see or hear anything last night?"

"One doesn't really hear anything from the bluff except the sound of the surf and the wind," she instructed the newcomer. "But I did see something last night."

Matt perked up. "What did you see, ma'am?"

"I saw a light on the beach. It flickered a few times and caught my eye while I was sitting near one of my windows. It looked like someone walking along the beach with a flashlight."

"Could you see who it was?"

She shook her head. "Too foggy to even see if there was a person attached to the light. All I saw was a flickering, and only for about five minutes, on and off." The stern line of Lydia's mouth softened a bit as her gaze drifted back toward the tunnel. "I…I wish I'd tried harder to see last night."

"You had no way of knowing, Mrs. Campbell," said Matt softly, following her eyes. "Do you have any idea about what time this was?"

"I know precisely what the time was," the older woman said. "I had been watching the *News Hour* for a while but it wasn't over, so between 7:30 and 8:00 p.m."

Matt wrote down in his notebook what Mrs. Campbell said.

"You're sure of the time?" he asked.

"Yes, Mr. Horning, I am quite certain of the time." Really.

"Did the flickering light look like it could have been in this general area?" He indicated the tunnel.

"I would say that, yes, this was about where I was looking. It's a little hard to judge from down here, but I could tell you for sure if I was standing at my window."

"Did you touch anything inside the tunnel?"

"I most certainly did not. And, I've already answered that question," she snapped. "Of course I didn't touch anything. It's rather terrifying to come across a dead child, wouldn't you say?"

"Yes, I would say that's true," Matt said. "I'm sorry." He looked into Lydia's eyes, sharing a moment to let themselves feel what they were feeling.

"Have you and your dog ever gone inside the tunnel before today?"

"Well, yes, I suppose we have," Lydia said with some hesitancy.

"Everyone in Port Stirling has walked through that tunnel," said Jay. "It's a fun thing to do. At least, it used to be." He looked sorrowful. The persistent wind made his ever-present cowlick stand straight up.

Matt nodded at Jay's remark. "Did you recognize the victim, Mrs. Campbell?"

"No, I didn't recognize her when I first saw her, but Officer Finley told me who she is, and once he'd said that, I did recall seeing her with our mayor's family."

"Have you ever talked to Emily Bushnell?" Matt pressed.

"No, I have not."

"Do you have any reason to want her dead?"

Lydia gaped at Matt.

"Am I a suspect, Chief Horning?" she said incredulously.

"No, no, of course you're not!" Abbott jumped in, taking Lydia's hands in his. "We're very grateful for your help, Lydia. The chief has to question everyone. Anyone who knows you knows you couldn't hurt a fly."

"Mr. Abbott's right," Matt said. "We appreciate what you did here this morning, but I have to start this investigation with the person who found the body. That's how we begin to rule out suspects. Please don't take it personally, ma'am, it's just part of our process." He spoke calmly and professionally, and then paused to let her catch her breath before continuing his questioning.

"How did you find her, Mrs. Campbell?"

Lydia pulled a tissue from her jacket pocket and quickly wiped her nose. "It was actually Mr. Darcy who discovered her. He was pulling quite hard on his leash in this direction, and I finally gave in and followed his lead. I didn't see her at first because of the tunnel. But Mr. Darcy knew she was in there, and he was aware that something was amiss."

At the sound of his name, Mr. Darcy looked from the seagull he'd been tracking and up at his owner. To Matt, who noticed the dog's movement, it looked like the border collie wanted to ask a question.

"Did you see anyone else on the beach this morning?"

"No, just Mr. Darcy and me. We like to go right at daybreak, and that's a little early for some people. Especially on a Saturday morning. People like to sleep in. Eat breakfast out. Read the newspaper. That sort of thing." Lydia realized she was rambling, but couldn't seem to stop herself.

"Please don't take offense, Mrs. Campbell, but I need to see your hands. Could you please slip off your gloves?"

She stared at the chief with a pursed mouth and a direct gaze, and, for a minute, Matt thought of that old countess on Downton Abbey.

"You cannot be serious." She sounded just like Maggie Smith, with a touch of John McEnroe thrown in.

"I would be derelict in my duty, ma'am, if I didn't investigate the person who discovered the body. It's routine. I'm sorry."

Bill Abbott, watching Lydia, held his breath for a moment before letting out a quiet puff of air, and almost imperceptibly shaking his head.

Lydia held Matt's eyes and glared at him while she removed her gloves in brisk, almost violent fashion. "Please hold onto Mr. Darcy's leash," she directed Jay, thrusting the leash in his direction.

Jay did as he was told.

Lydia stuck the gloves in her mouth. Then, she thrust both hands out at Matt, spread her fingers wide, held them still for a few seconds, and then crisply flipped them over and repeated the movement.

No marks of any kind or any blood, and, in fact, Lydia Campbell had an attractive manicure that looked fresh.

"Thank you." Matt pulled out his notebook to jot some notes in it, and Jay meekly handed the dog's leash back to its owner.

Lydia put her gloves back on, stared straight ahead, and stood stock still while Matt scribbled away.

Suddenly, Bill Abbott's cell phone rang loudly from his jacket pocket, and everyone jumped. Looking at the phone's surface, the blood rushed out of his face, and Abbott said to Matt, "It's Fred Bushnell. What do I do?"

Alarm and utter consternation were written all over Bill Abbott's face.

Matt said quickly, "If he says his daughter is missing, please tell him I'm here, and hand the phone to me. Got it?"

Twitching, Abbott nodded, and then answered his phone. After a brief exchange which indicated that the family just discovered their daughter was missing, he handed the phone to Matt.

"Mr. Bushnell, this is Matt Horning. I just landed in Port Stirling. Please tell me what's happened."

Matt's penetrating blue eyes followed two squawking seagulls in flight out to sea as he held the phone up to his ear and listened to the mayor. The sky, heavily laden with luxuriously-thick fast-moving clouds, was more robust here than in Dallas.

"I'm sorry, sir. Please stay calm, and I'll be over to your house soon. Stay out of your daughter's bedroom, don't touch anything near it, and keep all your family at home until I get there. No one is to leave the house. Do you understand? OK, thanks. I'll be there as fast as I can."

Jay and Matt locked eyes.

"Has the medical examiner been called?" Matt asked.

As Jay nodded affirmatively and started to answer the chief, Matt saw a woman waving from the bottom of the steps that he and Abbott had come down. She was a determined-looking 50-ish woman, and she was moving toward them with purpose, head down against the wind and the rain that was just beginning again. She tugged on the hood of her rust-colored raincoat, pulling it forward to keep the rain off her black-framed glasses.

Dr. Bernice Ryder went straight to Lydia, one of her private practice patients; there weren't enough dead bodies around Chinook County to keep Dr. Ryder busy on the ME side of things. She had been filled in by Pete Leonard, Port Stirling's 911 operator, and understood Lydia had found the girl's body.

"Oh, Lydia, I'm so sorry this happened to you," the woman said, hugging her. "Are you feeling OK?"

"For the umpteenth time," Lydia said, glancing at the two police-men, "I'm fine." But with that pronouncement, Lydia's knees buckled and she started to collapse. Matt, closest to her, swiftly reached out and cradled the fainting woman before she could hit the sand.

He and Dr. Ryder, working together, revived their witness. Jay, with a subtle glance at his new boss, who quietly indicated his approval, and Bill Abbott—along with, of course, Mr. Darcy, who was whimpering loudly and tagging along immediately next to Lydia, not letting her out of his sight—walked Lydia gingerly up the steps to her house. She would be of more use to them once she'd had a cup of strong tea, and a brief sit down.

* * *

After the three humans and one dog took off, Dr. Ryder and Matt examined Emily's body. They had introduced themselves to each other. "Without the benefit of an autopsy, I would say she died of multiple stab wounds to the abdomen with hemoperitoneum—that's blood in the cavity," Dr. Ryder said, as she hunched over the body. "With all this blood, it looks like probable hemorrhagic shock. She would have died quickly," she pointed out. "Once I can perform an autopsy, I'll have a good idea of the time of death, and should be able to tell you something about the murder weapon. It's been fairly recent, I would guess, not more than 10-15 hours. It doesn't look like she's been sexually assaulted because she's fully dressed, but I won't know that for sure until I can examine her."

Dr. Ryder stopped talking and leaned in closer to Emily's body, careful to not let her clothing touch anything. She lifted a strand of the girl's dripping wet hair, and pulled it outward away from her neck. She leaned in even closer, peering at Emily's neck.

"What?" asked Matt.

"There are bite marks on her neck and on her left arm. See here where her sweater has a tear?" She pointed to a spot just below Emily's left shoulder. "They are human bite marks, I believe," said Dr. Ryder. "I'll want to call in our DMD to confirm, but the impressions are pretty deep. Someone bit her repeatedly, and they were serious about it."

CHAPTER 3

Saturday, 9:10 a.m.

Dr. Ryder stood up and she and Matt stared at each other for a few moments over Emily's body. "This is a bad one," Bernice said, peeling off her latex gloves and breaking the silence. "How would you describe your karma, Chief? You've been here how long? We don't get many murders around here."

"I'm a nice guy, but, for some reason, my karma stinks lately," he said grimly. "Maybe my fortunes would improve if you just call me 'Matt.'"

"Sorry, Matt. I didn't mean to be a wise-ass. My way of dealing with horrific violence and stress is to be amusing. It doesn't always work. Like now."

Matt gave her a warm smile. "I've seen a lot of smart-asses in my career, and, believe me, doc, you don't qualify. Tell me, does my new hometown have a forensics team and an ambulance that can pick up this poor little thing's body?"

Port Stirling did not have forensics or an ambulance on site. The transport would arrive from Twisty River, the county seat, about thirty minutes away. Forensics would come with the ambulance to gather the physical evidence from the scene.

"Do they know to make it snappy because of the incoming tide?" asked Matt.

"Yeah. They're locals. My guy said 'Pedal to the metal—we left five minutes ago'. We'll take Emily to the morgue at Buck Bay Hospital and I'll perform the autopsy there," Dr. Ryder said. She watched Matt look anxiously back and forth between Emily's body and Lydia's house. "Go on up if you need to. We can't afford to waste time. I won't let anything happen to her." She reached out and touched Matt's arm.

"Thank you, Bernice. I need to get to the family, but I'll be in touch with you later today."

"No problem. Good luck to you. Get this asshole, OK?"

"We will, I promise. And Texans always keep their promises."

"I'd say as of today, you're an Oregonian," Bernice said, turning back toward the tunnel and waving good-bye over her head.

Protocol made Matt hesitant to leave the scene without a uniformed officer on guard, but Bernice was right, and no one could truly protect that little girl any longer. They were a small team facing a big case, and every minute mattered.

As Matt began to climb the weather-beaten stairs up the steep, rugged bluffs, it dawned on him that the ambulance couldn't access the beach, and Emily's body would have to be carried up on a gurney by the paramedics. This was, indeed, a new world for him after Texas. Would he ever fit in?

He met Jay, who was heading back down. Matt motioned for him to turn around and join him instead.

"Can I assume there is a crime team that we should bring in today?"

"Yes, sir, Chinook County has a team for big cases like this one. I didn't call all of them," Jay said, "but I did reach Ed Sonders. He's the Oregon State Police liaison for our area. He's on the way, but he was at the far end of the county when I talked to him. And, Pete, on the 911 desk, contacted Fern Byrne. She's one of the county's crime victim advocates. She lives in Port Stirling, and is waiting at City Hall until we need her."

"Fern Byrne?" asked Matt.

"Yep," Jay replied, his mouth turning up in a slight smile for the first time this morning, but quickly losing it. "And we should call Dr. Ryder's boss."

"Who's that?"

"David Dalrymple, Chinook County District Attorney," Jay answered. He leaned closer to Matt and lowered his voice before speaking again, not that there was anyone within earshot to hear them. "He doesn't like being left out of the loop. If you make the mistake of forgetting him once, he'll never forget that as long as you're in Port Stirling. You know the type?"

Matt did know the type. All too well.

"OK," Matt said as they finally reached the top step. "Please give Dalrymple and the others a shout and tell them what we've got here. Tell them we'll meet at Port Stirling City Hall this afternoon at 4:00 p.m., and they should notify anyone else on the team what's going on, but they should also keep a lid on the news. This is on a need-to-know basis only, and I do not want Emily's murder to leak out. Do not! Please make that clear. I'll tell Bill we're going to talk to the family first."

"I have the Bushnell's address," Jay said.

"Whether or not the family is involved in this child's murder," Matt continued, "this is going to be rough. I'd like your—our—victims' advocate to accompany us to the Bushnell home when we break the news. Is she a hand-holding type?"

"I think Fern is who you want for this. I've worked with her previously, and she's great at putting people at ease. She's never worked a murder either, though."

"I just need someone who can help us keep everyone calm. She doesn't have to solve the damn crime," Matt said, scowling at the universe in general.

"Fern can do that," Jay said to his boss. "Who else is going to the mayor's house with you, sir?"

"You are, of course. And quit calling me 'sir'. What's this state cop, Sonders, like? Could he help us interrogate the family?"

"Ed Sonders is my idol, a cool guy," Jay said. "He's also big. About my height, but with an extra 40 pounds of muscle. If we have any trouble with the family, he'll be the perfect guy. Ed's been around the block more than once."

"Sounds like the ideal sidekick. Will he be here soon?"

"Yes, I should think he's getting close. I'll call him again."

"The mayor knows you, right?"

"Yes, sir. I mean 'yes.'"

"Does Sonders know the family, too?"

"I think so, yeah. Ed's in Port Stirling fairly frequently, and he and the mayor have been in several meetings with us. I don't think they're friends or anything, but he'll be another familiar face. Fern knows the family, too."

"Sold," said Matt. "Call them both please, and give them the Bushnell residence address. Tell them to meet us there at 10:00 a.m., but not to go in until we arrive. I'll grab my luggage, and get the keys to my rental from Abbott, and then you can drive me there…I think it's close to here. I'd like to change into a jacket and tie before we call on the family. My uniform won't be issued until Tuesday, but I can at least look respectful." *Not like the cowboy I look like now.*

Matt started toward the house to fill in Abbott while Jay made the calls. Remembering Bernice on the beach, he gave Jay one more direction. "Can you get another one of our officers down here to guard the scene after Dr. Ryder and forensics take off with the ambulance?" Matt nodded to a couple in workout gear jogging toward the beach stairs at a good clip.

"Oh, crap!" said Jay, following his boss's stare.

Matt moved aggressively toward the couple as they neared. "I'm with the police, and this is a crime scene. You'll need to clear the area immediately, please."

His forceful voice and authoritative manner had the couple nodding in unison. After a quick glance down at the crime scene tape on the beach, and a jointly mumbled "Sorry", they turned and made a hasty retreat.

Jay arranged for one of his colleagues, the other on-duty patrol officer, to get to the scene quickly, and stand guard. "He's only five minutes away. I told him to hurry because word will get out fast."

"Yep, we need to get this party started and beat tracks to the family," Matt said. His heart skipped a beat as Matt thought about confronting another father. *Maybe this time it will turn out better than the last.*

*　*　*

Saturday, 9:35 a.m.

Before he'd left Port Stirling last month after his interview with Abbott, Matt had secured a small rental house on Ocean Bend Road from a list of available properties that Abbott's assistant, Mary Lou, had given him.

Although not the color he would have chosen, the buttercup-yellow cottage suited Matt. Between the two-bedroom house at the end of a short gravel lane, and the cliff-top fence was a quirky garden plot with four raised beds. It looked pretty ratty right now, but underneath the January rot, Matt could tell it had been tended in previous seasons. A lone, stumpy tree in one corner of the garden was bent back fiercely toward the cottage from many years of succumbing to the wind blowing hard off the ocean.

His new home was simple but cozy. It certainly didn't compare to the sprawling Texas ranch he'd grown up on, and that until one day ago he still shared with Beverly and Ross Horning, his parents. Matt's brother and sister, also in their 40's, still lived at the family compound too, and each sibling had their own separate wing. Sometimes days would pass without Matt laying eyes on any of his family. His new digs would fit entirely in the great room of just his wing of the family's ranch.

Matt paused just long enough to run his hand over the floor-to-ceiling river-rock fireplace at the heart of his new home. The big smooth rocks were now cold to his touch. That would change. The first thing Matt would do when he had the opportunity to settle in would be to build a big honkin' fire to ward off the damp winter chill that had seeped into the nooks and crannies of the empty house. The small cottage represented a clean break with his past, and that's all he needed currently.

A swift glance up the beach out the large picture windows that framed the Pacific brought Matt up short when he realized the tallest rock in the stack peeking up held Emily's tunnel. He hesitated for a moment, as the self-doubt he'd been dealing with the past couple of months crept back in. *What if I'm not good enough to catch this killer? What if my acceptance of this job puts the town at greater risk? What if whoever murdered Emily is smarter than me, and I'm putting my own life in danger in this strange new place? I sacrificed my comfort zone of family and birthplace to prove myself; what if I fail?*

No time to gaze out the windows or be paralyzed by fear right now. Moving into his bedroom, Matt threw his luggage down on the end of the bed, this time ignoring another ocean-front view. He pulled out a suit, white shirt, and tie. Putting on the navy wool Brooks Brothers jacket, he was—not for the first time—grateful for the southern-belle taste of his former wife, Susie Longworth. This suit had been a gift from her when she still thought she could turn him into something he wasn't.

He transferred his wallet and police notebook from his leather jacket to the suit's inside pocket, and, with a wistful look at the yawning fireplace opening, hurried back outside. When he rented the house last month, Matt could tell just by looking that his Yukon Denali wouldn't fit in the attached garage of the mid-50's structure, so it got left behind in Texas. He would buy a new car in Port Stirling, but that would have to wait until he put whoever killed that little girl behind bars.

* * *

Jay was happy for a few minutes alone in the police car while he waited for his new boss. It was a good time to collect his thoughts. While Matt had let himself into his new home to change clothes, Jay made two calls to Oregon State Police lieutenant Ed Sonders and Chinook County victims' advocate Fern Byrne. Both were horrified at Jay's news, and agreed to meet them at the Bushnell residence.

Jay was beyond grateful for Matt Horning's arrival in Port Stirling, and wondered what the hell the police department would have done today with old George still on the job—thank God he retired. Jay was not used to this kind of violence—he'd never been exposed to it and never expected it to happen in his town. A coked-out drug dealer ineffectively waving a hand gun around in the air was the worst thing he'd encountered in his years on the job.

Without completely understanding why, Jay already had a lot of faith in his new chief, even though he didn't know that much about him. The City Hall grapevine rumored that there had been some sort of trouble for Matt in Dallas, but Jay hadn't paid much attention to the gossip, figuring he would get the scoop directly from the chief if and when he wanted to share the details.

Before Matt had arrived, Jay had been expecting a stereotypical Texas cop as portrayed in the movies: beer belly, balding, red-faced, kind of stupid looking. Looking at Matt now, he realized he'd seen too many movies—his new boss was exactly the opposite of the stereotype.

"You married?" Jay asked, as Matt smoothly slid into the passenger's side of the patrol car.

"I was, but she didn't buy into being a cop's wife," Matt said. "When we first met, I was in the NFL, played for the Cowboys, but got hurt. It's a big leap from NFL wife to cop's wife."

"Get out!" Jay exclaimed. "You played in the NFL?"

"Yeah, I was a cornerback until I blew out my knee. Played under Mack Brown."

"You must have been pretty good. The Cowboys. Wow. I'm speechless."

"Yeah, even though I didn't last long, it was a cool experience," Matt said.

Chances were good that Jay would never look at his boss the same way again.

Back to business, Matt said, "How long will it take us to get to the mayor's house?"

"Oh, about two minutes, give or take a minute," Jay answered.

"Huh?"

"Everything in Port Stirling is close by. Your house is squarely in the middle of today's action. The mayor's house is back up Ocean Bend Road toward Lydia Campbell's house, and then off to our right.

Do you remember the sign for Whale Rock Wayside we passed on the way here?"

"Yeah." Matt's stomach growled loudly.

"Well, directly across the road from that is the street the mayor lives on—Cranberry Drive. Have you had anything to eat yet this morning? Do you want to stop and grab something real quick?"

"Nothin' but some peanuts on the plane out of Portland. But I'll get through notifying the family and then we can worry about food. Let's do this, pardner."

CHAPTER 4

Saturday, 10:05 a.m.

Cranberry Drive was a small development of homes on the east side of Ocean Bend Road opposite the entrance to Whale Rock Wayside, a state park. The Bushnell house sat at the end of a cul-de-sac. The Pacific was not visible from it, but it was an easy walk to the Wayside's beach staircase. Even though the family house was across the road from the clifftop, Matt guessed correctly that they could hear the ocean's bellow with their windows open.

A pale blue Volkswagen bug was parked in front of the Bushnell home when Jay and Matt arrived. The VW had a single red rose in its dashboard flower vase. *Of course it did. Had to be Fern Byrne's car,* Matt figured. *And what was up with that name?*

The wide-eyed female face that peered at Matt through the VW's rolled-up window had a scared-stiff look on it, similar to Jay's pasty pallor when they first met on the beach. But as Fern Byrne unfolded her long legs out of the compact car to meet the cops, she presented a calm, professional demeanor, if somewhat wary.

"I'm Matt Horning," he said, sticking out his hand, and locking on to Fern's direct gaze. "Thanks for coming. Not sure if this is your pay grade or not, but we could use a steady helping hand with the family about now." After what he'd just viewed on the beach below them, the red-haired, freckle-faced, tallish, slender woman in her

30's before him seemed to usher in a breath of fresh air right off the ocean. The blue sweater she wore fastidiously over a black slim skirt and boots reminded Matt of the color of the Pacific Ocean when he'd interviewed on that bright sunny day in December.

"Fern Byrne," she replied, giving Matt a firm handshake and a flitting smile. A little wave in Jay's direction. "No problem, Chief. I don't know if you're technically the chief yet, but I guess this"—she jerked her thumb toward the house—"makes you THE CHIEF."

"Yup, it does, ma'am. I understand that you know the family."

"Yes. Not well, but I've met them all, including little Emily," she said and her chin quivered for a moment. "Before we go in there, I want to make sure I have the facts correct. Emily's body was found in the tunnel in Whale Rock earlier this morning. She's dead, right? Are we sure?" Fern looked at Matt with hope in her eyes, trying to push out the dread.

"She's been stabbed multiple times, Ms. Byrne. Yes, I'm afraid Emily is dead. Her body is being moved to the morgue in Buck Bay, and the medical examiner will perform an autopsy this afternoon, once her family makes an official identification."

Fern gulped, and it came out rather loud sounding.

"And you don't know who the murderer is, correct?"

"That's correct. Emily was killed by person or persons unknown."

Fern put one hand up over her mouth, and took a deep breath. "You know this doesn't happen in Port Stirling, don't you?" she said.

"So I've been told."

"We protect our children. We don't kill them."

Although she was clearly upset, Matt detected competence and steel in Fern Byrne. Jay had been right; Fern was the perfect person to help the family get through the truly awful news they were about to deliver.

An Oregon State Police car, thankfully with its lights not flashing, pulled in right behind Jay's vehicle, and skidded to a stop.

Matt felt a strong hand on his back and turned around to see the uniformed officer from the state police. At 5'11" inches, Matt had to look up at the 6'4" cop.

"There goes my Saturday morning golf game," the big guy said, but under his breath and leaning in so only Matt could hear him. "Edward J. Sonders, Oregon State Police," he pronounced, and clasped Matt's extended hand in a death grip. "Heck of a first day on the job, Chief. Welcome to Port Stirling."

Sonders had a stern, barely-lined face, broad shoulders, and a barrel chest. He looked tough-as-nails in his spotless dark blue uniform and darker blue broad-brimmed hat with the state seal. He was wearing a tie, and a prominent badge on his chest, but Matt's eyes went right to the gun holstered around his not insubstantial waist. Sonders' eyes twinkled in spite of the grim circumstances and his intimidating appearance. Matt liked him on the spot.

The two-story Bushnell house was set back from the street on its pie-shaped lot, and had a pretty wishing well and what were probably colorful flowers in the spring and summer, set around a big lawn. The three cops and the county advocate gathered in an informal circle in front of the house's low, decorative gate. Fern had pulled a black rain-coat out of her car, and now wrapped it tightly around her, securing the coat's hood over her hair, which was threatening to frizz up. Fat raindrops dripped off the brim of the men's uniform hats, and Matt realized that his official chief's hat would likely be the key ingredient in his new Oregon uniform . . . hatless, he was getting soaked.

"OK, here's how this is going to work," Matt said to his rapt audience. "We'll take the family all in one room, and the four of us will stay together while I tell them we found Emily. Then, once I gauge the reaction of each person, I'll ask each of you to take a statement from one of them. One of us will be assigned to each parent, and I'll take mom or dad, probably dad. I will designate one of you to go with the other parent, and one will take the three siblings. Fern, we'll most likely want you to be in the room with the mother because she's usually the most upset and in need of care in cases like these. Sexist, I realize, but that's been my experience when a child dies."

Fern nodded.

"Lieutenant Sonders, do you know the mayor?" Matt asked.

"Yes, Chief, I do. But I've never met the family, only been in official meetings with Fred along with Jay here. I'm sorry for their loss, but you all need to know that there is a very good chance someone in that house is the perpetrator."

Matt looked first at Fern and then at Jay. "The lieutenant is right. The odds and statistics say when a child is murdered, it's usually a family member. One positive this morning is that I have no pre-conceived notions or judgments about the victim or her family—all I know is the crime scene. So, give them your condolences and empathy, as I will, but keep in mind we have a job to do, OK?"

Matt didn't wait for an answer, and strode up to the front porch. His three colleagues marched behind him. Drooping Christmas lights, still up ten days after the holiday, surrounded the red door. Matt rang the doorbell. A hearty gust of wind from the southwest blew some dead, wet leaves across his black Cole Haan loafers as he stared unblinking at the front door.

CHAPTER 5

Saturday, 10:10 a.m.

The mayor answered his door. Fred Bushnell was wearing khaki pants and a forest green sweater. His wife, Marjorie Bushnell, was standing slightly behind him in close-fitting, almost tight, jeans and a white, untucked blouse. She was wearing fuzzy turquoise slippers.

"Thank God you're finally here," Fred said sharply. "Are you Horning?"

"Let the poor man come in, Fred," said his wife, taking a step forward. "It's nice to meet you, Mr. Horning. Bill Abbott says wonderful things about you."

"It's nice to meet you, too, ma'am. Mr. Mayor." Matt shook both their hands in turn, and looked them in the eye. "I'm sorry the circumstances aren't better." He turned to indicate his colleagues. "I think you know Officer Jay Finley and Lieutenant Ed Sonders from the state police?" he asked the mayor, who nodded. "And this is Fern Byrne, who works for Chinook County. May we come in?"

Mayor Bushnell eyed the entourage, and held open his door for the visitors to enter. "What are you doing about my daughter's disappearance?" he demanded as the cops grouped in the foyer.

Matt ignored the mayor's question. "Let's all sit down somewhere," Matt said instead, his voice resolute.

Marjorie ushered the party into the sunken living room off to the right of the foyer, and pointed her guests to a seating area in front of the welcoming red-brick fireplace. Only Sonders remained standing, and he had positioned himself in the archway between the others and the front door, the top of his hat nearly brushing the arch. Fred and Marjorie sat opposite Matt and Jay on a newish-looking, ivory-colored sofa. A glass-topped coffee table was between them. Two large, coffee-table-ish books sat on top; one called "Cheese", and the second one "Great Links Golf Courses". In the center of the table was a spectacular four-flowered red amaryllis that must have politely bloomed right at Christmas time.

"Would any of you like some coffee?" Mrs. Bushnell offered. An odd question, considering why they were here, and Matt and Fern, who was seated in a floral chintz chair flanking the Bushnell's sofa, exchanged a quick glance.

"No thank you, ma'am. I'm afraid I have very bad news," Matt started. "The worst possible news." He let that sink in a moment before continuing.

Marjorie Horning rubbed the side of her nose and almost imperceptibly shook her head "no". One of Fred's legs seemed to have a mind of its own, and twitched up and down.

"What is it?" Marjorie said first, her fingers now tapping, impatiently, on the arm of the sofa.

"I'm afraid it's about your daughter, Emily." He paused, and lowered his voice to a gentler range. "I'm sorry to tell you that her body has been found on the beach this morning."

"Well, is she alright?" Fred asked, not understanding. He crossed his legs in a futile attempt to stop the twitching one.

"I'm afraid she's dead, Mr. Bushnell. I'm so sorry."

"That's not possible. I put her to bed myself last night." Fred's face turned pallid and he suddenly looked ill, as the reality of what Matt said was beginning to sink in.

"Emily can't be dead," cried Marjorie. "She's my baby. You must be mistaken." Tears started down both parents' cheeks, and they stared at Matt as if he had the power to fix this. Fern reached across the sofa arm, and tried to take Marjorie's hand, but she swatted her away, as if Fern were an annoying bee.

Undeterred, Fern stayed close and said to both parents, "I'm sorry, but Chief Horning is not mistaken. Jay has unofficially identified Emily's body, and he's sure it's your daughter." Fern rose and went over to the mayor, perching on the arm of the sofa, and putting her hand on his shoulder. "I can't tell you and your family how sorry we are," she said softly. "Please accept our deepest sympathies."

Fred looked up at Fern, his face a study in grief, and then bolted off the sofa and ran down the hallway on the other side of the entry foyer to his daughter's bedroom. His plaintive wail came from the end of the hall.

* * *

Marjorie rushed down the hallway to her husband, who was doubled over in his own personal pain, hands on his knees. Sonders let them go, but moved with an agility that contradicted his size, discreetly blocking the door of what he figured must be Emily's bedroom with his body. Matt and Fern followed the Bushnells down the hallway. Matt whispered to her, "Best to give them a moment before we tell them what happens next."

"Agreed," Fern nodded.

Instinctively, Jay hung around the home's front door…just in case. Emily's bedroom had two windows, and one of them was wide open, the sash thrown up to its limit. Delicate white eyelet curtains swayed in and out of the open window as the wind did its thing. The window sill was soaked, the carpet under it damp, and getting damper by the minute. Matt was somewhat surprised that neither parent had closed the window when they discovered their daughter was missing, even though he'd told them to not touch anything. Most people think that admonition doesn't apply to them, but he was relieved they apparently hadn't disturbed the scene.

Horning's eyes went to the little girl's bedside lamp, which featured a big pink butterfly on its base, and a pink shade with white daisies all over it. Mesmerized by that sweet lamp, Matt loved the little girl who had chosen it even more.

Emily's twin bed had a slightly rumpled appearance, and the lime green coverlet was thrown back to reveal white sheets and one pink blanket. The small pillow was in place at the head of the bed, and had a few wrinkles in it. A tiny nightgown was laying sadly on the floor at the foot of the bed. The overhead light in the ceiling was off, as was her bedside lamp, and the closet door was gaping open. A child-sized clothes-hanger laid on the closet's floor. Denim tennis shoes, one turned on its side, looked as if they had been carelessly discarded.

In a frenzied move, Fred slipped past Sonders, and advanced toward the open window. "Please don't touch anything," Matt said quickly, as Sonders moved to grab the mayor.

"I just want to see if Em is out here," Fred sobbed and tried to stick his head out the open window.

Sonders put both hands on the distraught father's upper arms, and physically lifted him away from the window.

"I'm sorry, Fred—can I call you Fred?" Matt started. Fred nodded mutely. "I would give anything if I could bring your daughter back to you, but that's not possible. She's dead." Matt looked over Fred's shoulder to where Marjorie stood with her hands over both ears, as if she couldn't bear to hear any more, and stared at the floor. Matt repeated, "Emily is dead, Marjorie. I need you both to tell me that you understand . . . Emily is not coming home."

Fred moved next to Marjorie, but didn't touch her. Marjorie said, "We understand, don't we, Fred?" Fred used the back of both hands to wipe tears from his face. Silently, he nodded.

"OK," Matt continued, speaking slowly and deliberately. "I can't think of a good way to tell you this, but it looks like your daughter was murdered. I'll need to get a forensics crew in this room as soon as possible. May I suggest that we move back to your living room?" *Try to be gentle*, Matt told himself. *The mayor. Jesus.*

Marjorie and Fred, who had simultaneously gasped at the word "murdered", moved silently and numbly down the hall, Fred's arm now around Marjorie's shoulder. Likely holding her up. On Fred's other side, Fern took his elbow and gently rubbed his back, and he, unlike his wife, seemed to appreciate Fern's comforting gesture.

A hall door opened up before they reached the foyer, and 14-year-old Jack Bushnell appeared in his PJ's, rubbing one eye. "What's going on?" he asked.

Marjorie rushed to wrap her arms around Jack, tears streaming down her face. She opened her mouth to speak, but the words didn't come out. Jack stood silently with his arms straight down at his sides, allowing his mother to hold him. He looked over her shoulder at his dad with a "What the hell is this?" look on his face.

"It's your sister, Jack. Emily." Fred choked out the name of his youngest daughter. "These people are from the police. They think something happened to her."

"How could something happen to Em? She's friggin' four years old," said Jack in the cops' direction.

Leave it to a teenager to state the obvious.

"Did you see your sister this morning?" Matt asked Jack.

Jack stared at Matt. He blinked slowly, surveyed his dad before turning back to Matt and saying "No. I just woke up." Marjorie released her grip on Jack, and Fred put his arm around her shoulder again to steady his wife. Fern took a firm hold of Marjorie's other arm and murmured something to her that was inaudible to the others.

"I'm sorry, but we need to ask you all some questions," Matt said. "Can we please all go back to the living room now?"

"Can I eat something first?" asked Jack. "I'm starving."

The adults looked at him as if he'd just announced he was flying to the moon. Even with his work experience with teenagers, Matt thought it an odd response to just learning that your baby sister was in serious trouble.

"I'll make him some quick toast," Marjorie said through gulps. Before Matt could reply, and shaking loose of Fern's grip, she made a beeline toward what he assumed must be the kitchen. Fern glanced over at Matt, and he gave her a nod. She trotted along closely behind Marjorie.

"I really need y'all to go back in the living room and take a seat, please. Now."

"Where are you from?" asked Jack, staring at Matt. He seemed genuinely curious. "You sound funny."

The corners of Matt's mouth turned up in a slight smile in spite of himself. The kid had no filter.

"Texas. I just moved here from Texas. Is it that obvious?"

"Yes, sir, it is." Jack threw in the "sir", suddenly realizing that it might be in his best interests to tone down his act. "I knew you weren't from Port Stirling."

"Mr. Horning is our new police chief, Jack," said his father. "In

41

fact, he just got to town and hasn't really taken over yet," added Fred, looking down at his shoes and the tears falling on them.

"Actually, Bill Abbott did swear me in this morning," said Matt. "I'm officially in charge of your daughter's case. I'm sorry to do this, Fred, but I've brought along Officer Finley and Lieutenant Sonders because we need to take statements from everyone in your family. We'll try to make this as brief as we can, sir."

Fred corralled his son, and together they moved to the sofa. All of a sudden, Fred looked more like Jack's grandfather than his father. Ashen-faced except for a red nose and red eyes, he shuffled down the hall and sat down gingerly, pulling the boy close to him.

Jack fidgeted and looked uncomfortable.

"Where are your other children? We need everyone in this room right now."

The mayor looked confused. Everything was happening too fast. Finally, he said, "Susan and Gary went to the farmer's market right before we called you. Susan wanted to get some food so we wouldn't have to go out later until after we'd found Emily. She got her driver's license last week, and we still like someone to ride with her, so Gary went along. They should be home soon."

"Call them please," directed Matt. "Tell them they need to come home immediately—no stops on the way."

"Where's my daughter, Mr. Horning?" He squeezed his son's hand as he looked up into Matt's face. Fred was openly crying and his voice was choked. "What happened to her? Where is she?"

Jay cleared his throat behind Matt as if he was trying to help the mayor clear his.

"Dr. Bernice Ryder—the Chinook County medical examiner . . ." Matt started.

"I know Bernice," Fred interrupted.

"Of course. Dr. Ryder and the ambulance attendants have taken Emily to the lab in Buck Bay, while we came here to talk to you. I'm so sorry, Fred. I don't know what else to say."

"Do you mean my sister is dead?" said a stone-faced Jack Bushnell.

"Yes, son, I'm afraid she is," said Matt as gently as he could. "Her body was found on the beach this morning."

"How did she die?" asked the boy.

"We don't know that yet, and won't until after your parents have identified her body for certain."

'Her body' hung in the heavy air for a moment. Matt took out his spiral-bound notebook from the pocket of his navy jacket.

"Where did you find her?" Jack persisted.

"I'd rather not go into that yet," Matt said sternly to the boy, and gave him his tough detective look in the hopes of silencing him.

"Shit like this doesn't happen in Port Stirling," argued Jack. His father did nothing to scold his language, and was again staring at his fascinating shoes. Fred appeared to be in shock.

Yeah, that's why I took this job. Because shit like this doesn't happen here.

Matt took note of father and son's appearances. Starting with his tan loafers and same-colored socks, everything about the mayor was clean and tidy, including his creased khakis and dark green sweater. An unobtrusive watch on his left wrist.

Jack had on mismatched PJ's and was barefoot. Without staring too hard, both males looked free of dirt, sand, blood, or any marks on their face or body.

"Please call Susan and Gary and tell them to come home," Matt said again to the mayor, this time more sharply. "Do you need Officer Finley to get a phone for you?"

"What? No. I have a phone," Fred said, fishing into his pants pocket.

The officers waited quietly while Fred phoned his son's mobile phone. Matt nodded his approval while Fred choked out that it was an emergency, and they needed to come home right now.

Once Fred had hung up, Matt said, "I need to ask you a few preliminary questions for the record, Fred. Are you OK to proceed?"

"Do your job, Chief," the mayor said quietly.

Matt turned to Jay and said, "Officer Finley, please go into the kitchen with Mrs. Bushnell and get her statement. Lieutenant Sonders, please take Jack into the dining room for questioning,"—he motioned to the room which led off the living room through a second archway—" and be on the lookout for the other two children. Any questions?"

Jay took off with a backward glance at Matt. Matt caught his apprehensive look, and he gave him a slight rise of his chin that said *"You can do this."*

Lieutenant Sonders nodded at Matt and said to Jack, "Let's go, young man." Jack, to Matt's relief, patted his dad's knee, got up, and followed Sonders silently into the adjacent room. Fred's eyes followed his son.

Once they were alone in the living room, Matt asked Fred, "When did you last see Emily?"

He looked at Matt with an anguished face for several excruciating moments before squeaking, "Between 6:30-7:00 p.m. last night when I put her to bed."

"How did she act? Anything unusual about her?"

"No. She didn't want to go to bed yet, but that was normal—Em never wants to go to bed. Afraid she'll miss something, I guess," Fred allowed.

"So, nothing odd about her behavior last night?"

"Nothing. Just my perfect little girl." Fred's shoulders began to shake, and Matt moved beside him on the sofa.

"Just a few more questions, Fred. I'm so sorry to have to do this."
Matt waited while Fred caught his breath. "Was anyone with you when
you put Emily to bed?"

Fred looked puzzled. "No. I always put her to bed when I'm home."

"So you were alone with her?"

"Yes. Yes, I suppose I was. I'm sure her mother would have gone
in at some point and given her a nighty-night kiss, but when I left
her she was alone."

"Did you turn out the light?"

"Of course. Like always." Fred took in a sharp intake of breath
and paused, looking directly at Matt. "Are you sure my daughter has
been killed?" he pleaded.

"Dr. Ryder said Emily died quickly and wouldn't have known
what was happening to her," Matt said softly. "I hope that helps some."

Fred put his face in his hands and sobbed. Matt sat patiently while
the mayor broke down, and then finally said, "Do you own a knife,
Fred?"

The change in topic and tone startled Fred and he turned to his
new police chief, a spooked look on his ravaged face.

"What do you mean? Was she stabbed?"

"Please answer my question, Mr. Bushnell."

Taken aback at being spoken to in this manner, Fred answered.
"I have a small pocket knife, and, of course, we have a set of kitchen
knives. Was Emily stabbed?"

"Do you have your pocket knife on your person now?" Matt asked,
ignoring Fred's question for the second time. "If so, may I see it, please?"

Fred reached into a side pants pocket and pulled out a small knife
sheathed in a camouflage design. He handed it to Matt, who grabbed
it with his clean handkerchief, and opened it up, splaying the three
different blades. The pocket knife wasn't big enough to do any real

damage, and all three blades were clean and looked barely used. Nevertheless, Matt opened Jay's police kit, and deposited the mayor's knife in a small plastic bag.

"I'll need to keep this for now," Matt explained, seeing the stricken look on Fred's face. "It's just procedure—nothing to worry about. We'll want to see your kitchen knives, too, but let's keep going for the time being. Who, exactly, other than you, your wife, and Jack live in this house currently?" Matt inquired. "Full names, ages, occupations, please."

"My other daughter, Susan, who will be sixteen tomorrow, lives with us. She's a junior at Port Stirling High School. And my oldest son, Gary, is home visiting from college. The U of O is on break. He's 18. Nineteen next week."

Just then, new voices came from the kitchen. Lieutenant Sonders got up from his dining room chair, instructing Jack to stay put, and went to the kitchen to collect Susan and Gary. He pointed out chairs for them around the dining table close to where Jack sat, and darted an "under control" look in Matt's direction.

Matt saluted back at him. Just then, Marjorie went into the dining room, and handed a plate and glass of orange juice to Jack. Her hands shook so badly the juice sloshed around in the glass.

"Thanks, mom" said Jack, grabbing for his breakfast before it ended up on the floor.

Jay escorted Marjorie back into the kitchen, out of Matt's sight. Jack wolfed down his food.

"Did all five of you sleep here last night?" Matt continued his interrogation of the mayor.

"Yes," said Fred. "Oh, no, wait. Susan was at her friend Chloe's house for a slumber party. All the girls stayed the night."

"But both of your sons and you and Marjorie slept here?"

"That's correct."

"Did the four of you leave the house at any point during the evening?"

"Well, Marjorie and I were here all night. All six of us had dinner together, and..."

"What time was that?" Matt interrupted.

"I don't know. Early. Probably about 5:30 p.m. Jack was going to the movies with a friend, and Susan was eager to get to her party, so I know we ate pretty early. Gary was going out later too. Meeting up with some of his old high school buddies."

From the adjacent room, likely hearing his name mentioned, Jack said loudly, "I went to the movies!" Or maybe it only sounded loud in the muted, glum atmosphere of the two rooms.

"But you slept here, Jack," corrected his father. "That's what Chief Horning asked."

"Yeah, I slept here. I get it," the boy said. "Sorry, dad."

"Were you awake when your sons came home?" Matt asked. "What time did each get back?"

Fred stared at Matt for a longish moment before answering. "I'm afraid I was asleep. It had been a long week, the wife and I had a martini and watched a movie, and I fell asleep during it."

"What time was that?"

"Not sure. 10:00 p.m. maybe?"

"Did you look in on the kids' rooms? Did you check on Emily?"

Again, Fred met Matt's direct gaze before speaking. "We have to walk by all of their rooms to the end of the hall to go upstairs," Fred said. "Emily and Jack's doors were both closed and Emily's lights were off, like normal. Jack's light was still on, which was also normal. We assumed that Emily was asleep, and Jack was doing whatever Jack does at night." Fred sounded defensive.

"What about Gary's room? Was he home?"

"I don't think so. His door was open, and he always closes it when he's in his room. It's not unusual for Gary to stay out late. We didn't think anything of it. He's old enough to do what he wants." Prickly tone.

"You didn't check to see if he might be in the kitchen or someplace else in the house?"

"No."

"Did you wake up at any time during the night? Did you hear anything unusual?"

"No. I told you, I was tired."

"So you didn't hear anything all night?"

"Look, Horning," Fred said, his voice rising. "I've told you everything was normal, I didn't hear or see anything during the night. If I did, I would tell you."

Ignoring Fred's outburst, Matt said, "Did your wife go to bed when you did?"

"Yes. She probably read for a while, she usually does. I went to sleep the minute my head hit the pillow."

"Do you know if Marjorie left your bedroom during the night?"

"I don't think so—she told me this morning she didn't hear anything all night either." Fred paused before adding, "But I guess I don't know that for sure, do I?"

"If you were sound asleep all night," Matt answered, "no, I guess you don't know for sure."

CHAPTER 6

Saturday, 11:00 a.m.

"I've got what I need from you now, Fred," Matt said. "I'll want to talk to you again later after you've identified your daughter's body. More about Emily's activities and your family's whereabouts in the last few days. Understood?"

"Yes."

Matt stood up and walked into the dining room. He introduced himself to Gary and Susan, and they both stood to shake his hand. Both of them were crying.

"I'm sorry for your loss," Matt said to the siblings. "We'll find out what happened to your little sister, I promise you. Lieutenant Sonders, are you about ready to wrap up here?"

"Yes, Chief. I have statements from all three."

"OK, good. Let's see how Officer Finley is doing in the kitchen. If he's ready, we'll take Mr. and Mrs. Bushnell to Buck Bay now."

Matt moved into the kitchen, which was separated from the dining room by a low wall with a built-in buffet. Jay and Fern sat at a small round kitchen table, where Jay was still questioning Marjorie. Fern caught Matt's eye and slowly shook her head "no".

Matt sauntered behind Marjorie over to the kitchen countertop next to the sink that overlooked a large, nicely-landscaped back yard. He appeared to be checking out the view, but was really inspecting the set of knives in a wooden block between the sink and the cooktop. The set had twelve slots, and there were ten knives resting in their proper slots. He glanced into the farmhouse-style antique copper sink to see if perhaps it held two dirty knives, but there were no dishes or cutlery at all—clean as a whistle. Matt started to surreptitiously open the dishwasher, but then thought better of it. *If there is a knife in there and I take it without a search warrant, it might screw up the case.*

"We're about finished here, Chief," Jay said. "I've got Mrs. Bushnell's statement for now." Lieutenant Sonders had joined them in the kitchen, and the three kids were lurking behind him.

"OK, thank you all for your time, and, again, please accept our condolences on your family's loss," said Matt. "Here's what's going to happen next. Fern, did you get ahold of that pastor you mentioned?"

"Yes, I did. Pastor Winston and his wife Patricia are on their way here now. It should be just a few minutes."

"OK, good. Kids, Pastor Winston and his wife are going to stay with the three of you while Ms. Byrne, Officer Finley and I escort your parents to Buck Bay to identify Emily's body. The three of you are not to leave this house. And no one is to enter Emily's bedroom. Do you understand me?"

The three siblings nodded silently.

"I need a verbal answer from each of you," Matt said firmly, staring them down.

They all said "yes" simultaneously.

"Lieutenant Sonders, please get the forensics team here and supervise their work. This is now a crime scene. Am I clear?"

Matt walked over to Ed Sonders and with his back to Fred and Marjorie, whispered "And please get a search warrant from whatever judge has to issue it as quick as you can." Sonders nodded and whispered back, "Consider it done."

The doorbell rang, a loud, jarring buzzer, and everyone jumped. Fern Byrne composed herself first and said, "That must be the Winstons. I'll get the door."

Once Pastor John and his wife Patricia expressed their grief and comforted the Bushnell family, Matt addressed them. "Thank you for coming on such short notice. I'd really appreciate it if you would stay here with the kids and Lieutenant Sonders while our forensic team does its work in Emily's bedroom. We'll take Fred and Marjorie over to Buck Bay to see their daughter, and then we will drop them off back here. We'll likely be gone about 90 minutes. Are you good with that?"

"This is a terrible tragedy, and the Lord works in mysterious ways," droned Pastor Winston. "The good wife and I will do what we can to bring solace to this stricken house. At this time of sadness and . . ."

"Thanks," interrupted Matt. "We'll be back as soon as possible. Mr. and Mrs. Bushnell, please get your coats. We'll go in the Port Stirling police car."

Fern went quickly to Susan Bushnell who was sobbing loudly in the doorway of the kitchen. She gave the girl a firm hug, and said "Go lay down for a while, and I'll be back soon. We can talk, OK?" Susan looked at Fern through teary eyes and nodded her assent, grateful for Fern's kindness.

* * *

Jay nosed the police car out of Cranberry Drive and headed north on Ocean Bend Road. Fern sat in the front seat next to Jay, while Matt got in back with Marjorie and Fred. He didn't think the Bushnells were the type to bail out of a moving car, but he didn't want to take any chances.

To break the awkward silence in the vehicle, which was starting to get lengthy, Fern looked over her shoulder and asked Matt when he got to town.

"Just this morning," he replied. "I was supposed to start work on Tuesday."

"You're from Texas, I understand," Fern said, but it came out sounding like a question.

"Yes, ma'am. The Dallas area. Lived there all my life."

"What made you come to Port Stirling?" she asked. "Our little town seems like quite a departure from Dallas."

"Chief Horning got into a little trouble in Texas," Fred Bushnell said. There was a hint of malice in his voice. "Isn't that right, Chief?"

Matt stared at the mayor for a split second before answering, "You could say that. I prefer to think I was doing my job. The Grand Jury agreed with me." *No sense dodging the question; clearly the mayor was told my story before I was hired.*

"But the girl's parents didn't agree with your version of what happened, did they?" Fred persisted.

"It was a tragic accident, and they were understandably upset to lose their daughter," Matt bristled. "I'm sure you can understand how they felt."

"Texas' loss is Port Stirling's gain," Fern said quickly in an attempt to de-escalate whatever in hell was happening in the back seat. "Where will you be living, Chief?"

"I rented a nice little bungalow on Ocean Bend Road. It's small, but it suits me just fine." *Thank you, Fern Byrne.*

"It's that cottage that belongs to Carol Newland, the teacher who retired and moved to California," Jay piped in. "She didn't want to sell it in case she ever wants to come back to Port Stirling. You're going to love living on the beach."

The mention of the beach brought an abrupt halt to all conversation, and the five adults rode in silence the rest of the way to the morgue.

* * *

Friday night, 8:12 p.m.

In death, I can now live. Watch me walk across the sea. The shark is in the tree! Eat! High on dying! Eat! Bite! Bite!

Is this real? All this blood! I'm covered in death. Bite!

Better think about getting rid of Emily's blood. Never liked this sweater anyway. Throw it in trash. Saturday pickup! Bite!

Head hurts. Hands shaking. The shark! Tide coming in. Strong! Knife in my eye! Eat! Eat!

CHAPTER 7

Saturday, 1:00 p.m.

Matt, Jay, and Fern had been caught in a downpour leaving the Bushnell house after dropping off the mayor and his wife following the trip to the morgue. They left an unfortunate puddle inside Matt's City Hall office. OSP Lieutenant Ed Sonders followed them back to City Hall, and the four sat around a table in Matt's new office, munching on the sandwiches that Bill Abbott's trusty admin assistant had fetched for them. Mary Lou, stunned by such a frightful crime in her hometown, had insisted on coming in to work on Saturday to help out any way she could.

It had stopped raining, and the sun was peeking out occasionally through fast-moving clouds. The view Matt had valued in December was beginning to materialize through his rain-spattered windows. He removed his suit jacket, loosened his tie, and took a big bite of the turkey and cranberry sauce sandwich.

"What happened when Fred and Marjorie went to the morgue and identified the body?" asked Sonders.

"All of us went in with the parents," Matt said between bites, indicating Jay and Fern. "Bernice was already there with the body. Marjorie gave the official confirmation that it was Emily. Both parents were relatively calm, considering the circumstances. I've seen much worse," Matt added. "They both cried, but it was a soft cry, not a loud, sobbing scene," he continued. "Would you agree with that, Fern? What was your take?"

"I agree. The only thing I would add—because I thought it was odd—is that at one point Fred moved to put his arm around Marjorie's shoulders and she shook him off. It was subtle, but I caught it."

"You know, you're right," Matt said. "I don't think they touched each other the entire time they were in the room with their daughter's body."

"That does seem odd," noted Sonders. "Most parents would cling to each other in this situation, you'd think. Wouldn't you?"

"People are different," Matt said. "I've seen all sorts of reactions to violence. Some people rant and rave, and some go absolutely silent. It's difficult to make any judgments based on grief levels."

Sonders nodded. "Every marriage is different, too. We don't know anything about the Bushnell's except how they appear in public. I haven't been around Mrs. Bushnell that much, but Fred always struck me as a normal guy. If one or the other didn't kill their daughter, they would be in shock."

"Yeah," agreed Matt. "We dropped them back at their house and told them to get some rest this afternoon. They are not to leave the house until I tell them it's OK. Bernice was to start the autopsy after we left."

"It's important for the family to pull together now," said Fern. "No matter how this turns out, they all need to support each other. I encouraged them to not talk about their statements to us, or to try to figure out what happened to Emily, but, instead, to rest and try to distract themselves from reality as best they can. At least, for a few hours until it really sinks in."

"I stationed an OSP patrolman at the end of their driveway," said Ed Sonders. "In case anyone gets any funny ideas."

The difference between Fern's approach and Ed's was stark, but the two shared a friendly smile. They had worked together recently on a drug case when the single mother of two young children was arrested. Ed handled mom, and Fern took care of the children, and they respected each other's work.

"I should have thought of that, Ed, thanks," said Matt. "Let's compare the family's statements, shall we? Do you want to start with the kids?"

"The kids are all weird," Ed said with a straight face, not joking in the least. "Gary hates Port Stirling, can't wait to be back at U of O, and isn't overly fond of either parent. He was, however, close to Emily, and seemed upset at her death. Maybe the most distraught of the three siblings. Susan is out to lunch…"

"What do you mean by that?" Matt broke in.

"She's upset about her sister, of course, but at times during my interrogation she seemed just as upset about the fact that Emily managed to get herself killed on her birthday weekend."

"That's a teenage girl, me-first thought process," Fern inserted. "It's normal and should be discounted."

"What about Jack?" Matt asked the lieutenant.

"Jack handled himself well for a 14-year-old. In fact, he seemed like 14 going on 35. He's smarter than his two siblings. He said all the right things, but my bullshit meter was high. I kept getting the feeling that he was playing me."

"Hmm. Do the three have alibis?" Matt asked. "It seems like Susan's is probably the easiest to confirm; she either was or wasn't at her friend's slumber party all night."

"Yeah," agreed Sonders. "I will check that out as soon as we're done here. Both of the boys' alibis are a little shakier, especially in regards to timing. They were supposedly both out with friends in public locales, but that will take some tracking down."

"First we need to hear the time of death more definitively from

Bernice, and then we can pursue the boys' stories more efficiently," said Matt. "But, yes, talk to Susan's friend and her parents to make sure they were all in the house all night. Let's start by eliminating suspects with air-tight alibis. In your view, Ed, does Susan seem capable of planning and executing a murder like Emily's? Is she "out to lunch" as you say in general, or just because of the circumstances?"

"I don't think Susan is smart enough to premeditate a crime like this, if that's what you're asking me. Maybe it was a spur of the moment deal, but I don't believe she has the focus or the brain power to carefully plan her sister's death in advance. No."

"Check out her alibi anyway. We'll go from there. Tell us about your interview with Gary. The timing of Emily's homicide and Gary's being home is coincidental. And I never cared much for coincidences. Where did he go last night?" Matt asked.

"Said he left right after the family dinner to catch up with some of his former high school pals. Told me they met up at the Stirling Tavern, where they played pool for hours."

"That jives with what Marjorie said when I asked her what she could tell me about Gary's activities last night," Jay interjected.

"I didn't want to butt in when Marjorie said that," said Fern, switching gears, "but I thought you had to be 21 years old to be in there. Gary can't be that old yet, can he?"

"No, he's only 18," said Sonders, his cheeks turning a little rosy. "Gary said the mom of one of his friends owns the place, and she lets them hang out in the back. Apparently she turns a blind eye as long as the boys are just playing pool. That shit's gotta stop," he fumed.

"Agreed," said Matt. "Good catch. If he's 18, he shouldn't have been anywhere near that tavern. The law's the law. Did Gary say if they had anything to drink?"

"I asked him that question, and he said that they had a "couple of beers" each. My guess is they had a lot more than a couple because Gary told me he didn't get back home until almost 1:00 a.m. He asked me to not tell the owner that he told me they were served alcohol," Ed said, shaking his head. "Do I look like a guy who's not going to talk to the owner about this?"

They all laughed. "No, lieutenant, you do not. We're going to clean that up. You have my guarantee," Matt promised.

"You're a breath of fresh air, Chief," said Sonders. "I love ol' George, but I swear he's been asleep the past ten years."

Jay snorted.

"Did Gary say when he'd last seen Emily?"

"At the family dinner table. They all had an early dinner together before the three oldest kids split for their activities. That was the last time he saw her."

"Fred told me they'd all had dinner together, too. Jay?"

"Yep. Marjorie said the same thing. She told us that both parents and the four children had a "Friday night crab feed" at home to celebrate Susan's sixteenth birthday. The crab feed was a family tradition, and Marjorie thought it would be a fun way to mark them all being together."

"I can confirm that the dinner fare part of their story is true," said Fern. "I ran into the mayor at the Crab Shack yesterday. He was buying several big crabs."

"Why were you there?" Matt asked.

"Because it was Friday, and I wanted some clams for the weekend. Is there a law against that?"

"You are now an accomplice in the crustacean conspiracy," Jay smirked, trying to lighten the room's atmosphere.

"Just curious," Matt said.

"Did Gary mention if anything about Emily's behavior at dinner seemed odd or unusual?" Matt said, moving on.

"He said she was her normal, sweet self, and that they'd all had a good time together," Ed said. "Gary answered all my questions directly, and didn't seem to be hiding anything. I think he was telling the truth, and that he honestly wants to help us find the killer. We'll see if his alibi checks out."

Matt's cell phone rang, and, looking at his phone, he said to the group, "I have to take this—it's Dr. Ryder."

"Chief Horning? It's Bernice Ryder."

"Dr. Ryder."

They both would have been more comfortable with "Matt" and "Bernice", but, somehow, the gravity of the situation seemed to call for a degree of formality. Bernice jumped right in.

"Emily Bushnell died of a front-to-back, right-to-left stab wound to the abdomen, between 7:00 and 11:00 p.m. last night," she reported. "Her liver, small intestine, and descending aorta were perforated. Your murder weapon is likely a knife with approximately an eight-inch blade, serrated like a kitchen utility knife. Like I told you yesterday, hemoperitoneum, hemorrhage and a quick death."

"Was she sexually assaulted?" Matt asked.

"No. No sign of any molestation at all."

"You're sure?"

"Yes. I'm sure. There were slight bruises on both of her upper arms, and one two-inch scrape near her right ankle. Otherwise, the only other damage to the body are the bite wounds I showed you on her neck and upper arm, and two more I discovered on her chest. They are human bites."

"Good God," said Matt.

"Yes," replied Bernice. "If it helps, I don't think there was much of a struggle. I suspect she lost consciousness almost immediately. It was over quickly."

"Who would kill a little girl if they hadn't sexually assaulted her?" Matt said rhetorically. "It doesn't make sense."

"Maybe she saw something she wasn't supposed to see."

"Like what?"

"Hell if I know. You're the cop. Oops, that came out a little snippier than I intended. Sorry," Bernice apologized. "My mouth does that."

Matt ignored it. "Did she have any drugs or alcohol in her system?"

"No. Just her dinner. And, there was an absence of any significant natural disease."

"So, no drugs, no molestation, no motive to kill this little girl. But human bite marks on the body." Matt was frustrated. He heard a small moan escape from Fern.

"I'm sorry I can't give you more," Bernice said. "This one doesn't make any sense whatsoever."

"Do you send me a written report?" he asked.

"Yes. I've given you the highlights, and my report will include all the technical details. I'll write it up immediately, and get it to you today before our meeting. Do you have a city email address yet?"

Matt smiled through the wires. "Hell if I know. Probably not. I'll work on that. Thanks, Dr. Ryder. I really appreciate your diligence here."

Hitting the "end" button, Matt looked up at his colleagues who were all staring at him wide-eyed. "We've got nothing, friends. Nothing. And I'm scared."

CHAPTER 8

Saturday, 2:00 p.m.

Jay recounted that his statement from Marjorie differed slightly from what Gary told Ed Sonders, and both he and Fern had felt more uneasy about her as their interview progressed. Jay described to the chief and Ed how the interrogation of Marjorie had unfolded.

Marjorie told them she had spread newspaper over the dining room table, like when the children were little, and rounded up a couple of small hammers. She and the girls used the handle of a hefty flatware knife to crack the crabs, but the boys in her family liked to use a hammer, she shared with them.

It had been a rollicking affair, and they ate crab, along with her homemade tomato soup and bread until they were all stuffed. Ice cream for dessert, of course. Gary had regaled his family with tales from his first semester in Eugene at U of O. They laughed at his description of the "hippie culture", and thrilled to the newness of his dorm life in Bean Hall.

After dinner, they had all parted ways. Marjorie and Fred stayed at home, and watched a Netflix movie. Jay did the questioning, but Fern popped in occasionally in an attempt to keep Marjorie at ease, and was proud of herself for asking what they'd seen. Turns out, they'd watched an old "Poirot" mystery about an actor who had been killed on stage.

Jack had gone to the movies in town, like he'd said. Marjorie didn't know which movie he'd seen, and wrung her hands together at that admission. "I should know what movie my son is seeing, shouldn't I?" she said, biting her lip. "It was a last-minute decision by Jack, and he rushed out the door before I thought to ask him what he was going to see." She sounded a titch guarded to Fern.

"How did he get to the movie?" asked Jay. "He's not driving yet, is he? How old is Jack?"

"He's 14, and, no, not driving yet. He's dying to, though, and Fred is teaching him. They go to the Community Center parking lot after closing and Fred lets him drive around there. He's getting pretty good at it, Fred says. Don't tell," she said as an afterthought.

"The boy's got to learn somehow, doesn't he?" Jay smiled. He was genuine, but it couldn't hurt to get on Marjorie's good side until they got through this.

Susan had dropped Jack off at the town's only movie theater about 6:30 p.m. She was on her way to her friend Chloe's house for a slumber party which started then, and the theater—less than a mile from the Bushnell residence—was on Susan's route. Chloe was hosting the party to celebrate her BFF Susan's upcoming sixteenth birthday, and there were to be seven friends at the sleepover.

Jack was to catch a ride home with a buddy after the movie. Marjorie assumed that plan had hatched successfully, but she couldn't say for sure as both she and Fred had fallen asleep on the couch during their movie.

Because they had both been groggy, they didn't check on the kids' rooms. But Marjorie remembered that the light from Jack's room showed under his door, so she knew he was home but still up—he was always persnickety about turning out his light when he wasn't in his room. Fred had put Emily to bed right after Susan and Jack left, and Marjorie noticed that her light was off and the bedroom was quiet when she and Fred turned the corner at the end of the hallway and went upstairs to their bedroom.

They had quickly performed their bedtime hygiene, and gone right to sleep. They hadn't heard Gary come in.

"No reading?" Jay asked, keeping his eyes down on his notebook; it seemed like an awfully intimate question to ask.

"No. It had been a long week for Fred at work. Lots to catch up on after the holidays, meetings, budgets, that sort of thing. We were both happy to see this Friday night and we were tired. I barely remember turning out my light," she added.

"Was Fred asleep when you turned out your light?"

Marjorie looked down at her clasped hands. "I don't know if he was asleep or not, but he turned out his light first." Her voice was barely above a whisper.

"Did he kiss you goodnight?"

"Of course he did. He always does. Not that it's any of your business." Feisty words, but still a whisper. Downcast eyes.

"Did you wake up at any point during the night?" Jay continued.

"No."

"So you didn't hear or see anything suspicious?"

"No."

"Was the mayor still in bed when you woke up?"

"No. He was in the kitchen. He'd made coffee."

"Was he dressed?"

"Yes."

"So, he'd been up for a while?" Jay pried.

"I have no idea." Marjorie paused, turned her head, and looked up at her wallpaper with disdain, muttering something to herself about it needing to go—Jay didn't quite catch her entire remark. Fern followed Marjorie's gaze into the dining room to her left. She interrupted Jay to ask Marjorie what she was thinking about. Marjorie replied that she thought the Ralph Lauren Cottage Rose wallpaper in the dining room that had seemed so sophisticated when she bought it, now looked tired. She added that she had made a mental note to replace it soon.

Fern glanced quickly in Jay's direction to see if he was at all disturbed by this thought diversion. The astonished look on his face told Fern she wasn't alone.

"Where is my daughter, Jay?" Marjorie asked.

Jay lifted his eyes from his notepad, and met Marjorie's vague eyes. "She's in Buck Bay, with the Medical Examiner," he said as softly as he could. Fern was relieved that Jay had avoided using the word "morgue".

Out of respect, Jay waited a heartbeat or two before proceeding with a new tack. "What can you tell me about Gary's activities last night?"

"He left right after our crab feed, too. He was going to catch up with some of his town friends, and they were going to meet up at the Stirling Tavern and play pool."

They'd had a brief discussion at this point about the age of Gary and his friends, but Jay steered the conversation back to Gary's activities.

"Paula kicked them out about 1:00 a.m. Gary said, and he came directly home," Marjorie said.

"How did he seem this morning?"

"He was his usual self at breakfast. Nothing out of the ordinary. He slept in a little later, but I imagine that was because he was out late."

"What was Gary wearing when he left the house last night?"

"Why do you want to know that?" Marjorie asked, her tone sharp.

"Listen, Mrs. Bushnell, I've never done this before—questioned the family of a homicide victim," Jay admitted. "I'm sorry to have to ask you these personal questions, but I'm afraid I'll screw it up and make it harder for Chief Horning to figure it all out."

Fern leaned in, put her hands face down on the table between them, and spoke gently to Marjorie. "Jay doesn't want to not ask what might turn out to be an important question down the road in this investigation. We all want to do what we can to find out who did this terrible thing to your family. Can you understand and help us, Marjorie?"

"Well, I still don't see why Gary's clothes could make any possible difference. He was playing pool with his friends and wasn't involved at all."

"How do you know that for sure?" Jay asked. "You said yourself that you didn't hear him come in."

In an instant, Marjorie lunged forward and slapped her fist on the table, startling both Jay and Fern. "Because I know my son!" she shrieked. "He loves his little sister. Loves her to pieces. You are out of line, Jay." She leaned back in her chair and crossed her arms in front of her chest.

Oh, don't play mayor's wife with me, Jay said to himself. He felt so, so sorry for the woman, but he wasn't about to be hung out to dry. He looked over at Fern, and she calmly took a wayward lock of her shoulder-length auburn hair and placed it firmly behind her ear, as if Marjorie's outburst had physically ruffled her. To Jay, it signified that he should proceed.

"What was Gary wearing when he left the house last night, Mrs. Bushnell?" Jay repeated.

A period of quiet while Jay and Marjorie stared at each other. Mrs. Bushnell blinked first.

"He had on jeans, and a green Ducks sweatshirt."

Jay had a bizarre urge to say "Go Ducks!" He resisted it.

"Was he wearing a cap?"

"No, Gary has beautiful hair and rarely wears a cap."

"What kind of shoes did he have on?"

"I don't know—I didn't look at his shoes. Probably some kind of sneaker."

"What about Jack? What was he wearing when he went to the movies?" *Just answer the question,* Jay thought. *Let's don't go there again.*

"Also jeans. And, I think he had on a sweater and his Port Stirling lettermen's jacket. He got it for track, he's on the varsity team. He's a good distance runner, especially for his age. He's proud of that jacket and wears it everywhere. Jack always wears the same shoes, black and silver Nikes. They're almost worn out. I must remember to take him to buy some new ones."

"Was Fred with you the entire evening?"

The quick change of subject appeared to throw Marjorie for a split second.

"What do you mean?"

"What time did Fred get home from work, and was he within your sight all night?" Jay studied Marjorie's face carefully as he rephrased his question.

Marjorie didn't flinch, but she did look puzzled. She looked away from Jay and Fern, and briefly put her hand under her chin, while she gazed off into space, thinking. She coughed.

"The usual time, about 5:30 p.m. We had a cocktail while he helped me prepare the crab."

"Was that normal? The drink?"

"Yes, we always have a cocktail on Friday night to celebrate the end of the week. We try to not have liquor any other night of the week."

"Ah, a worthy goal," inserted Fern. One which Fern herself rarely met.

"Is it safe for me to assume that Fred was home all night?" asked Jay. "Through dinner and afterwards during your movie? Was he ever out of your sight?"

"My husband was with me the entire evening." Frigid.

"Was Emily at home when Fred arrived?" Jay continued.

"Yes, she was coloring at the kitchen table. She asked her father if she could have a martooni, too," Marjorie smiled weakly at the memory. The end of her nose got red, and her lower lip started to quiver.

"I know this is hard, Marjorie," said Fern, "but we need to get all the facts if we're going to find out who killed your daughter. You OK?"

Marjorie nodded.

"Did Emily act normal?" Jay continued. "Did anything seem out of place?"

"She was the same as always. A happy child." Tears were streaming down Marjorie's face, but they were silent tears. Fern, trying to hide it from Jay, discreetly wiped away a tear from her cheek, too.

"Tell me about your family dinner. What did you talk about?" Jay asked.

"You know, the usual—Fred's work, Jack and Susan's school day, whether or not they had homework for the weekend . . . that sort of thing. Gary told us he was being recruited to join a fraternity on campus, and asked our opinion. We explained to the kids about Greek life."

"How long is Gary to be home? When does he go back?"

"He came home a couple of days before Christmas, and I think his classes start up again on January 15. He'll probably go back to Eugene a day or two before that."

"I'll bet it's been nice having him home again."

"Yes," said Marjorie. "In some ways, it feels like he never left, but in other ways, it's completely different. It's like he's an adult now."

"What's been his mood since he's been here?"

"Fine. Pleasant. He was pretty tired when he got here. He sleeps a lot."

"Has he been any moodier than when he lived here full-time?" Jay pressed.

"I just told you. Gary is pleasant and happy." Again with the icy demeanor.

"Were there any sharp words at dinner?" Jay said, determined to keep going.

"No."

"Really? No sibling rivalries? Nobody in trouble with you or Fred?"

Marjorie thought for a minute. "Well, Susan accused Gary of acting like a big shot in front of her girlfriends yesterday at the Dairy Queen, but Gary laughed it off. Fred told Gary to quit embarrassing Susan in front of her friends, but it was more like "boys will be boys".

"Anything else?"

"Emily wanted Susan to help her crack a piece of crab, and Gary and Jack told her to quit being such a baby. She threw a piece of crab at Jack."

Jay stopped writing and paused with his pen in the air.

"What?" said an agitated Marjorie, noticing the change in Jay's posture. "She was just being playful with the boys. It was perfectly natural. Gary laughed and wagged his finger at her and said something in a fake stern voice like 'We don't throw food in this house, young lady.' Everyone laughed and it was over."

CHAPTER 9

Saturday, 3:45 p.m.

"Before we bring in the county crime team, there's something I want to be clear about," Matt said to Ed, Jay, and Fern, who were still gathered in the Chief's office. "Y'all don't know me very well yet, but I am a team player. However, because of the nature of this investigation and who is involved, and also because I'm new, we'll keep this headquartered with us. I want this town to feel confident they got the right guy when they hired me. I want to make that clear up front in the meeting. What I want from you guys is to tell me if I'll be running into any buzz saws on the crime team."

"Understood, Chief," Jay said, Ed and Fern nodding in agreement. "The only member to watch out for is David Dalrymple, the county DA. He knows his stuff, but he's a jerk."

Ed snickered. "Jay's correct, Dalrymple's the only guy who will give you grief."

"Is he the guy Dr. Ryder mentioned? Her boss?"

"Yep," Jay answered.

"And while, technically, I report to the CVA Program Director," added Fern, "I also have a dotted line to Dalrymple. I'm automatically assigned to any case he files."

"Do you think he's a jerk, too?" asked Matt.

Fern folded her hands primly in her lap, looked directly at Matt, and didn't say a word.

"OK, I get it," he smiled. "I'm writing 'Dalrymple, watch out'. Do you know all of the crime team folks, Jay?"

"I know them all, if it's the usual call out," Jay said. "It will be the Chief and his main investigator from the Buck Bay PD since it's a homicide. Buck Bay is the largest police force in the county, and they can provide lots of boots on the ground for us. I'd also expect the Chinook County Sheriff...all good guys. The Sheriff is Earl Johnson—been sheriff for years. And then Bernice if the situation calls for her."

Matt scribbled names.

"I also called the investigator from Twisty River PD since we're dealing with a homicide," added Sonders. "Twisty River is a woman, Patty Perkins, and she's sharp, really a first-rate investigator. The best we've got in the county, in my opinion."

"Are they all good to work with in your experience?" Matt asked all three colleagues.

Jay leaned back in his chair. "I would say 'yes'," he answered. "Bernice is tough and doesn't suffer fools gladly."

"I noticed that already," Matt said with a wry smile. "Tell me more about her boss."

"Dalrymple is smart and driven," Jay answered. "More so than most people around these parts. He worries more about the PR than the rest of us. He'll be apoplectic when he learns it's the mayor's daughter."

"Yeah, I talked to Dalrymple before I met you at the Bushnell residence, and the victim definitely got his attention," Sonders said. "He'll be here."

"What's his backstory?" asked Matt.

"He's originally from Los Angeles," replied Sonders. "L.A, for

God's sake," he concluded, shaking his head, as if that was all Matt needed to know.

Jay fidgeted in his chair and added, "You might want to be on the lookout, sir, for Dalrymple to make a move to take over. He tried to assert himself in a case we had with a tourist who went missing at the golf course last summer. The guy was found down in Silver River the next day recovering from a toot. Dalrymple insisted on running the show for those 24 hours."

"Even though it was a Port Stirling PD case?" Matt asked, dumbfounded.

"Yep. But it was high-profile—a major league baseball player—and Dalrymple wanted the entire country to know he was in charge."

"Just what I need," Matt muttered. "Thanks for the warning. Don't worry, guys, I'm not about to let a politician take over."

"Patty is amazing," said Fern. "In my experience, she's dogged, and thinks of details no one else does. She's going to take the death of this child hard, and will want to help us."

"Agreed," said Sonders. "Turn Patty loose and let her do her thing."

"What about the county sheriff?" asked Matt.

"Earl Johnson is deliberate and a hard worker," said Jay. "Between us, I don't think much of his department on the whole, but Earl's a good guy."

"Earl is Dalrymple's right-hand man on the South Coast Inter-agency Narcotics Team and he's great on drug dealers. He hates the bad guys," added Sonders. "Between him and me, we know where all the vermin are."

"Good to know," said Matt. "If our killer turns out to not be one of the family, we'll have to go vermin-huntin.'"

"Speaking of the family again," Fern said with a shaky half-smile, "there were two things that seemed odd to me. The first was Jack's wanting breakfast and wolfing it down. My experience is that this kind of trauma causes a general lack of appetite. But he's a teenager, so . . . ."

"Do you think Jack fully understands the situation?"

"Yes, I believe he does. Like Ed said, he struck me as a smart kid."

"You mentioned two things. What's the other?"

Fern shot a quick look at Jay. "Well, I thought parts of Marjorie's response to Jay's questioning were downright bizarre."

"How so?" Matt noticed that Jay nodded his agreement with Fern.

"Well, she veered from deeply upset and agitated—which would be a normal response—to snappish, followed by haughty, as if she was too good to be questioned by Jay in this manner. She also made some vague, off-hand remark about her wallpaper at one point—under her breath, as if to herself - which I thought to be curious under the circumstances."

"Yeah, that was totally weird," agreed Jay.

"So," Fern continued, "her daughter is dead, and Marjorie didn't even ask where Emily's body was until late in Jay's interview. I would have thought that was the first thing she would want to know. When told where Emily was, I expected a series of questions about when she could see her, what happens next, and so on. But Marjorie just said "Oh", followed by an uncomfortably long pause while Jay and I waited for her follow-up questions that never came."

"Did she seem in control of her faculties?"

"Yes, it didn't seem that she was demented in any way. Do you agree Jay?"

"Her behavior was unsettling to me," Jay said. "But she's not a psycho, I don't think. After all, we know the mayor and his family, and it's hard to imagine any of them killing Emily."

"Jay's right. It doesn't seem possible," agreed Fern.

"You're both telling me that Marjorie Bushnell acted a little deranged today," said Matt, his voice calm and even. "Do not let your personal knowledge of the family hold you back from what your instincts are telling you. Do you understand what I'm getting at?"

Both Jay and Fern stared at Matt.

"Whether you want to believe it or not, our killer is likely to be one of the family. You must throw out any preconceived notions about what you think you know about the Bushnells. Today is the first day of your relationship with them, and you need to pay attention to your gut feelings. Especially you, Fern, because you're trained in psychological make-up."

"I understand what you're saying, Chief," said Fern. "It's just difficult to get my head around a mother killing her own child. A mother who's married to our mayor."

"Mothers kill their children, Fern," said Ed Sonders. "It's happened here in Oregon more than you want to believe. Anyone remember Diane Downs?"

"Oh, Jesus, that was in Oregon, wasn't it?" said Matt.

"Yes," said Ed. "Happened in Springfield. My wife was an ER nurse at the hospital when she came in with her shot children. Said Downs was strange from the get-go."

"Still, we know Marjorie," argued Jay. "It can't happen here."

"It can happen anywhere, Jay," said Matt softly. "We have to keep open minds and follow the evidence. Both of you need to get rid of the tapes in your head, and listen to Lieutenant Sonders—he's right."

"My money's on mom," Ed said, his face deliberately impassive.

Fern reached out and lightly slugged him in the arm.

Matt pushed back his chair and stood up. "Let's do this meeting, kids."

* * *

Saturday, 4:00 p.m.

Even though it was only 4:00 p.m. on this gloomy January day, dusk was already approaching by the time Bill Abbott let in the team at the side door.

Matt had found the room earlier today, and knew it would work as their command center throughout the duration of this case. The large erasable white board, along with the big mahogany conference table and ten faux-leather chairs would serve nicely as his War Room. One rather sad, faded oil painting of the Twisty River lighthouse decorated one wall, like it was trying to make up for the lack of a view in this windowless, institutional room.

Standing to greet them, Matt said "I'm Matt Horning, Port Stirling Police Chief. I'm new," he added in what he hoped was a droll, self-effacing tone.

"Did you bring this trouble with you from Texas?" said Chinook County District Attorney David Dalrymple, frowning.

OK, here we go, thought Matt, giving the DA a hard look. He ignored the rude question, and nodded to the other colleagues.

"Welcome, Chief," the others chimed in, as they all took seats.

"Thank you. And thank y'all for coming on such short notice. This briefing will be unpleasant—I have to warn you," Matt started. "We're here because the body of four-year-old Emily Bushnell was found in a rock tunnel on the beach this morning. Emily is Port Stirling's mayor's daughter—Fred Bushnell's little girl. She died of multiple stab wounds on her torso, and we're dealing with a homicide by an unknown person or persons."

"Have you even been sworn in yet?" interrupted Dalrymple, leaning forward theatrically with his hands clasped on the table in front of him. The DA looked to be in his early 50s, fit, with seriously thinning blondish hair. He was sharply dressed, and a slight fragrance emanated from him. There was a hint of scorn in his question, and he had what Matt would call a sneer on his face.

"Yes, sir, I have," Matt replied matter-of-factly. "Bill Abbott gave me the oath this morning on the beach. Officer Finley here and Lydia Campbell, the lady who found the child's body, were the witnesses. I'm legal."

"Isn't that a bit non-traditional?" Dalrymple said. "Shouldn't there be a public ceremony so we all know you're officially on the job? It feels a little too 'fly-by-the-seat-of-your-pants' for my liking."

"Mr. Abbott and I felt that, under the circumstances, there wasn't time to do it the traditional way, plus, it wouldn't be appropriate. I'm official, and this investigation has begun under my auspices." Matt stared him down.

"So, Officer Finley, Lieutenant Sonders and I will brief you on what happened this morning after Emily's body was found," Matt continued on as if there had been no interruption. "I think you all know Jay Finley and Ed Sonders. This"—he indicated Fern on his immediate left with an upturned hand—"is Fern Byrne. For those of you who haven't worked with Fern previously, she works for Chinook County as a crime victims' advocate, and she was on the scene with us this morning to help with the mayor and his family. I was grateful to have her on site to comfort the family, and Fern's insight as a psychologist will help our team with profiling suspects as we move forward." Matt smiled at Fern, and she looked nervously around the room, trying her best to smile. To those who knew her, it was obvious that Fern was agitated.

"A case of this magnitude should be handled by the County," DA Dalrymple cut in. "Especially since you've just arrived in town,

Chief. I'm sure you have a strong resumé from your work in Texas, but those of us around this table know the area well, and you can't be expected to be up to speed yet. It's too much to ask of you, no matter how well-intentioned you are."

Matt could tell by the smug look on Dalrymple's face that the DA knew what had happened to him in Texas. Dead girl in Texas. Dead girl in Oregon. Maybe he did bring trouble with him.

"I got this job because of my experience as a lead investigator with dozens of crime team operations, David," Matt said, using the DA's first name on purpose. "I appreciate your concern, but with the help of Dr. Ryder", (Matt inclined his head in Bernice's direction, across the table from her boss), "Jay, Ed, and Fern, we got through the initial investigative phase just fine this morning. This crime occurred in Port Stirling, and the Port Stirling PD will lead the investigation. We'll be OK if I can count on all of you for your help as needed."

The silence in the room was broken by Twisty River lead investigator Patty Perkins who said, "Alright then, let's go. How can we help you, Chief?" She clicked her ball-point pen, and looked in the Chief's direction.

CHAPTER 10

Matt shared the facts of the case with the county team, admonishing them upfront that the details were not to leave the room, and should only be shared on an "as needed" basis with other investigators they would bring in to assist.

"I know that tunnel," said the DA, when Matt asked for their questions and comments.

"We all know that tunnel," said Patty Perkins. She sounded brusque and a little dismissive of Dalrymple's remark. "Is there any physical evidence?" she asked Matt.

Shaking his head, Matt answered, "No, none so far. Forensics is looking at fingerprints in Emily's bedroom. There was blood at the crime scene, but it all belongs to Emily. No murder weapon. There was a high tide at 4:10am, and it looked like the tug of it had shifted Emily's body some."

"It was a modest high tide," added Jay. "Not enough to carry her out to sea, but high enough to move her around, and destroy footprints or any other evidence." He looked morose.

"How long had she been there?" Dalrymple asked.

"Dr. Ryder?" Matt said, looking at the ME.

"Based on the results of my autopsy," Bernice said, looking at her boss Dalrymple, "I think she was killed sometime between 7:00 and 11:00 p.m. last night. Rigor mortis was almost complete when I first viewed the body this morning—she was stiff. The Rigid Stage takes eight-to-twelve hours. The lividity—gravity-pulled blood—indicates that she was killed where she was found. The impressions against her skin displayed as indentations from the surface of the tunnel. The details of how she died are in my report."

Pin-drop silence around the table.

"And no one in her family noticed she was missing all night?" Dalrymple asked, incredulous.

"Based on our interviews with the family earlier, they put Emily to bed and thought she was there all night," Matt said. "Apparently, neither parent checked on her before they retired for the night."

"Unbelievable," said Sonders shaking his head. "Four years old and you don't at least poke your head in the door?"

"Yeah," Matt said. His remark hung in the air.

"Why didn't you call out the crime team before you interrogated the family?" demanded Dalrymple.

"Fair question," Matt responded. "We felt it was crucial to secure both crime scenes—on the beach and Emily's bedroom—immediately, which we did. And, in my experience, it's important to interrogate the family right away, which we also did. We needed to arrange for the mayor and his wife to formally identify the body. Jay knew to call in Dr. Ryder and get her on the scene."

Dalrymple glared at Bernice. "You should have called me at once."

"That was my fault, David," Matt said. "I asked Dr. Ryder to not notify anyone else until I'd had a chance to inform the family." He paused. "I'm not sure it would have gone down any differently if we'd had this meeting first."

"Our protocol is to call out the crime team instantaneously," Dalrymple said pompously, drawing himself up straight in his chair. "And, we're dealing with a prominent family."

"Well, I'm sorry if I've offended any of you," Matt said, looking around the table. "But I didn't want the family to get a head start on getting their stories straight while we waited around to assemble y'all."

"Good Lord, Chief, we're talking about the mayor of Port Stirling," said Earl Johnson. It was the first time the county sheriff had spoken.

"No one knows that better than I do," Matt said. "He's my boss's boss. Believe me, Sheriff, I understand the political ramifications."

"You can't believe that Fred is a suspect," said the DA.

"Of course he's a suspect," huffed Patty. "And so is Fred's entire family. The chief is right. Unless the girl was sexually assaulted, or witnessed something she wasn't meant to see, odds are it was a family member who did her in."

Patty turned to Dr. Ryder. "Was the poor little thing assaulted, Bernice?"

"No. And there wasn't much sign of even a struggle. Here's my autopsy report." Bernice distributed her report to all team members. "My conclusion is that someone—probably someone she knew and trusted because there was no sign of a struggle—stabbed her before she barely knew what was happening. You will also note there were bite marks on Emily's body."

"Human or animal?" asked Dalrymple of his ME.

"Human, I'm afraid," said Bernice. "I called in Lawrence Bush to have a look, and he confirmed. Dr. Bush is the county's dental expert," she clarified for Matt.

"Good God," said Patty. She brought her hand up to cover her mouth as she skimmed Bernice's report.

"What the hell are we dealing with?" said a stricken Sheriff Johnson.

"Was Emily fully dressed?" asked Dalrymple. It was clear that the DA was determined to remain calm, but he, too, had paled while glancing at the report.

"Yes," Jay said. "When her body was found, she was wearing jeans, a white tee shirt, a pink sweater, white socks, and one pink shoe on her left foot—we don't know what happened to her right shoe. It wasn't on the beach, and it wasn't in her room. Oh, and she also had a barrette in her hair. Her mother told Fern that Emily always insisted on wearing the barrette, even to bed."

Matt struck a business tone. "Once you've all had a chance to read Bernice's autopsy report, and our statements from the family, we'll need to divvy up some investigative duties. My thinking is that Sheriff Johnson and Lieutenant Sonders should begin checking out their sources, and see what they can learn about any incidents or arrests in the past week around the county. Any new bad guys around? Buck Bay PD, could you guys begin checking area hotels and motels for any strangers in town that might be of interest. Fern tells me that because it's January, there shouldn't be that many tourists in town."

"She's correct, it's a slow time," interrupted Dalrymple. "Thank goodness for that, at least. But before you go any further, Chief, I insist that we reconsider running this investigation out of my office at the county. It's nothing personal, and you seem to have a good handle on how to proceed, but we have more resources at the county level than Port Stirling has. It's more practical."

"Maybe," Matt agreed. "But, in my view, we have all the resources we need sitting around this table. I'm confident I'll have the help I need to find this killer. This is our town, this is my mayor, and this office will coordinate the investigation. We'll meet in this room on an as-needed basis," Matt said, his voice firm and professional. "If any of you have any pressing responsibilities elsewhere that will limit your participation on Emily's case, please let me know now. Otherwise, I'll count on you and the agencies you represent to assist."

They went around the table and everyone indicated "we're in". Beaten, at least for the moment, Dalrymple nodded in agreement.

"OK," Matt continued. "Sheriff, if your guys could work with the Buck Bay PD and canvas the county's transient lodgings for suspicious strangers, I'll have my department check out Port Stirling accommodations, out-of-state license plates and so on. Ed, Jay, and I will stay on the family and related issues—checking their alibis, their whereabouts and activities in the days leading up to the murder, etc. Fern, once we learn where we are on the family's alibis, I'd like a psychological profile on any of the five who can't be definitely ruled out. That's probably going to be everyone but Susan, who either was or wasn't at that slumber party all night."

"OK," Fern agreed.

"Patty, I've heard you're an excellent investigator," Matt said to the Twisty River representative.

"True," she deadpanned.

"OK, then. How 'bout you interrogate Lydia Campbell and see what you can learn about her neighbors. Anyone on Ocean Bend Road who may have seen or heard something last night."

"In the interest of full disclosure," Patty said, her voice now serious, "Lydia is a friend of mine. But she is an observant, intelligent woman, and knowing her as I do, she will do anything she can to help us get to the bottom of this."

"I don't have a problem with that," said Matt. "As long as you stay objective and realize that the person who found the body is always a suspect until ruled out."

"Absolutely, Chief," Patty said. She asked Jay, "Did Lydia indicate whether or not she'd seen anything last night?"

Jay related to Patty and the team Lydia's story about seeing the light on the beach and the timing.

"So, if Lydia saw something last night, there's a good chance that someone else on Ocean Bend Road may have, too," said Patty. "I'll start with her, and then go door-to-door and see if the chickens lay any eggs for me."

Matt smiled at her. "Thank you, ma'am. I'll find out if anyone locally had any grudges against the mayor or his family for any reason. If anything turns up there beyond what my department can handle, I'll ask the county and the state police to assist—sound good, Ed and Earl? Mr. Dalrymple, can you stand by to help us with any search warrants we may need?" Matt said. "I want to proceed with one for the Bushnell residence now, and then we'll wait and see what the rest of you turn up."

"Don't you think you should check in with Bill Abbott first and see if he agrees to a Bushnell warrant?" said the DA. "Your boss might not concur with you that that's a good idea."

"I have Bill's full support to run this investigation as I see fit," Matt said. "You can't possibly be suggesting that we don't need to search the family home, David. Get the warrant, please."

"I hope to hell you know what you're doing," said the DA. "I'll call Judge Hedges when I get back to Twisty River."

"Is he local?" asked Matt.

"She," said Dalrymple, impatiently shuffling the reports in front of him, and stuffing them in his briefcase.

"Oops, sorry," said Matt. "I guess that's my Texas law and order background showing."

"You're not in Texas any more, Chief Horning. Which is why I still feel that this homicide investigation should be handled out of my office." Dalrymple's voice was as icy as they come.

"Not gonna happen, David," Matt said.

"Are you two finished comparing dick size?" asked Patty sweetly, as she looked between Dalrymple and Horning, and pushed her chair back. "Can we get started on this investigation?"

Matt stood up, too. "OK people, that's it for now. We will stay in close communication. If anything turns up, or you have any doubts or questions, call me immediately. Here's my mobile number. When word gets out, everyone's likely to be scared to death, and we need to wrap this up quickly."

Before they dispersed to put the wheels in motion, the ten people in the War Room agreed to meet again Sunday at 4:00 p.m., and every day next week, if necessary, at that same appointed hour. Matt hoped no further meetings would be necessary.

He had passed his first test. But Matt had the distinct feeling that the next one would be along shortly.

* * *

Saturday, 9:55 a.m.

Janey Crawley, the checker at Goodie's Market who sold Matt his coffee, immediately phoned her friend Sara after Matt paid her, and left through the store's automatic double doors, a coffee in each hand.

"Either there is a lone tourist who only now arrived, or I just met the new police chief," Janey reported. "Word is he's single, ya know?"

"What's he look like?" Sara asked her childhood friend.

"I would have to say 'awesome sauce'. Oh, and kinda like a cop."

"Are you telling me we replaced that old fart Simonson with a cute guy?"

"Yeah. He's not that young, probably about our age," said the 37-year-old checker. "He's a sweetheart. Called me 'ma'am' when I asked him if he wanted his receipt. Has a sweet little Texas twang—that's how I knew it was him."

"Hello! It's about time this poor old town got something fresh other than those douchebag golfers."

"Wait'll you see him. He looks like a movie star. Or some hot athlete. No shit. Hair that kinda curls around his ears, baby blues that look right through you, dimple in his chin, and he was rockin' a suit."

"On Saturday morning? In Port Stirling? Kinda weird, don't you think? But he sounds yummy. Where do you think he's livin'?"

"Well, I didn't want to appear too, ya know, forward, so I, like, didn't ask him. The two best rentals right now are the old Tatlock farm house out on the Twisty River road, and that Ocean Bend house that belongs to that teacher who moved to California. My bet is he wouldn't want to be stuck out in the boonies, so he's probably got the Ocean Bend house."

"That little yellow one right on the bluff?" Sara asked.

"Yeah. Plus, if he's from Texas, he probably ain't never seen the ocean," Janey surmised, pushing her slightly greasy bangs back off her forehead. "Oops, customer. Gotta go."

CHAPTER 11

Saturday, 5:30 p.m.

Once he'd received the written statements of the family members from Ed and Jay, Matt collated them with the write-up of his interrogation of Fred Bushnell, and made copies for the six-member Port Stirling police department, who had all been called in to work by their new chief.

One of his off-duty patrol officers told Matt that he'd just had a beer, and wondered if he should drive to City Hall.

"One beer?" asked Matt.

"Yes, sir."

"How far away do you live?"

"Less than a mile."

"Risk it. This is important." Matt thought Officer Ralph Newman didn't seem very excited about coming to work on Saturday evening. *Tough.*

Matt also made a call to brief Bill Abbott on the crime team meeting, and the city manager asked his new police chief if he should come back to City Hall and make the introductions to the rest of his department. Matt told him it wasn't necessary, and that he could handle it with an assist from Jay.

The small assembled group was seated and quiet in anticipation of what had precipitated this sudden turn of events. Jay did the honors, introducing a somewhat tense Matt to his staff, one by one: Patrol

Sergeant Walt Perret, Patrol Officers Doug Lewis, Rudy Huggins, and Ralph Newman. Only Sergeant Perret had on a department uniform; the officers were dressed in jeans, as only Jay was officially on-duty today. Officer Newman was wearing a Philadelphia Eagles sweatshirt, which offended Matt's Cowboys loyalty. *A lazy police officer who likes the Eagles?* Matt would have to set him straight in more ways than one.

"And this is the department's records clerk, Sylvia Hofstetter," Jay continued, motioning to a silver-haired, petite woman dressed all in purple who was 70 if she was a day. Her hairdo would have been right at home in Dallas, and was bigger than her slim body.

"How do you do, ma'am?" Matt said, shaking her hand, as he had with the officers in turn.

"I'm doing fine now that you're here, honey!" Sylvia said loudly as she pumped Matt's hand in both of hers. Everyone laughed, and it broke the tension in the room. Matt could have kissed her.

Matt filled them in on the particulars of the case. He asked for their confidentiality, and only shared the bare bones of the homicide. At this stage, until he knew his staff better, the fewer investigators who knew all the grim details, the better.

He instructed Sergeant Perret and the officers to do a license plate search on every car parked along Ocean Bend Road, both residential and commercial establishments, and to gather all the hotel/motel registrations for last night. The chief requested that they start immediately, and no one objected, at least to his face.

"Do you think the mayor and his family are involved?" asked Walt. Elephant in the room.

"We don't know yet," Matt answered honestly. "We took initial statements from the family and Lydia Campbell, who found the body. All of the Bushnells are accounted for on Friday night, but we haven't started checking their alibis. That will happen soon. Please tell your families that there has been a violent crime, and that you have to put in a few hours tonight," Matt commanded. "Don't mention the victim at this point—word will get out soon enough, but I want to keep it within our circle as long as I can. Understood?"

Everyone nodded.

"For your ears only, the family disavowed any knowledge of the crime, and they all say they thought Emily was in her bedroom all night."

"Did you call Patty Perkins from over in Twisty River?" asked Perret. "She's really good at shit like this."

"Language, Walt," admonished Sylvia.

"Yes. Patty was in the county team meeting, and she's going to help us investigate. I've asked her to start by interviewing Lydia Campbell in more depth than we did on the beach, and then to poke around at other Ocean Bend Road neighbors. Ed Sonders from the Oregon State Police is also helping us and will be one of the key guys, along with Jay here and Fern Byrne who's helping us with the family."

Sergeant Perret looked relieved. In fact, they all looked relieved. "That sounds good, boss," said Perret. "We'll do whatever you tell us to, but none of us ain't never investigated a homicide before."

"I have," said Sylvia gruffly. "We had one back in '66, but it was a drug kill, not a poor child's murder. This will be quite different, I presume." She looked expectantly at Matt.

"It will be hard," Matt confirmed. "I'm not going to sugarcoat it. Any time a young person goes before their time, it's tough." He paused and took a breath. "Let's see what y'all can gather about who was in the near vicinity last night. I don't have a department phone yet, but here's my personal mobile number. Do not hesitate to call me for any reason."

"I'll get you a real phone, dearie," said Sylvia, and she traipsed out of the squad room and headed down the hallway, trailing purple fabric behind her.

* * *

Saturday, 5:45 p.m.

Twisty River PD investigator Patty Perkins used the lions-head door knocker on Lydia Campbell's front door. Looking through the door's glass panel to the ocean beyond, Patty noted that off to the southwest, darker, more ominous clouds were forming as the last wisp of daylight disappeared below the horizon. The air had turned blustery.

Although the beach at Port Stirling was certainly dramatic and had its appeal to the senses, Patty preferred the more pastoral Twisty River valley. Her home on five acres just across the Twisty River Bridge from town—and twenty miles upstream from the Pacific Ocean - provided a tranquil respite from the rigors of her job. Warmer and less windy than Port Stirling, Twisty River felt more harmonious to Patty. She had lived there for over 30 years, the past six alone since her husband, Pat, died of a heart attack while trout fishing on the Hornbuckle River.

Patty and Pat had been happy throughout their marriage, but Patty didn't mind being alone. She was good with solitude, and while she missed Pat, she was satisfied with her life now. She grew vegetables and flowers on her acreage, listened to classical music, and read every night. She had great friends in the area, and took advantage of her paid time off to travel the world. In the summer, she hiked through-out the county and swam in the river. In the winter, she watched that same river and prayed it wouldn't flood over her backyard patio. Most winters, God did not listen to her prayers.

Patty's main passion was her job. She disliked "the villains", and was tenacious in pursuit. Chief Kramer had long ago designated Patty as his department's representative on the county's crime team. More often than not it was Patty's legwork and smarts that lead to an arrest. Yeah, she could be a bit prickly, but it was a small price to pay for her job performance.

Lydia opened her front door with a puny "Come on in, Patty", as she stepped aside to allow the detective to enter. Lydia and Patty played in the same bridge league, and had known each other for several years. Familiarity could only help in these circumstances; Patty knew that Lydia would try as hard as she could to recall anything that might help her friend and the crime team.

Mr. Darcy greeted their guest with enthusiasm, jumping up on Patty's leg in the hopes of a petting. "Oh, for heaven's sake, Mr. Darcy," said Lydia with exasperation. "You know better than to jump up. Go to your bed this instant." She pointed at his bed near the fireplace, and he trotted off obediently.

"It's been an unsettling day for both of us," Lydia added. "Have a seat." Patty went for one of the beige rockers near the window. Lydia took its mate across from Patty. "Can I get you anything?" Lydia asked. "Coffee?"

"A cup of coffee would be great," Patty smiled. She took out her tatty old notebook and fished in her bag for a pen while Lydia produced two coffees.

"This is a most unpleasant experience for you," Patty said. "How are you holding up under the strain?" Patty thought the older woman looked pale and drawn. Lydia was usually rosy-cheeked and full of energy, especially for a woman well into her 70's.

"I'm doing OK, I guess—better this afternoon," Lydia said. "I won't lie to you, Patty, this morning was difficult. I keep seeing that poor girl's sad little face. I've been cold all day, just can't get warm, and every time I try to drift off in a little nap, that damnable wind rattles the house and keeps me awake. Not a fun day."

"I keep telling you to sell this pile of bricks and move to Twisty River," Patty said warmly. "I don't hear a sound in my house. Maybe some occasional frogs croaking."

"And leave this view?" Lydia motioned toward the window. Her view up and down the beach was spectacular, Patty had to admit.

"Your new police chief, Matt Horning, sent me to ask you a few questions about the case. Do you feel up to it?"

"Of course. I'm glad he sent you, although he seems like a nice young man."

"He's a good guy, I think," Patty agreed. "Knows his stuff. Smart as a whip."

"Certainly easy on the eyes, isn't he?" Lydia smiled.

"I suppose he is, now that you mention it," Patty smiled back. "I was so busy being impressed and relieved by his professional demeanor in our meeting this afternoon, I'm not sure I even noticed his looks. He really took charge. It was good to see. You should have seen him stand his ground with our gasbag district attorney. Shut Dalrymple right up."

"I hear that's not always easy to do," said Lydia.

"Don't you know it . . . but you didn't hear that from me. I can't count the times I've been in a room with him and bit my tongue to keep from saying 'Put a sock in it.'"

Lydia laughed at her friend's colorful language. "I've never said 'Put a sock in it' to another human being in my lifetime, but I'm not at all surprised that you might have."

"We need to talk about last night," Patty changed the subject. "Were you home?"

"Yes, I was here. Cooking and watching TV."

"Did you go out at all?"

"Only to walk Mr. Darcy."

"What time was that?"

"About 5:00 p.m."

"Where did you go?"

"Well, it was a foggy, drizzly afternoon - it was already almost dark by then, if I recall—and neither he nor I were interested in a lengthy walk on the beach, so we walked down the road for a bit. He did his business, and we turned around and hustled back inside."

"Were you home the rest of the evening?"

"Yes."

"Can anyone attest to that?" Patty had to ask.

"Do you mean can anyone confirm that I was home? I'm not sure what you mean." Lydia did indeed look confused.

"Did anyone stop by? Or phone? Did you talk to anyone at all Friday night?"

"Well . . ." Lydia paused to think. "No, I didn't talk to a single soul. I cooked a stew, watched TV, and worked on my jigsaw puzzle." She indicated the card table set up behind Patty's chair at the other end of the big window. "Do I have a problem?" Lydia asked, staring directly into Patty's eyes.

"No, of course not," Patty assured her. "I just have to get all the facts down. It's routine. This is important, however: Did you see anything on the beach Friday afternoon or last night? What can you remember about any activity, especially anything unusual or out of the ordinary?"

"It got dark early, as I mentioned. I hate this time of year when the days are so short. Depressing," Lydia said.

"I hear you", Patty sympathized. "I go to work in the dark and come home in the dark."

"Before Mr. Darcy and I went for our potty walk, and before it got completely dark, there were a couple of people down on the beach, but they didn't linger long. The fog was coming in, and it was damp and disagreeable."

"Did you recognize anyone?"

"I think one couple was Fritz and Heidi Ericksen, who live down past the Pacific View Motel. They are die-hards and don't seem to let the bad weather deter them. I'm not 100 percent positive it was them, though, as they were wearing jackets with hoods pulled up over their heads. But they often walk the beach in the late afternoon, and the size and shape looked like them."

"Anyone else?"

Lydia thought. "There was one man walking alone shortly after I saw the Ericksens. He walked at a fast clip, and disappeared down around the promontory."

"Do you know who it was?" Patty asked.

"No. Never seen him before."

"What was he wearing?"

"Kind of a black tracksuit thing, or it might have been one of those waterproof golf outfits—pants and a windbreaker."

"Short? Tall? Skinny? Fat?"

"I would say he was on the tall side, and slender. Dark hair—it looked black from here."

"He wasn't wearing a cap or hat?" Patty asked.

"No, of that I'm sure because I remember thinking 'you idiot to go bare-headed in this soggy weather'. He didn't look prepared for a January afternoon on Port Stirling beach."

"Do you remember seeing anyone else?"

"Not before it got dark," Lydia answered. "But there was one strange thing later on; it must have been between 7:00 and 8:00 p.m. because The News Hour was on. Probably closer to 8:00 p.m. because I was ready to eat. Anyway, I saw a light flickering on the beach. You see that sometimes in the summer when the kids are partying after dark, but I rarely see anyone down there after dark in the winter."

"What kind of light was it?" Patty asked, sitting up straighter and clutching her notebook.

"I'd say it was a flashlight of some sort. I first saw it flickering in close to land a couple of times. Then I went into the kitchen to get a glass of wine, and when I came back to my window, I saw it flicker again, this time closer to the shoreline." Lydia paused and gazed out to the sea. "I think it was close to the tunnel."

"How long did it last?"

"Only a few moments, and then it went dark and I didn't see it again."

"Did you keep looking out the window?" Patty asked.

"No, I can't really say that I did. As I mentioned, I was working on and off in the kitchen, and not really paying attention to the window. I was watching TV mostly."

"Could you see who was holding the light?"

"Heavens no. It was black as molasses, and foggy as all get out."

"What did you think when you saw the light?"

"I thought 'Another idiot'. Who would be down on the beach on a dark, foggy night like this one?" Lydia said. "And then, I thought 'I hope it's not crazy old Ted Frolick' . . ." Lydia's voice trailed off and she sat mutely with her hands clasped on her lap.

"Who is Ted Frolick?" Patty asked gently, so as not to agitate her friend.

Lydia didn't immediately answer the question. Patty didn't press her, but held her gaze until Lydia finally spoke.

"Ted might be a little bit off his rocker, but he's just old and has lived alone too long. Probably will happen to me, too," Lydia attempted a smile. "There's no way Ted could ever do something like this. He's very sweet. He just gets a little confused at times."

"What made you think of him first when you saw the light?" asked Patty.

"Well, I guess because I've seen him down on the beach in nasty weather before. And because he walks around here a lot."

"Where does he live?" Patty asked as she jotted down notes.

"He lives next door to Fauntleroy Restaurant's parking lot. His property abuts the lot."

"You mean that shack with all the driftwood and glass floats out in front of it?"

"That's his house, yes," Lydia replied. Her left thumb was busy working her old wedding ring, twirling it around her finger. Patty pressed forward.

"How long has he lived here?"

"I don't know. Probably forever. I really don't know him well; we stop and chat when we see each other out walking. He loves to pet Mr. Darcy, and Mr. Darcy loves him, too. I take him some leftovers occasionally, an extra loaf of my banana bread—that kind of thing. I like to give him something hot to eat once in a while."

"That's nice of you, dear," Patty said.

"He can be a little muddled at times, and I worry that he doesn't always remember to eat a balanced diet. And, he often brings me flowers from his back garden. You can't see it from the road, but he's got a beautiful garden behind his house." Lydia nodded to a vase of rose hips and dried hydrangeas on her kitchen table. "He brought me those last week."

"Very nice."

"Everyone around here knows Ted, and we all watch out for him. He's a lovely man, and it's the neighborly thing to do. It's not possible that he could have hurt that child. Just not possible," Lydia said shaking her head.

"I'll have to talk to him—you know that, don't you?"

"I suppose that you will do what you will do," Lydia replied.

The two women sat staring at each other for a moment.

"Let's talk about this morning," said Patty.

"No doubt you've seen plenty of dead bodies," Lydia said, staring out to the ocean, "but I've only seen two. My Harold the morning he didn't wake up, and this poor little girl. Emily. I remember thinking that I hoped she wasn't cold, laying there in the wet sand."

"Dr. Ryder said it happened fast, and that she wouldn't have felt much," Patty told her.

"Still. She would have known that whoever it was wanted her dead. That's got to be a bad last thought no matter how old you are."

"How did you discover her body?"

"I've told all this to the police," Lydia said, but there was no sharpness in her voice, only resignation.

"I know, honey. But we need to go over it again to make sure you haven't forgotten something that might be important. OK?"

"Mr. Darcy and I went down our access steps to the beach right after it got light out. We turned south and started walking close to the shoreline in the packed sand."

"Do you always go south?" Patty asked.

"No, it depends on which way the wind is blowing. I like to start out with it blowing in my face so we have it at our back on the way home when we get tired. Yesterday morning the wind was coming off the ocean from the southwest, so we headed into it first. The tide was out and it wasn't necessary to use the tunnel to get through, so I started to head around it. But Mr. Darcy pulled on his leash and wanted to go in the tunnel. I let him, and he went straight up to the child, and that's how we found her."

Patty reached across the small table between their rockers and took Lydia's hands in her own. Mr. Darcy, asleep in front of the fireplace in his doggy bed, raised his head at the sound of his name.

"It was so awful," Lydia said. Her eyes were moist and her nose and cheeks were reddening. "Mr. Darcy sat right down next to her body, and I looked at her, willing her to move. But she didn't."

"Officer Finley said you had the presence of mind to not touch her, and that you called 911 on your cell phone. Is that correct?"

"It wasn't presence of mind," Lydia said sadly, "I was afraid to touch her. Scared out of my wits. I'm embarrassed to say that I left Mr. Darcy with her, and I turned my back and went outside the tunnel to make the call. It feels like perfectly dreadful behavior on my part. Leaving her alone like that."

"People respond to violence in different ways, Lydia. Your response was normal." Patty paused to let her friend compose herself.

"Did you notice anything unusual around her body or in the tunnel?"

"Like a murder weapon? No," Lydia said shaking her head. "The only thing other than Emily that I noticed was a couple of big bullwhips at the far end of the tunnel—the end closest to the ocean, not the end we entered. I noticed them because they hadn't been there a couple of days earlier. Likely they washed in with the high tide last night."

"Did you see any footprints in the sand?"

"No. Only Mr. Darcy's paw prints. It was low tide, but the sand around the girl was still wet, and there were puddles."

"Did you notice any writing on the tunnel walls? Or anything clinging to them?"

"I didn't inspect the rest of the tunnel—thought it better to stay away and let the police do their thing. But, no, I didn't see anything else out of the ordinary. The tunnel looked like it always does. Only with a dead child in it. Do you think she was killed there?"

"Too soon to know for sure, but it looks that way. Chief Horning told us in our briefing that there didn't appear to be any sign of a struggle in Emily's bedroom. It looks like she got up, got dressed, and climbed out her window."

"Why on earth would she have done that?" Lydia puzzled.

"That's the sixty-four-thousand-dollar question," Patty replied.

CHAPTER 12

Saturday, 7:00 p.m.

All in one motion, Fern Byrne kicked off her shoes and tossed her purse and keys on the hall table just inside her garage door. She had never felt so wiped out in her life.

Drink? Bubble bath? Jammies? What should come first?

After the crime team meeting ended, Fern had driven back to the Bushnell residence, stopping first to pick up a couple of large pizzas at the local joint. She needed to know that the family was doing OK. Pastor Winston and his wife were there, and planning to stay the night in the guest room. Fern offered her assistance and comfort to all the family members, but there were no takers. She got tepid hugs from Susan and Jack, but no one's heart was in it. Everyone was drained dry, not surprisingly. It was clear that they were strung out emotionally, and that nothing else would happen tonight. Dropping her business card on their foyer table, Fern urged them to call her if they needed anything, and took her leave.

Although Fern's psychology education included dealing with death, she had no real-life prior experience in murder interrogations, and sitting in with Jay while he took Marjorie Bushnell's statement had been eye-opening. Fern hadn't a clue what she was supposed to be feeling tonight, but her initial sentiment had been confirmed by Jay and the new police chief; she felt some of the family's response to Emily's death to be a bit odd.

Most peculiar in Fern's eyes, Marjorie had turned rude and angry during Jay's questioning; not at the injustice of her daughter's death, but seemingly at being put upon by having Jay and Fern present. Like they were ruining her day or something.

It felt off to Fern. Not that she had ever been around parents of dead children, but she was pretty good at human nature, and how normal people reacted in a time of tragedy. And, after the first hour or so of their arrival at the house, Marjorie Bushnell did not act like the mother of a dead child.

Maybe, thought Fern, Marjorie was overwhelmed. Or really tired. Or just a disagreeable woman.

Or maybe she's a murderer.

Fern went into her bathroom to wash up before heading to the kitchen. She looked paler than usual, and her dripping wet, long red hair made her look bedraggled. Her hair was usually her best feature, long, thick and naturally wavy in a luxurious auburn color. Fern also had nice skin, although dark circles were beginning to form tonight under her green eyes, and her paleness was more pronounced than usual under her scattered freckles.

You need to get your act together, girlfriend, she said to herself in the mirror. She toweled off her wet head, rinsed her face clean, and applied her favorite moisturizer, which was being discontinued according to the lady at the mall counter. Eventually Fern would have to face facts. Moisturizer change. Drowned-rat look. Dark circles.

Dead little girl.

Let's have a drink. A big, fat drink.

Usually a moderate drinker of mostly Oregon pinot noir—it was practically a state law—Fern headed for her liquor cabinet tonight. She wasn't sure what she might find there, but it seemed like the right call. Her house felt emptier than usual with a stillness about it, and she felt jumpy. To be expected.

She poured herself a hefty glass of Beefeater Gin and threw in some ice, and a couple of plump green olives; if it was good enough for the Queen Mother, it was good enough for Irish Fern Byrne.

After a couple of sips of the potent gin, Fern's stomach started growling. She didn't have much extra fat on her 5'8" lanky body, and not a lot of reserves when it came to missing meals. She'd planned to go to the farmer's market this morning and get some Petrale sole from her favorite fishermen's booth, and some veggies from Mikey's Organic Farm for tonight's dinner, but that didn't happen.

Fern grabbed a frozen pizza from her freezer, and said a quick thanks to Paul Newman for his company's fine product. A fresh tomato sliced on top of Paul's pepperoni would have to do as her vegetable tonight. *Back on the straight and narrow tomorrow,* she promised herself. Tonight, gin and pizza seemed like a great idea.

Fern had lived in Port Stirling all of her life, which was strange, because she didn't seem to fit. She was well-educated, having received a M.A. in Psychology and a B.A. in Art History from Stanford University. Her intention when she left Port Stirling was to stay in San Francisco after college, and get a job in a government agency or a corporate setting. She was practical enough to realize that, even though she loved art and painting, she wasn't good enough at it to make it her career. While she searched for the right permanent job for her psychology degree, Fern took a temporary job as lead preparator on exhibition projects at the city's Asian Art Museum.

What Fern hadn't counted on was a bad relationship with one Thomas Chesley. She'd met Tom, a member of the Asian Art Commission and a seriously generous donor to the museum, about one month into her new job.

Long story, short: Tom was charming, handsome, rich. He was also very married, which he somehow forgot to mention during their whirlwind six-month courtship.

Fern learned of this fact one Friday evening when she and Tom had gone to his residence at the Ritz-Carlton Club to have dinner and spend the night, which they often did. Tom explained that his "real" home, to which Fern had never been invited, was in Sausalito, and it was too much trouble to get there after late nights in the city.

Tom poured them both a glass of the chilled wine his concierge had left for them, and they studied the room service menu together.

But before they could place their order, a key turned in the door lock, and in came Mrs. Thomas Chesley. Tom jumped up from the sofa and moved quickly away from Fern.

"Darling, I thought you flew to New York this morning?" Tom said.

"Yes. Apparently that's what you thought," Deidre Chesley said. She spoke to Tom, but her eyes were on Fern.

And, Fern's eyes were on Deidre Chesley. It was like looking in the mirror twenty years from now.

Turns out, Thomas Chesley not only collected Asian art, he also collected redheads. Also turns out, Fern was No. 4.

Unfortunately, what happened next was rather cliché. Thomas—and/or Deidre—made Fern's life at the museum difficult. She went crying home to Rory and Catherine Byrne in Port Stirling. The Byrnes, who exhibited their sense of humor when naming their daughter, welcomed her back with open arms.

That was five years ago, and here she was. Although she was jolted hard by Emily's death, and felt completely disheveled by the day's pursuits, today had been the single most exciting thing that had happened to Fern during those intervening years. For the first time, she was a truly valuable member of the crime team. Thank goodness the new police chief was here to lead the investigation, and, why-oh-why had no one bothered to share with her how gorgeous Matt Horning was? That curly hair, those cheekbones.

But Fern couldn't keep the happy image of Matt Horning in her brain for long; it kept returning to Marjorie Bushnell and her behavior that morning. Fern recalled that Marjorie had mentioned her dining room wallpaper during their interrogation, and while she figured Marjorie's line of thinking was due to shock, it still jarred both her and Jay at the time. When Fern had followed Marjorie's gaze, she noted the beautiful dining room with its gorgeous furniture and expensive crystal chandelier. What on earth could make Marjorie think about wallpaper at a time like this?!? It was peculiar behavior for a grief-stricken mother.

Now in her own modest but clean contemporary home, Fern tried not to compare the Bushnell's elegant dining room with its fancy-pants wallpaper and pricey crystal chandelier to her own. She'd bought a perfectly serviceable oak dining table that sat eight, with its leaf, and added some cool laminated placemats and cloth napkins she'd bought years ago at an outdoor market in France. One coat of light grey paint on the walls. Done.

Maybe she'd start a new cookie-jar fund for a small, but tasteful chandelier to replace her standard bowl fixture that was becoming uglier by the minute as she thought about it and compared it to the Bushnell's.

As Fern trudged down her hallway to her bedroom, she glanced in the dining room and caught sight of her pedestrian light fixture centered above the table. "Damn you," she, or, perhaps the gin, said to it.

As Fern drifted off to a dead-to-the-world sleep, she wondered what tomorrow would bring. She thought about Matt's request to profile the family, and she knew exactly how she would proceed. Fern was not in the least bit intimidated by this role suddenly thrust upon her. She had, after all, watched plenty of crime dramas on TV.

* * *

Saturday, 7:45 p.m.

When his officers dispersed to begin scouring the Ocean Bend Road area, Matt went to his office. He flicked on the light switch inside his door, but only long enough to get his bearings and find his desk chair. Sitting in the dark, facing his big picture window, he watched the lights quivering on the jetty and beyond. The lighthouse, although now officially decommissioned, was still brightly lit, and served as a beacon guarding the shoreline. Matt had always hated the early twilight and darkness that January brought in Texas, but here it seemed appropriate. Maybe it was just the circumstances of the day, but it needed to be dark, and he needed to sit alone in the inky light and think.

Matt's training had taught him that when it came to the homicide of a child, the murderer always—always—came from one of three groups: the victim's family, a known "crazy", or someone trying to cover up something the child had seen or heard. Because the ME determined that Emily hadn't been sexually assaulted, he didn't know the primary motivation for her death, sitting here twelve hours after her body was discovered.

Matt would, before the night was out, return to the War Room, and write on the big board the case's questions that needed answering, just like every homicide detective ever had done before him. But first, he wanted to flesh them out in his own mind here in the darkness.

Who, exactly, was Emily Bushnell?

Why was she killed? Did someone have a grudge against her or her family? Did she see something she shouldn't have? Know something she shouldn't know? Were they dealing with a "crazy" or a serial killer?

Is there any previous violence in the Bushnell family? Any other children in the region dead or missing? Didn't sound like it, according to his officers, but Matt would check the records to be sure.

Where was she killed? And, if it was the tunnel in which her body was found, why was that spot chosen?

What was the murder weapon and where is it now?

Why did no one—that they knew of so far—hear or see anything last night?

Who killed her? Family member, acquaintance, or stranger?

Lots of questions and no real answers, not yet anyway. But proper investigations, often tedious in nature, had a way of unearthing the truth in Matt's experience. Follow the facts and evidence, and don't overlook anything or anyone because 'conventional wisdom' caused others to look in the other direction.

He would have to be watchful of letting the town's preconceptions influence the investigation. That became apparent to Matt in his earlier meeting with Fern, Jay, and Ed. Fern was a smart professional, but she'd already made up her mind that Marjorie couldn't possibly be their killer, even in light of what her own, trained hunches were whispering to her. Even Jay, an intelligent, earnest cop, was letting his personal feelings and relationship with the mayor and his family color his perception. Matt had hoped for a quieter beginning to his new life, but, deep down, he thought perhaps it was a good thing the universe had brought him here now to steer this investigation of that poor little thing's death.

His personal motto was "Don't get bogged down in the bullshit." There might be less bullshit in Port Stirling than in Plano, but Matt knew without a doubt there would still be bullshit. He hoped it wouldn't get as deep as his last situation with a dead girl.

Eventually, he went down the dark hallway to the War Room, and wrote the unanswered questions, leaving room below each one for the answers that he was confident would come soon. His cell phone buzzed, and he saw that it was a "541" call, his new area code. Picking up, Patty Perkins said, "Chief, do you have a minute?"

"Yes, ma'am, I do. I'm writing down all the case questions, and I hope you have an answer or two."

"No answers yet, but I do have an update for you on my conversation with Lydia Campbell." Patty recounted the particulars of her talk with Lydia, and told him about her mention of Ted Frolick, her Ocean Bend Road neighbor.

"Oh?" Matt said. "Why did she think of Frolick when she saw the light?"

"I asked her that very question, and she said he often wanders about, and is known to be on the beach after dark. She was worried that it might have been him down there on a dark night. But when she realized what she was saying, she backtracked in a hurry, and told me that he wouldn't hurt a fly, and he couldn't possibly be a suspect."

"That's what they always say, right?"

"Yes, that's what they always say, right up until the time we slap cuffs on them. This might be our first lead. I'll go see him first thing tomorrow morning. Does that meet with your approval?"

Matt, looking at his watch, saw that it was almost 8:30 p.m. "Yeah, that sounds good. It's getting kinda late to be knocking on doors tonight. What time do you think you'll visit Mr. Frolick tomorrow?"

"Us old people get up early. I'll knock on his door about 8:00 a.m."

Matt had to chuckle in spite of the circumstances. "Ah, an early bird. Love it."

They rang off, agreeing to talk again tomorrow morning after Patty got a bead on crazy old Ted Frolick.

Jay poked his head in the War Room and said, "There you are. I came to tell you that Abbott has assigned you official wheels."

He threw a set of car keys to Matt, who caught them easily.

"I was wondering how I was going to get to my new home tonight," Matt said.

"I'm happy to drive you, but Abbott's thought of everything. He said to tell you that your squad car is parked out in the far corner of the lot. Also said that Mary Lou and he took your boxes from Texas that arrived two days ago, and put them inside the door to your cottage—the realtor has the only other key, and she let them in. Mary Lou wanted to unpack them for you, but Abbott put the kibosh on that," he smiled.

"Not that I have anything remotely interesting in those boxes. Or that I'm going to have any time soon to unpack them."

"No. Guess not. Say, do you want to go grab a bite? What are you going to do for food?"

"No, you go on home, Jay. I'm almost finished here, and then I'll head home, too. We'll start bright and early tomorrow morning. I'd like you here by 7:00 a.m."

"Sure thing. You know how to get to your place, right?"

"It's dark as hell around here, but, yeah, I'll find it eventually."

* * *

In the dense fog, Matt missed the turnoff to his cottage, but it worked out. When he realized his mistake, he'd pulled into the parking lot of the Inn at Whale Rock hotel and restaurant just down the road from where he now knew his house to be. When he saw the neon sign of a martini and a crab in the restaurant's front window, it dawned on him how hungry he was.

The restaurant was done up in nautical style with natural wood walls and a carpet with an anchors design. The bar was the first thing one came to, with the restaurant beyond. It was two-level, with tables along the upper railing, and booths down five steps into a glass-walled room looking out to the Pacific. Relieved to find the restaurant still open, he'd slipped alone into a booth when the hostess said "sit any-where you like".

Dead tired and weak with hunger, Matt reflected on this life-chang-ing move he was making. He felt comfortable in Port Stirling with its slow vibe, but was he nuts to take this job? He knew virtually no one in Oregon except his professional colleagues. No friends here. Completely different weather. Unfamiliar business environment. Even the food was different from home, he thought, as he browsed the restaurant's menu.

"Can I get you a drink to start with?" asked his waitress. She smiled and slapped down a cocktail napkin on the table in front of him. Her nametag read "Vicki". She looked to be about his age, and was sporting an older-model, dark brown version of a Farrah Fawcett hairdo. Matt recognized it because he had "that" poster in his college fraternity room at Texas. Vicki was dressed in brown slacks and a too-tight animal print sweater.

"I'll have a beer," Matt responded. "How about a Coors?"

"Really?" Vicki said. "Wouldn't you rather try one of our craft beers?" She looked at Matt like he was a foreigner. In a way, he was.

"Should I?"

"Well, Coors was what we used to drink before we started making all these terrific beers around here. Seems a shame to go back in time, don't it? Can I recommend one or two for you?" She did seem helpful.

"Tell you what, Vicki. Why don't you bring me a beer you think I should drink, and we'll go from there?"

"Smart man."

Vicki reappeared in a heartbeat with a pint of Pelican Silverspot IPA. "Taste this, and you'll never touch a Coors again in your lifetime," she said smugly.

He did, and allowed that Vicki might be right.

"OK, Miss Know-it-all, what should I eat?" he said, and closed his menu. Honestly, he was too tired to pore over the four-page menu.

"Where you from?"

"Texas."

"Oh, lord," she rolled her eyes. "I had fish there once, and I swear it took three weeks for it to get from the water to my table. You sit back and I'll bring you what you don't know you need." She trotted off before Matt could answer.

While he waited for his surprise dinner, Matt at least was contented in the knowledge that everyone in town had been friendly and accommodating to this stranger. He felt welcome, and, in a strange fashion, taken care of. It was nice for a change, but he wondered if it would last.

All Matt knew was that after his dinner of thick, creamy clam chowder, two whole Dungeness crabs, homemade sour dough bread, and a salad of wild greens, fresh cranberries, and hazelnuts, plus a second Pelican beer, he felt more taken care of than at any time in his recent life. He made it the few blocks to his new home in a fog as thick as his chowder, blissful for the first time on this dreadful day.

* * *

Saturday, 9:30 a.m.

Look at them down there. All idiots. Love standing up here in a state park, one of several gawkers wondering what's going on down on the beach.

What do they think they're going to find in that tunnel after last night's high tide? Whatever was there, like a dead body, will be far out to sea by now.

She will never be able to open her stupid little mouth again. Bite! Eat!

They'll never find her. Mystery in this shithole town forever and ever. Whatever do you think happened to little sugary Emily? They'll ask each other in the stores and at the gas stations. The old biddies should thank me. Bite! Shark in tree! I've given them something to flap their yaps at for years. Talk about as they go about their small lives.

How I killed her. Wonder if the killer is one of them. Ha! Hadn't thought about that. Suspect each other. Eat! Bite! Afraid every night when they turn out the light. Never figure out it was me. Never. Shark! Tree! Cops in this town couldn't find their shithole if it was sitting on a plate in front of them.

Never find the twat. Never know it was me who put that knife in her belly. Went in so easily, like cutting a cake. Almost too easy.

Took some fun out of it.

Why is the ambulance here? What are those guys doing, for fuck's sake? What are they carrying?

Shit! Shit! Shit! The tide didn't take her away! How is that possible? Bite! Bite! It was supposed to be the highest tide of the month. How could she still be in that tunnel? Fuck happened?

Where are they taking you, Emily—where? You're dead. I know you're dead. Made sure of that.

Eat! Bite! Bite!

CHAPTER 13

Sunday, 6:00 a.m.

Wind and rain lashing at his window woke Matt just before dawn on Sunday. He felt as if he'd been born in this town perched on the rocky headland of the mighty Pacific Ocean, and had been dealing with the mystery of this child's death for weeks, instead of the mere twenty-four hours since the discovery of Emily's body.

He showered, shaved, dressed and made a pot of coffee, all before the sky lightened enough to see the water. He'd been too tuckered out—and too full of food and beer—last night to unpack anything, and would live out of his suitcase another day. It was chilly in his cottage, and the wood floor in his bedroom was cold to his bare feet, even through the scattered area rugs. Matt looked forward to building his first fire in the massive stone fireplace, but that pleasure would have to wait, so, for now, he cranked up the electric baseboard heat.

Now that dawn was breaking, he was drawn to the big picture window that overlooked the sea. Through the rain, he watched the white-capped pounders slamming onto the beach as he drank his coffee and thought about how he wanted today to unfold. Even on this crappy morning, the view was breathtaking.

In spite of yesterday's rocky start to his new life, Matt was falling for Port Stirling. The majesty of his view made him feel inconsequential on one hand, but that his life held significance on the other. He was a speck on the great Pacific, but he was here for a reason. Watching the gulls swooping and the relentless waves making their high tide inroads further onto the deserted beach, Matt knew he was going to have a tough time returning to Texas when the time came.

Something near the shoreline caught his eye. At first Matt thought it was a log drifting in the shallow waters just offshore, but then he saw a pair of eyes. A seal was bobbing along, staring up at Matt above him on the bluff. For a split second, he was sure he and the seal made eye contact, and his new amigo was saying "What are you doing about Emily's murder?"

I'm trying to solve it, my friend.

"You got this," the seal said back to him, and he might have winked before disappearing under the surf.

As much as he hated to pull himself away from the window, knowledgeable of what the day ahead of him was likely to bring, and fearful of the opportunity for regular meals, Matt went back into the kitchen to see what he could dig up. Someone, likely Mary Lou, stocked his frig and cupboards with some essentials. *Who does nice things like that anymore?* He found bacon and eggs, and fried them up, pouring a second cup of coffee to wash it down.

With a quick glance out the window to see if his new pet had returned—alas, no—Matt gathered up his notes off the dining room table, grabbed his jacket off the hook by the door, and headed out to his office on this bleak, gray, and very wet Sunday morning.

* * *

Sunday, 7:00 a.m.

Matt figured to be the first one in City Hall this morning, but he figured wrong. Jay was there, which wasn't a complete surprise, but so was Fern, who pulled into the parking lot just ahead of Matt and was locking her car as he drove up.

"Couldn't sleep," she smiled in greeting. "You?"

"I always sleep. Just never quite as much as I want to, and, besides, we can sleep after we catch our killer. Thanks for getting here early on a Sunday morning."

"It's my job, Chief. Doesn't matter what day of the week it is. I have a plan for how to proceed on the family profiling you need, and I want to run it by you before we go back to the Bushnell house."

Matt swiped his key card to City Hall's side entrance, and held open the door for Fern. He took note of how the merciless rain beaded up on her raspberry pink raincoat, and realized he needed to buy a new coat sooner rather than later; his lightweight jacket wasn't cutting it in this climate. *Two days, two different raincoats on Fern; maybe that's all I need.* They went straight to his office, and found Jay standing at the big window looking out to the lighthouse with his hands on his waist.

"Another fine January day in western Oregon," he said, turning to greet his new boss and Fern.

"Yeah, I'm beginning to think I've been hoodwinked about the weather here," Matt said. He thought Jay looked a little worse for wear than he did last night when they went home. The horror of what he saw yesterday had clearly fully kicked in.

"You OK?" Matt asked him.

"I'm OK. Just."

"It's natural to be upset by violence of this nature," said Fern. "I didn't see Emily's body, and I still had visions of her all night. I can't imagine how you must feel today." She walked over to Jay and patted his back.

"She's right," said Matt. "It never gets easier, and you will never forget yesterday morning, I'm sorry to say. The only way to help the pain go away is to expose the killer. It won't help Emily, but it will help us to feel that we made it up to her somehow. Let's talk about where we are after Day 1."

Matt updated them on Patty Perkins' phone call after her interrogation of Lydia Campbell. "Do either of you know Ted Frolick? He lives down Ocean Bend Road from Lydia."

"Is he that crazy old coot who lives in the dump with all the junk out in front?" Jay asked.

"I don't know," admitted Matt. "I'm asking you. Lydia told Patty that he was the first person she thought of when she saw the light on the beach Friday night. Patty's paying him a visit this morning."

"Oh my God," Jay said, his eyes widening. "I should have thought of Frolick immediately. He lives right above where Emily was found, and he's always down on the beach."

"Is he really crazy, or are you using the word lightly?"

"He's probably not really crazy," Jay answered, his voice serious. "I don't know him all that well. He just seems a little offbeat. And I don't understand all the junk he collects and deposits in his front yard. It's an eyesore if you ask me."

"Well, let's see what Patty gets this morning. Our first job is to try to establish a motive," said Matt. "Unfortunately, we're running on empty when it comes to who had a reason to want her dead. The one thing we already know is that it wasn't the result of a sexual assault, so somebody had to have another beef with this girl. I think we can rule out financial motive because we're talking about a 4-year-old. It's possible we're dealing with a serial killer who kills for the thrill of it, or some other form of psychological gratification."

None of them were willing to address that possibility yet, and it seemed highly unlikely in such a small town, but it had creeped into the far reaches of the brains in Matt's office.

"Hmm," said Fern, whose interest was piqued. "Well, except for the children who have been swept out to sea by sneaker waves, we haven't had any other child deaths in Chinook County for over ten years that I can think of. Don't serial killers always kill in a similar fashion—kids, gender, blondes, etc.?"

"Usually there is some sort of link, with a cooling-off period in between murders," Matt said. "I'll need a list of every non-natural death in the area for the past five years, children and adults."

"Even those swept out to sea?" asked Jay.

"Yes, even if their deaths were declared 'accidental.'" Matt asked. "I want to read the files."

"I can dig them up fast for you."

"Great. Thanks, Jay. We're probably not dealing with a serial child killer, unless Emily was his first. It's far more likely it's one of the Bushnells. Fern, tell us how you intend to go about profiling the family."

"Well, first, you need to know I haven't done this yet in the real world, only in school," Fern started. "And I probably won't do it the same way an FBI agent, or whoever else you might have worked with previously does it. Instead of trying to develop a criminal profile for a possible murderer, I'm going to focus on the family's personality traits and examine their behavior. You seem to think it's one of them, so that's where I think I can help the most."

"Go on," said Matt.

"I'm going to focus on the most unusual aspect of Emily's case, and that's the human bite marks that Bernice found on her body," said Fern, swallowing hard and brushing a wayward hair away from her face. "I'll do a study on individuals who have committed similar offenses across the country, and then I'll compare the Bushnells' personality traits that may parallel traits of these other killers. I'll be closely observing the family today and making my own notes."

"That sounds good," said Matt, nodding his head. "Do you know of any previous cases, dead or wounded, in the area with human bites?"

"No," answered Jay. "I've never seen or heard of anything like this. It's so gross."

"OK, let's move down to the War Room and go through the questions I came up with last night. I want these fresh in your minds when we go back to the family today, and I want to be able to fill in some answers by tonight. Here's how we're going to handle the family."

CHAPTER 14

Sunday, 8:10 a.m.

Patty Perkins found Ted Frolick's house easily from Lydia's directions. Truly, one couldn't miss it. What looked like decades of beachcombing had ended up in his front yard, which nestled right up against Ocean Bend Road. Only a gravel walkway—no sidewalks here—separated his low, rickety fence from the road.

A wispy smoke curled out of the chimney, and the curtains were drawn closed over the two wide windows that flanked the cottage's front door. Patty couldn't tell if anyone was home or not. She hadn't tried to call Ted Frolick first, thinking she would surprise him with her visit. But now, as she approached the gray, weather-beaten door on the uneven stone pathway, she felt a stab of trepidation.

There were no cars going by on Ocean Bend Road. This morning's earlier rain and wind had passed by, and the air was still. The clouds coming off the sea were moving lickety-split overhead, and, looking up, Patty was happy to see occasional patches of blue sky. She could hear the waves breaking below the clifftop, and the occasional squawk of a gull, but, otherwise, it was eerily quiet. Perhaps she should call for backup? *Nonsense.* Her beleaguered colleagues on the crime team all had their hands full with their own investigations. Wary or not, she would have to put on her big-girl panties, and see precisely what was up with Mr. Frolick.

She stepped up on the one rickety step in front of the door and rapped sharply with her knuckles. Then, she stepped back and listened.

Nothing.

Decades of experience taught her to look at the windows and see if she might detect any movement behind the curtains, but she saw nothing or no one. She stepped up and knocked again. And waited again.

Still nothing.

OK, now what?

Lydia had mentioned Frolick's garden in the back of the house. Patty thought it possible that he might be out there on this calm morning. She noticed a somewhat dilapidated gate to the right of the house, and gave it a try. It opened easily, and she found a slightly overgrown path close to the south side of the cottage.

Patty started gingerly walking forward, going slowly and with her ears perked up.

"Who the hell are you?" a man's voice bellowed from the far end of the path.

Startled, Patty stopped in her tracks. Ted Frolick stood facing her with a trowel in his hand about ten feet away. He was wearing overalls over a deep purple long-sleeved tee shirt. Bare-headed, his shock of silver hair was disheveled, and he had a rumpled air about him. His face was lean and clean shaven, and his intelligent eyes stared calmly at Patty. It was hard to guess his age, but Patty thought he was some-where in his late-60's—just a few years older than her—and definitely younger than she had expected since people referred to him as "old Ted Frolick".

Collecting her wits, Patty said, "I'm looking for Mr. Ted Frolick. Might that be you?" She smiled to let him know she was on a friendly mission.

"You found him. Who are you?" He did not return her smile.

"My name is Patricia Perkins, and I work for the Twisty River Police Department," she said, while simultaneously holding up her police ID. "Can I take a few minutes of your time to talk?"

"You're trespassing." Just a statement of fact—no malice or threat in his voice.

"I'm sorry about that. Your friend Lydia Campbell told me you might be working in your garden. I knocked on your front door, and then decided to see if you were in your back yard."

"You know Lydia?"

"Yes, she and I play in a bridge club together. I've known her for years. I'm surprised you and I haven't met."

Abruptly, he turned his back on Patty, and walked to a bare bed of dirt a few feet away.

"Can we talk, Mr. Frolick?" she persisted.

"Come on, if you like. I have to get these bulbs in the ground. Already late with them."

He wasn't so much unfriendly as he was distracted. Patty had been warned that he was 'crazy', but, so far, Frolick didn't strike her that way. He might be eccentric, definitely, but there was a quiet intelligence in his manner.

"What are you planting?"

"Hyacinth. Should have been in the ground in November. Forgot I had them."

"Well, it's been pretty mild this winter . . . you're probably OK with them."

Patty looked around the space and wondered at how different it looked than his front yard. Frolick's garden was tidy, even on this day in mid-winter. There wasn't much grass, just a couple of pathways that were lined with neatly-placed rocks. The bulk of the space was filled with flowerbeds, surrounded by shrubs, mostly hydrangeas, she thought, although they were in January stick mode. One carved-out bed at the left was full of rose bushes, five or six of them, all pruned and primed for early spring growth. It was easy to imagine this garden in the full flush of summer beauty. It occurred to Patty that Frolick might delight in presenting a ramshackle appearance to the world out front, while keeping this jewelry-box garden all to himself. She felt like an intruder, but she had a job to do.

"What do you want to ask me about?" Frolick asked as he continued to spade the ground. A paper bag holding his bulbs sat open near his right knee.

"Do you know Emily Bushnell?" Patty asked to Frolick's back. She tried to maneuver herself around him so she could see his face.

"You mean Marjorie and Fred's girl? Yes, I know the family." Dig. Dig. Dig.

"Could you stop working for just a minute, please?"

Frolick put down his trowel, and wiped his hands on the front of his overalls. He stood and faced Patty with his full attention. "What is it, Ms. Perkins?"

"Thank you. Emily Bushnell was found dead on the beach below here yesterday"—she gestured out to the beach beyond the road—"and we think she was murdered. I'd like to ask you a few questions."

"Is she the young one?" His voice was calm and steady. If he felt any emotion, his face didn't betray it.

"Yes, four years old. Where were you on Friday evening?" she asked, all business now.

"I have no idea."

"Were you at home?"

"I can't remember what I had for breakfast this morning, how do you expect me to remember back to Friday? But, yes, I was likely at home. I'm here most of the time."

"Friday night was particularly foggy and rather drippy…do you remember?"

"You know, I do remember that. I went out to the store to get some food from the deli. Great invention, delis, don't you think?"

Patty smiled. "Yes, I have to agree with you. One doesn't always feel like cooking, does one?"

"No, one doesn't." A hint of a smile. "I'm sorry to hear about that little girl. She's a little charmer, that one."

"She was stabbed." Patty let that truth hang in the air.

"And you think I did it?" he asked, and seemed keenly interested to know.

"Did you?"

"I don't think so," he replied. "You would think I'd remember that."

Patty stared at him. *Was he pulling her leg?*

"Did you walk on the beach Friday night?"

"Doubt it. Likely stayed in with my deli dinner and turned in early. This time of year I go to bed early and get up early."

"Do you walk on the beach most days?"

"Yes, I would say so. No point in living here if you don't enjoy the ocean."

"But you didn't go down there on Friday?"

"That's not what I said."

She gave him a puzzled look.

"I said I didn't go for a walk on Friday *night*. I was down there earlier in the day. Picking up a piece of driftwood I'd spotted from the bluff." He ran his hand through his ruffled hair.

"Do you remember if you saw anything strange or out of the ordinary?"

"Didn't see another soul, if I recall."

"Do you have a police record, Mr. Frolick?" Patty asked, changing tactics.

"No, I don't believe I do. Seems as though I'd recall that, too."

This man was as crazy as she was.

"You remember some things and don't remember others. Is that a pattern with you?"

"Do I have dementia, you mean?"

"Yes, that's what I'm getting at. Do you think you weave in and out of reality at times?"

"Quite possible," he replied matter-of-factly.

"Does that frighten you?"

"Yes, it does. That's why I try to stick to my routine. And, I don't believe it's part of my routine to kill little girls." He was serious, and Patty believed him. She also liked him, and felt a twinge of regret for his situation.

"Can anyone verify that you were home on Friday night?" she asked.

"Doubt it. They know me at the deli, though. If you need to check that what I'm telling you is the truth, Sandy over there would probably remember that I stopped by."

"What did you buy?"

"Rotisserie chicken and a fruit salad," he said without hesitating.

"How can you remember that from two nights ago?" She truly wanted to know.

Frolick shrugged. "Not sure how. But it's what I bought."

"OK. How well do you know the Bushnells?" Another change of direction.

"About like everybody else, I guess," he replied. "Fred's the mayor."

"Yes, he's the mayor. Do you ever talk to him?"

"I see him sometimes down on the beach, and sometimes at the post office. Can't say that I do more than talk about the weather with him. There are things I could tell him, though."

"What do you mean?"

"Do you think he knows his uppity wife fools around with one of our firemen? Or that all of his kids smoke pot. Not the little girl," he clarified, "she's an innocent. Was an innocent."

Patty stood rooted to the spot. She was momentarily stunned.

"Marjorie Bushnell is having an affair?"

"Yes, I believe that she is."

"How on earth would you know that?" Patty asked. She was incredulous.

"Saw 'em."

"You saw Marjorie Bushnell and another man together? Who is he?"

"Craig Kenton, he's a volunteer fireman. Also works at the hardware store. I saw them coming out of the A-frame cabin below the Pacific View Motel. They were cozy."

"When was this?"

"I've seen them twice. The time at the A-frame was about a month ago, middle of the day. Can't remember what day of the week it was. Then, I saw them last week with their cars pulled up next to each other in back of the market. They were both driving and pulled up in opposite directions to talk. She had the little girl in the back seat."

"Why were you behind the market?"

"I was looking for a trash can to dump my lunch bag."

"They could just be friends and were catching up," Patty suggested.

"Just friends don't plant a big, lengthy smooch on the lips leaving a beach cabin together."

"You saw them kiss?" Patty felt a chill, and it wasn't only the cool January air.

"Yes. I had just come around the corner by the cave and was

probably hidden from their view behind the rocks. There was no one else around, and they probably thought they were all alone. Surprise!" he grinned, and threw his hands up in the air.

"This is hard to believe, Mr. Frolick."

"Believe it or not, I can't help you there. Marjorie and Craig, sitting in a tree, K-I-S-S-I-N-G!"

"But how could they think they could get away with a relationship in a small town like this?" Patty couldn't remember ever being more surprised at a nugget of information from an interview.

"Maybe they don't care if they get caught." Frolick said.

"But it's crazy—she's the mayor's wife."

"Craig Kenton is a nice-looking young man." He was amused at Patty's obvious discomfort with this topic.

"Still," she said.

"The stirrings below don't always cause man or woman to stop and think."

CHAPTER 15

Sunday, 8:30 a.m.

In the War Room, Matt, Jay, Fern, and recently-arrived Ed Sonders discussed verifying the alibis of each Bushnell. Jay and Ed were in uniform, looking starched. Matt already knew them well enough to understand that they both made a habit of being professional. Fern was wearing a black dress and the same knee-high boots as yesterday. Matt liked her better in yesterday's blue sweater, but accepted that the black dress was the appropriate choice for today.

"Before I left here last night, I phoned the Port Stirling Cinema and spoke to the manager," Matt told his colleagues. "She says that Jack Bushnell and his pal Joey Hawthorne were at the movies Friday night, although she couldn't verify how long they stayed—she only sold them tickets and saw them in their seats before the movie started."

"Did she say what the movie was?" asked Ed.

"Yeah, it was the Star Wars film."

"OK, that's what Jack told me they saw," confirmed Ed.

"I also tracked down Joey's parents—they're the only Hawthorne in the book—and talked to his dad," said Matt. "He corroborated that the two boys went to the movies. Said his son walked home afterward, and was actually home a little earlier than he expected."

"Did Mr. Hawthorne know about Emily's murder?" asked Fern.

"No, he wanted to know why I was calling, of course. I told him that we were investigating a crime, and needed to verify where the kids were Friday night. I could tell he didn't know what was going on. So, if Joey and Jack killed Emily, Joey did a good job hiding it from his parents. One thing—we're going to get into it a little deeper with the three siblings today, and because two of them are still minors, we'll need to have one of their parents in the room to make sure we stay on the up and up. Gary is eighteen and if we want to interrogate him separately we can."

"How do you see this morning working?" asked Jay.

"From a logistical standpoint, the four of us are going in at the same time as our search warrant crew—we got the warrant last night from Judge Hedges. Thank you Mr. District Attorney."

"Oh, man, the mayor and his wife are not going to like this," said Jay, shaking his head.

"No, they're not," Matt agreed. "But it's going to happen and they will have to face up to reality. We're looking for a serrated kitchen knife, and any bloody clothes, in particular. Once the search is underway, I want you and Fern to continue with Marjorie, but let's add Susan to the mix. Today we need to press on their alibis, really quiz them about Friday night. Ask for any verification you can get to nail down the details. Also, you'll want to ask them both about their activities and whereabouts during the past week…see if anything unusual stands out. What did the family do all week? Was Emily within someone's sight every day? Because we don't have a motive yet, we need to establish Emily's whereabouts, mood, health, everything about her in the days leading up to her death. We also need contacts for all the girls at Susan's slumber party, and the parents of the home involved."

"I would like to know if either Susan or her mother kept a diary," added Fern. "Can we add that to the search warrant? Girls and women often put their daily thoughts down somewhere, and it might offer up some insight."

"It depends. I had to state the things constituting the object of the search—the knife, bloody clothes, and all computers - and get authorization to seize those items. If the DA prepared the affidavit to include language like "and any other evidence related to said crime", then we have more leeway. He did tell me that Oregon law is tougher than the federal 4th amendment requirements for search and seizure. It's an excellent thought though, Fern—can you call Dalrymple and ask him the specific language of the affidavit? I'm waiting for my copy of it; he said I'd have it first thing this morning."

"I'll go call him right now," said Fern, getting up.

"Jay, are you clear on how to proceed?" Matt asked his officer.

"I think so. We're trying to get straight on where everyone was all week and what they were doing. I'm also assuming that Marjorie was Emily's primary caretaker since Fred spends a lot of time here and out in the community, so she should be able to shed the most light on Emily's movements."

"Right. Ed, I want you to drill down with Gary. I didn't make it over to the Stirling Tavern in person last night, but I did have a phone call with Paula, the owner, before I left here, and she said she couldn't swear to it that Gary never left the tavern Friday night. She said she didn't keep a close eye on their group. When I asked her if he could have slipped out for an hour and then slipped back in, she said it was possible, and she might not have noticed. She had a big crowd Friday night. I want you to share that with Gary and note his response, OK?"

"Interesting," replied Ed. "I should be able to tell from his reaction if he's telling the truth or not."

"Also, I'm going to pop into the tavern tonight and surprise her.

We'll see if there are any minors present. I hate to admit it, but I was too tired last night to do a raid justice."

"What?" said Ed. "You mean you're a human after all?"

"Very funny."

"I'll go with you tonight and we'll check IDs together. It will be a bonding experience for us."

"That's a plan, Mr. Smartass. In the meantime, I will take Fred and Jack together this morning. I need to know more about their alibis, their relationships with Emily, and how the previous week unfolded for both of them. I woke up wondering if anyone in town held any grudges against the mayor. Any history? Anyone know?"

"You might ask the mayor about Fergus Dunbar," said Jay. "He's a local farmer who lit into him at the last city council meeting. He's harmless in my opinion, but we should know Fred's thoughts on him."

"What was his beef?" said Matt, jotting down the name.

"I can't remember exactly. Something about telling tourists about the local farmers' CSA program, I think. Fergus wanted the mayor to help promote it, and he said no. Something like that."

"Anything else I should know about our mayor's dealings with the town folks?"

"Not that I can think of."

"Mr. Dalrymple says the search warrant is on its way, and a copy of the affidavit he wrote should be on your FAX machine," said Fern, coming back into the room. "Also, all of your officers are here and ready to go when we are."

"Great," said Matt. "I'll call the mayor and tell him we're on the way. I want y'all to remember that the Bushnell house is a potential crime scene, and that one or more of the family is our likely perpetrator. If any of you are uncomfortable going back in there this morning, this is the time to let me know. I know this is new for you, Jay, and you,

Fern. It's normal to feel apprehensive, but if you think it will get in the way of our investigation, I need to know that now."

"I'm uncomfortable as hell, Chief," Jay spoke first. "But I'm clear on what I need to do, and it's my friggin' job," he said, his voice strong and convincing.

"What he said," said Fern, pointing at Jay, and attempting a timid smile.

"Let's go," said Ed.

* * *

Sunday, 8:30 a.m.

Gary Bushnell got out of his childhood bed, stretched, and looked outside the window. *What a fucking nightmare.* He was happy to see that last night's storm had passed on, and they might actually get some sunshine in this God-forsaken shithole.

He should have stayed in Eugene for the holidays. His family was fucked up, for sure. He wanted to stay at school and make a move on this hot bitch that was in his freshman sociology class. She was from San Diego, and was planning to stay in her dorm between semesters. Gary thought she might be dead broke, and couldn't afford the plane fare home. He'd been planning to move on her by spending some dough on restaurants and acting like a big-shot mayor's son.

What a fucking joke his parents are. His lunatic mother insisted that he come to Port Stirling for Christmas, and his clueless dad reminded him that they were paying his bills, and that it was the "least he could for his mother". So now, instead of fucking the lights out of Miss San Diego, here he was stuck with these crazies for another two weeks.

Long blonde hair, even longer legs, and big, bouncing titties. Wasted.

Great. Just great.

* * *

Susan Bushnell rolled over and noticed a ray of sun peeking through the slit in her curtains. *Unbelievable,* she thought. *How could this be happening?* Instead of lazing around today and enjoying her sixteenth birthday weekend with her friends, she would have to get up and endure her ridiculous parents.

Susan deeply loved her little sister and would miss her, of course. But—hello!—life goes on, does it not? She wasn't sure if she could handle more of that lame Fern Byrne and that huge cop asking her more questions about Friday night. Now, if that scrumptious new police chief with his sexy Texas voice would take over, she'd tell him everything she knew. Which was a lot.

* * *

Jack Bushnell was still sleeping on this eerily quiet Sunday morning. He always could sleep with the best of them.

Marjorie Bushnell knew she should get up and start the coffee. But she laid in bed staring at the ceiling, trying to remember what was wrong. She'd woken up with a bad feeling, but couldn't quite put her finger on it.

Oh, yes. Emily was dead.

* * *

The mayor had been up since dawn. Coming downstairs to the living room, he was relieved to see that that irritating blowhard Pastor John and his silly wife were gone. They had insisted on staying until the entire family had gone to bed last night and were resting. *I'm an atheist, you idiot,* Fred felt like saying to them. But he knew it wouldn't do any good. Their kind never had a clue.

Fred couldn't bring himself to go for his usual morning constitutional down on the beach. He didn't really want to see the tunnel where his daughter's body had been found, and it was high tide this morning anyway.

Instead, Fred Bushnell made the coffee, and then turned on his computer to see if there was any word yet on Emily's death. A story like this one would ignite everyone in his town, and he needed some time this morning to decide how he would handle it.

He went first to the *Buck Bay News'* website. Nothing. What a relief. He had asked Bernice Ryder when they went to view the body in the morgue last night to not say anything yet. Bernice had looked at him strangely, but nodded her agreement.

It was weird to see his usually livewire daughter laying there still and pale. He recalled that both he and Marjorie had been curiously detached, almost as if they were looking at the body of someone else's child, someone they knew only vaguely.

When Bernice asked them both "Is this your daughter, Emily Bushnell?" Marjorie had piped up first and said 'Yes'. Fred had felt offended at Marjorie's haste, feeling that it should be up to the man of the house to respond to a question like that. Yes, he was definitely put out by being upstaged.

He would have to talk to Marjorie about that.

CHAPTER 16

Sunday, 9:30 a.m.

The three cops and Fern headed for the City Hall parking lot. On this partly sunny, cool morning not much was stirring in Port Stirling. There was a calmness in the air, but plenty of tension in the group.

"Fern, you ride with me," Matt said, heading for his squad car. "Jay, go with Ed in his OSP car. We don't want to overrun the Bushnell property with vehicles. We'll follow you, Ed."

"What if everyone tells the same stories again?" asked Fern, as she buckled up.

"If mom and dad tell the same story again, we'll have a tough time disproving it."

"Because it's impossible to verify?"

"Right. It will be easier for Ed to nail down the kids' alibis. We'll know by this afternoon if Gary, Susan, and Jack were where they said they were. That's why I want you to focus on Marjorie this morning."

"It's hard to imagine kids doing something like this," Fern said quietly. "I understand that it happens, but it's so hard to picture in this case."

"Would it help you get your head around the possibility if I tell you that I've seen teenage violence on a personal level? Because I have. It happens."

"What happened to you?"

"I'd rather not go into the gory details right now, if you don't mind," Matt said. "Just know that drugs, mental illness, depression, and a raft of other problems can sweep up kids these days just as easily as adults."

"Did this happen in a case in Texas that caused you to seek a fresh start? Is that why you're here?" Fern persisted.

"This conversation needs to happen later, not now," Matt said, his voice steely, but polite. "We need to focus. I will tell you to not overlook Susan because she's a girl."

"I won't overlook anyone in that house." Fern paused. "You know, Chief, trust is a powerful thing. If we're going to work together on this case, I need to trust you and you need to trust me. If whatever happened to you in Texas is coloring your view of Emily's death, I want to know."

"It's not, and I'm not hiding anything from you. It's just not the right time to be telling you a sad story. If anything, my recent experience has broadened my viewpoint. I won't be assuming anyone is innocent; they'll all have to prove it to me."

Fern looked sideways at Matt, who was staring straight ahead at the road. She saw his jaw clench. "That sounds good." She made a conscious decision to leave it there, but she could tell that Matt was struggling with his past. Whatever secret he carried with him to Port Stirling would eventually come out, but Fern could only go by how Matt had handled the investigation so far. And, internal demons or no, Matt instilled confidence in the team. Their new police chief knew what he was doing, and Fern had every belief that their killer was up against a serious adversary.

Fern would leave Matt's story alone—for now—but if his past started interfering with the present situation, she would act.

* * *

Before they knocked on the door, Matt said to Ed and Jay, "Let's take a look at Emily's bedroom window from the outside." The three cops walked around to the end of the house, where Emily's bedroom window faced north.

"There's no sign of forced entry," Ed noted. "Nothing broken—window or lock."

Matt ran his hand along the window casing and the siding below it. "Nothing out of the ordinary." He looked down and gently stroked a fern directly below the window. "A couple of fronds broken." He lifted up the fern's branches, and said, "No real footprints, just mud." Matt's own shoes were now covered in mud. "Why wouldn't the lock be broken?"

"It's a small town," said Jay. "We don't always lock our doors and windows.

"Or," said Matt, "it was an inside job, not an outside job," he said. "I think the window was opened from the inside."

The mayor answered the door. Not surprisingly, he looked even more haggard than he had yesterday. But he was neatly dressed in black slacks and a black V-neck sweater worn over a white dress shirt.

"Please come in, all of you," Fred said, opening the door wide. "Is there any progress on your investigation, Chief?" he asked.

"It's continuing, Mr. Mayor," Matt said. "As part of it," he said, handing the signed search warrant to Fred, "a team composed of men from my police department is here with us to conduct a search of the premises." The Port Stirling P.D. officers stood just outside the front door, waiting for the go-ahead from their chief.

"What the hell do you think you're doing?" asked a clearly astonished Fred, and he stood his ground in front of the officers. He essentially blocked their entrance, and the Port Stirling P.D. stood still, not eager to take on their mayor.

"The affidavit was prepared by District Attorney David Dalrymple, and signed by Judge Cynthia Hedges," Matt replied. "It gives me authorization to administer a thorough search of the house and grounds, and to seize any evidence that might pertain to the homicide of your daughter."

"Give me that!" Marjorie yelled, coming up behind Fred and snatching it out of his hand. Like her husband, Marjorie looked tired, too, but had made an effort with her appearance. She was wearing a black tweed skirt with a stone-colored jewel-neck sweater and black kitten heels. Her hair was carefully brushed and held back with a black velvet headband that looked a little too young for her, and a little too saucy for the occasion. She wore small gold earrings. Her lipstick looked too bright for her pale skin.

"You have no right to do this, Mister Horning," she snarled, drawing out the "Mister" in mocking fashion. Her hand trembled and the warrant shook.

"I do have the right, Mrs. Bushnell. I'm sorry to put you and your family through this, but my men are going to perform this search, starting right now. Officers, come in," Matt ordered them, using his right arm to create a barrier between them and the Bushnells.

Fred grabbed the warrant back from his wife and skimmed it quickly. His shoulders slumped, and he handed it back to Matt, resigning himself.

"Do what you have to do, but I need answers to some questions."

"Fair enough, Fred. But first, here's how this is going to work this morning. You and Jack are going into the kitchen to talk with me. Marjorie and Susan, you will go with Jay and Fern into the dining room, and Ed will take Gary into the living room for further questioning. Your rights were read to you yesterday, and still apply today unless you object and want to call a lawyer."

"We don't need a lawyer," said Fred. Marjorie was silent.

"OK, then the officers will start their search. Jack," Matt said, "please come with your dad and me into the kitchen." The three siblings had gathered behind their parents. Everyone quietly moved to their appointed areas, and the PSPD officers started off down the hallway.

"Who is involved in Emily's investigation, Horning?" asked Fred. "I'm her father, I have a right to know."

"We've called in the Chinook County major crime team, and I believe you know most of them. In addition to Ed representing the Oregon State Police, and Jay on the Port Stirling side, we're being helped out by the DA and Fern from the county, Patty Perkins representing the Twisty River P.D., the county sheriff, Earl Johnson. The Buck Bay P.D. are marshalling their force to provide me with more investigative help. Oh, and Dr. Bernice Ryder in her role as the county's Medical Examiner. The team met yesterday, and all will have an active role in helping me bring your daughter's killer to justice. And, they all wanted me to express their condolences to you and your family. Everyone is so sorry."

"We're a close-knit town," said Fred sadly, putting his arm around Jack's shoulder. "This is a shock to everyone."

"Yes, sir."

"Who's checking to see if there are any strangers in town? Nobody we know would want to hurt my little girl."

"My department is running checks on license plates and local hotels and motels, and the Buck Bay officers are scoping out the rest of the county with Sheriff Johnson's deputies."

"It must have been some pervert staying at Port Stirling Links," Fred said, his voice shaking with anger.

"Why do you say that?"

"Because they fly in here with their millions in the bank, and don't give a thought to the townspeople. It's surprising we haven't had more trouble from them since this damnable course was built. Was Emily abused?" His eyes looked haunted.

"No, she was not. Dr. Ryder said she was stabbed, and it was over quickly." Matt saw no reason at this point to share the information about the bite marks found on his daughter's body. Fred sobbed into his hands.

"Like with a knife?" asked Jack.

"Yes, son, with a knife. That's one of the things my officers are hunting for this morning. You don't have one in your room, do you?" Matt asked Jack, searching his face for any telltale signs of guilt.

"No."

"Did you hide one Friday night, Jack? Maybe you hid it in the rocks on the beach somewhere?"

"Look, Horning," Fred got a hold of himself. "You can turn this house upside down for all I care, but you're not going to badger my son."

"Everyone in this house is a suspect, Fred. I've got to question your family. We'll rule people out when we can verify alibis, but until that happens, you need to let me do my job. Now, let's you and Jack and I go into the kitchen, please."

"I don't have a knife," Jack said, sitting down quietly at the kitchen table. Fred sat in the chair next to him, while Matt took a seat opposite the two.

"I believe you, Jack." Matt said. "Let's talk more about what you did Friday night. Would that be OK with you?"

"I told that other guy yesterday, I went to the movies with Joey." Jack waved his hand in the direction of Ed.

"Where exactly did you go?"

Jack looked at Matt liked he thought that was the dumbest question ever. "The Port Stirling Cinema. It's the only place in town."

"Oh, that's right. I forgot there is only one theater. What did you see?" Matt asked in a friendly voice.

"The new *Star Wars*."

"Was it cool?"

"I guess so. It was kinda hard to follow at first."

"What's the title mean? I haven't seen it."

"I think it was a starship, but I'm not sure. They never really explained it. Kinda dopey. They screwed this one up."

"How did it end? Did all the bad guys get killed?"

Jack hesitated. "Well, we didn't really see the end. It got kinda boring, so me and Joey bounced over to the other screen, and by the time we came back, it was over."

"Oh, I didn't realize there are two screens at the Cinema," Matt said. "What was playing in the other room?"

"*Deadpool*. It was kinda dorky."

"Who was in it?"

"That Ryan guy was the main dude."

"So you went back to the first movie?"

"That's what I just said."

"Just answer Chief Horning's questions, Jack," inserted Fred.

"Sure, dad."

Jack twitched. "Yeah, we got some popcorn and then snuck back into it, but the credits were rolling."

"I understand that your sister dropped you off. How'd you get home? Did Joey give you a lift?"

Jack paused and looked at a spot on the wall like he was trying to remember.

"Uh, no, I walked."

"You walked home?" Matt asked. His eyebrows may have shot up. "How far is it from the theater to your house?"

"Dunno. I jogged most of the way, so it didn't take me long. It's probably, like, a mile or something."

"How did Joey get home?"

"His dumb mother was going to pick him up. That's why I walked. I don't like her and she doesn't like me."

"Oh? Why is that?" Matt asked.

"She's stupid," Jack replied, as if it were the most natural thing in the world.

"How do you know she doesn't like you?"

"Joey told me. He said she said that I was too smart for my own good, and that I have a big head cuz dad's the mayor. Like being mayor of this place is anything special." Jack let out a little snort. "Sorry, dad," he said sheepishly, looking up at his father.

"It's OK, Jack. You're right; it's just a job." Fred looked very sad.

"Does Joey think that?" Matt went on as if he hadn't heard Fred.

"Nah, we got a good laugh," Jack smiled. "I think Joey knows his mom is kinda stupid. Sorry, but it's the truth." He rubbed his chin, as if he was searching for non-existent stubble.

Matt paused and waited for Fred to admonish Jack about calling his friend's mother stupid, but Fred sat there looking at his lap.

Changing gears. "Did you go into Emily's room when you got home?" Matt asked quickly, staring hard at Jack's face.

"Nope."

"Did you see her?"

"Nope."

"Did you see anyone?"

"No."

"Did you hear anything?"

"Nope. I think mom and dad were in the family room, but I just went to my room."

"So, you didn't see your parents when you came in?" Matt asked.

"No. I don't usually. I go to my room."

"We could see the light under his door when Marjorie and I went to bed," Fred said quietly, "so we knew he was home. Jack likes to read late, and we don't have a problem with that."

Matt turned to Fred. "But you didn't actually see him?"

"No. But it was just like every other night," Fred said defensively.

"Do you—did you—like your little sister, Jack?" Matt said.

Jack looked hard at Matt for a split second. "I like all my family," he finally replied. "And, I would like to know who hurt Emily. Will you find out?" He looked like he might be about to tear up, so Matt thought that was probably enough for today.

"Yes, son, I will find out," Matt answered, patting Jack on the shoulder. *I hope to hell and high water I do find out.*

* * *

Turning to Fred, Matt asked, "Anyone ever threatened you or any members of your family?"

"Not that I can recall," said Fred. "There are the occasional lunatics who don't like a zoning decision or my actions on the vagrants or the like, but they're harmless. People here speak out when they don't like something; it's the way we do things."

"Do they show up at City Council meetings, or how do you know when someone is unhappy?" Matt asked.

"Most of the time, people call me up on the phone and give me a piece of their mind."

"When is the last time that happened?"

Fred massaged his temples. "Not for several weeks. Probably the last time the water went off. City crew hit a pipe."

"Has anyone been upset with you recently?" Matt continued. "Anyone display any anger toward you, or said anything in the past week or so?"

"What about that nutcase Fergus who brought you the vegetables?" Jack asked his father. "He seemed pretty ticked off that you weren't helping him build his dopey business."

"Fergus Dunbar? No, he's a gentle soul," Fred said. "He was a little perturbed because I won't mention the farmers' CSA program in a City Council meeting, that's all. He didn't really expect me to promote the business, I don't think. Just wanted to make sure I was talking it up whenever I had the chance to do so. And we don't use the word "nutcase", Jack, OK?"

"Sorry, dad."

"Has he ever been 'perturbed' toward you previously?" Matt asked Fred.

"No, not really. Fergus is a good guy. It's just that this time of year, without an abundance of fresh crops and fresh tourists, all the farmers around these parts get a little antsy."

"Does Fergus live in town?"

"Sort of. He lives north a bit. You take 101 out of town, and then turn right on the north side of the river. Probably about four miles. I don't think Fergus meant any harm," said Fred. "He's a pretty good guy."

"But he blew a gasket at you, dad," insisted Jack.

"Yes, he yelled, but he was just frustrated because he's not making much money this winter," Fred said. "You'll understand that when you're older. I don't think he was mad at me, specifically."

"Just kind of a 'mad at the universe' thing, you think?" asked Matt.

"Exactly."

"Is there anyone else you can think of who would want to harm you or your family?"

"I'll think more about it, but, no, I can't think of anyone," Fred said. "At least, no one who could be disturbed enough to hurt Emily. It doesn't make any sense," he said staring at Matt with dead eyes.

"No, it doesn't," Matt agreed. "But someone killed her, and we have to figure out who had the means, motive, and opportunity."

CHAPTER 17

Sunday, 9:30 a.m.

Jay, Fern, Marjorie, and Susan took up positions at the dining room table. Fern made a note that the mother and daughter seated opposite her were not sitting particularly close to one another.

Jay walked Marjorie and Susan through their alibis, and nothing substantial had changed in the telling of their stories. He followed up on names and contact information for the girls at Susan's slumber party.

"Will they all have to know what happened to Em?" asked a distraught Susan.

"Eventually, yes," answered Jay. "But we're going to try to keep the details of our investigation as private as we can for now."

"Thank you for that, Jay," said Marjorie.

"The fewer people who know what happened, the easier it is for us to catch potential suspects by surprise."

"And it buys your family some time to cope with your grief," added Fern. "The news will get out. It always does in Port Stirling, but we'll try to protect your privacy as long as we can."

"I want to talk about your whereabouts and activities earlier this week," said Jay. "And whether you had any angry or unpleasant encounters with anyone in town. Let's start with that last part—any run-ins with anyone? Anybody mad at you or your family for any reason?"

Marjorie squeezed the bridge of her nose. "Well, I saw Ted Frolick wandering too close to the road a couple of days ago when I drove into town," Marjorie said. "He was walking with traffic and could have easily been hit from behind, so I rolled down my window and told him he was too close to the road. He flipped me the bird and kept walking. Can you believe it? I'm trying to help the old geezer and he gives me the finger," she said shaking her head in disbelief.

"Does he know who you are?" Jay asked.

"Well, of course, he knows who I am. I'm the mayor's wife; everyone knows who I am." She looked at Jay and he knew she was thinking: *What kind of foolish question is that?*

"Why do you think he reacted that way?" Jay persisted. "It would seem to me that he would thank you and move away from the road."

"Who knows?" Marjorie said. "Ted has bats in the belfry. Next time I'll let him get hit."

"Anyone else you can think of who seemed angry at you or Fred this week?"

"Well, there are always people unhappy with Fred because of city policies, but it never amounts to anything. One did come to the house this week—Fergus Dunbar, he's a farmer, and we buy a weekly produce basket from him. He was raging at Fred about something."

"When was this?"

"I think it was Tuesday evening."

"What exactly did he say to Fred? Did he threaten him?"

"I didn't pay any attention, sorry," said Marjorie. "Fergus is a hippie and I don't have patience with those people. I do like his vegetables, however," she added.

"He was mad at dad because dad won't do more to help the farmers," said Susan. She was slumped in her chair, and her breathing was a little shallow. "I listened to him. Dad got him calmed down, and Mr. Dunbar left. I don't think he would hurt Em, he's a nice man. I like him."

"O.K, I'll note his name just in case," said Jay. "Anyone else?"

"No, Fergus and old Frolick are the only ones I can think of," Marjorie said.

"Moving on then, who took care of Emily on Friday?"

Marjorie answered, "She was with me the entire day."

"What did the two of you do?"

"Oh, you know, the usual—shopping, errands, cooking."

"Did Emily act different than normal?"

"No."

"Nothing unusual at all in her behavior?" Jay asked.

"Nothing."

"While you were out and about town, is there a chance that Emily saw something she wasn't meant to see?" Fern asked Marjorie.

"Like what?" asked Marjorie.

"You know, mom, like a big drug deal going down," said Susan.

"Yeah, something like that," Fern said looking at Susan.

"Certainly not," said Marjorie. "Don't be ridiculous, Susan. We didn't see or do anything out of the ordinary. It was just another day."

"What about Thursday?" Jay continued. "Where was Emily the day before?"

"I took her to the doctor on Thursday morning," Marjorie said. "She had a little cough, and I wanted to make sure it wasn't anything to worry about."

"Was it?" asked Jay.

"Was it what?" Marjorie said.

"Something to worry about?"

"No, she was just getting over a case of the sniffles. Our doctor said she simply needed another day or two of rest. He said to keep her as quiet as I could, and she'd be fine."

"What else did you do on Thursday?" Jay asked.

"We went to Summers' Pharmacy, and to Toni's Threads to shop."

"I love that store, too," said Fern. "What did you buy?"

"I bought a cashmere sweater."

"It's real pretty," added Susan. "That was the new red sweater you were wearing Friday, right?"

"Yes, sweetie. One needs a bright color to get through January sometimes."

"Did you leave Emily in the car at any time when you were shopping?" Jay asked.

Marjorie shifted her weight in her chair. "I might have left her just for a minute when I ran into the pharmacy to pick up a prescription," she said, her voice thin and defensive.

"Where was that?" Jay asked.

"At Summer's Pharmacy. I'm not about to go to that new impersonal Rite Aid," Marjorie huffed. Jay thought he saw the tip of her nose raise up in the air slightly. *OK, we're not going to Rite Aid. Got it.*

"Any other time Emily might have been alone for a few minutes?"

"No, I don't think so. At least, not while we were out of the house. She played in her room and watched TV in the family room. She was curled up on the floor with her blankie. The Muppets were on."

"How did she act when you came out of the pharmacy? Any different than when you'd left her?" Jay continued.

Marjorie looked over at the painting on the wall behind Jay's left shoulder. He didn't know his British castles all that well, but he thought it might be an oil painting of Windsor Castle. It looked like it had hung there forever.

"She might have been a little subdued," Marjorie said. "But she did have a cold, and it was getting late in the afternoon, so she was probably a little pooped out."

"Did she say anything when you returned to the car?"

"Just 'are we going home now, mommy?' That's what she always says when we come back to the car."

"Were you in the habit of leaving her alone in the car?" Fern asked.

Marjorie glared at her. "Do you have children, Fern?" she said.

"No, Mrs. Bushnell, I don't."

"Then your question is out of line."

"We are trying to investigate your daughter's death," said Fern. "I would think you would want us to understand any family patterns that might help Jay and the Chief get to the bottom of your tragedy."

"Was that all Emily said: 'are we going home now'?" Jay inserted. "Did she say anything like 'I saw Billy and Wendy', or I saw Mr. Huggins'? Anything like that?"

"No. Nothing else. If she saw anything strange, she didn't mention it. Emily was essentially with me entirely on both days - Thursday and Friday," Marjorie's jaw quivered. "If she saw something she shouldn't have, she never told me."

* * *

Sunday, 10:00 a.m.

In the Bushnell kitchen, Matt's cell phone rang, and he recognized Patty Perkins' number.

"Excuse me for a minute," he said to Fred and Jack, and slipped out through the sliding glass door that led to a cement patio.

"Hi, Patty. What's up?"

"Thank you for picking up. I've uncovered something intriguing during my questioning of Ted Frolick."

"Are you still at his place?"

"No, I've got a statement from him, and I'm in City Hall writing up my report, but I wanted to get to you while you are still with the Bushnells. Get ready - this is a bombshell," Patty continued.

"OK, you've got my attention," Matt said.

"It seems that one of our local firemen, Craig Kenton, might be having an affair with Marjorie Bushnell. Ted Frolick has seen them together twice, once in compromising circumstances."

Matt, stunned, grunted, "Huh? Would she dare do anything that dumb in a village this size, the mayor's wife? Everyone would know, wouldn't they?"

"That's exactly what I thought when I first heard about it," said Patty. "Marjorie is a lot of things, but I never pegged her for dumb. Frolick told me he first saw Marjorie and Kenton coming out of the A-frame cabin below the Pacific View Motel. Frolick was down on the beach directly below them, and recognized them both. They stood clutching each other and kissing. Frolick said they looked like they were saying 'good-bye.'"

"But Frolick has a reputation for being a little—how shall I say—quirky, doesn't he?"

"I know, I know," said Patty, waving one hand in the air for emphasis, even though she was the only person in the War Room. "Frolick might not be the most reliable witness, but he's not as crazy as people say. It's possible that he's got some dementia starting, but he's aware of his situation, and he knows when he's in the moment and when he isn't. He knows both Marjorie and Kenton, and swears it was them. He told me they didn't see him because he was on the far side of two big rocks, and he hid when he saw them."

"You said he saw them together twice; when was the time at the cabin, and when and where was the second time?" Matt asked, at full attention.

"He saw them leaving the cabin about a month ago—he couldn't remember the exact day. But he said it was mid-morning on a weekday.

And then he saw them again last week in the parking lot behind Goodie's Market, pulled up in both of their cars and talking out the windows." Patty looked down at the table and shuffled through her notes. "Frolick also said that Emily was with her mother in the car's back seat in the parking lot," she added in a quieter voice. "He thought it might have been on Thursday afternoon."

"So you think Marjorie might have been worried that Emily would say something to her dad about 'mommy talking to a strange man'?"

"It's a real possibility, don't you think?" Patty answered.

"Holy shit," Matt said. "Yes, it's a possibility. Four-year-olds often say whatever pops into their head. Another possibility is that maybe Emily told her daddy about 'mommy and the strange man in the parking lot', and daddy decided he didn't want that story getting out."

"Also a possibility," Patty had to admit.

"What if Frolick was trying to deflect your attention away from him?"

"I considered that, Chief. But if he did, it was fast thinking on his part. I surprised him at his house while he was working in his garden. Unless he prepared this story in case we got on to him, it was fairly elaborate considering he didn't know I was coming to talk to him. And it didn't feel rehearsed to me—it just came up in our conversation. I'm—probably like you—a hard evidence kind of gal. But I also rely on my gut instincts, especially in the early stages of an investigation. I've been doing this a long time, Chief, and my gut on Frolick is that he was telling me the truth. There were too many details that someone making up a story on the spot wouldn't have included."

"Marjorie is a key player in this case," Matt said. "Whether Frolick is telling the truth or lying, this is still an important lead we need to follow, Patty. We need to know if it's true, and, if it is true, did Fred know about the affair. This will be fun…not," said Matt, shaking his head.

"Yeah," Patty agreed.

"In any event, I'll check it out. If Frolick is telling the truth, it's our first possible motive in this ugly case," Matt said. "I won't quiz Marjorie about it yet. We'll want to find this Kenton guy, and talk to him simultaneously when we confront Marjorie. If it's true, we don't want the two lovebirds to get their stories straight. Can you hang out at City Hall until we wrap up this round here?"

"Sure. I'll finish my report, and then eat lunch if you're not back."

"Do you have any idea where we might find Mr. Kenton?"

"Frolick said in addition to being a fireman, he also works at the hardware store. He's probably working today. Do you want me to go talk to him?"

Matt reflected for a moment. "Not yet, Patty. I'm inclined to send Ed to question Kenton. I think a big, strong state cop might be a bit more intimidating than you or me to a fireman. I'll stick with Marjorie while we see what Ed turns up."

Patty laughed. "If I had something to hide, yeah, Ed would intimidate me. Good choice. I'll do some background checking on Frolick, and I'll catch you later."

"One more thing, and I'm looking for your gut instinct here. Is Ted Frolick a suspect, in your view?" Matt asked her.

"Possibly. He's a bit of an odd duck, but if I had to bet the farm on it, I'd say no, I don't think Frolick killed Emily. He doesn't seem like the violent type. He'd rather outsmart you."

"Good work here, Patty. I'm on it, and we'll see you back at the ranch. Thanks."

Before Matt re-entered the kitchen, he caught a glimpse of Fred and Jack. Jack leaned forward with his arms crossed on the kitchen table, and his head resting on them. He faced away from his father, and his eyes were closed. Fred rested one hand on the boy's back, and stared solemnly at the back of his son's head. Either one of them might be a murderer, but, for now, if they had lost a daughter and a sister, Matt felt a stab of sorrow and pain for both of them.

* * *

Sunday, 9:30 a.m.

While Ed believed Gary's explanation of his Friday night, and still felt he was telling the truth, he felt a bit more uneasy about Gary this morning. *There's something a little off here,* he thought. *It's like he's not really who he pretends to be, or he has more to tell.*

"What time did you get home?" Ed asked the oldest Bushnell sibling, who kept pulling on a stray hair sticking out from a mole on his left jaw.

"It was late, man," Gary answered with a self-conscious smile. "Two o'clock, maybe, 2:30, something like that."

"We talked to the woman who owns the Stirling Tavern—Paula—and she said she couldn't swear to it that you never left the tavern Friday night. Said she didn't keep her eye on you and your friends all night. When I asked her if you could have slipped out for an hour and then slipped back in, she said it was possible, and she might not have noticed. She had a big crowd Friday, and didn't keep tabs on everyone. What do you say to that?"

"Aww, she knows I was there all night," Gary argued. "I talked to her off and on the whole time. I don't know why she'd say a thing like that. That's bullshit."

"We are going to interrogate your pals next. Is there anything you want to tell me before we see if they confirm your alibi...or not?"

"Like what?" Gary snarled, finally dropping the 'I'm such a good soul' façade. "That I killed my baby sister? Is that what you want me to say? Well, I didn't. I loved her. She was the only good thing in this fucked-up family. She was sweet and loving, and I loved her back. I would never hurt a hair on her beautiful head." He started to cry, openly and without reserve.

Ed was taken aback. "What's so fucked up about your family?" he asked.

"Everything," Gary said through sobs. "For starters, don't you wonder why Susan, Jack and me all look alike, and Emily doesn't look like any of us? And she came along ten years after us?" he challenged.

"I hadn't noticed that she didn't look like any of you," Ed admitted. "Why do you mention it now?"

"The three of us look like the perfect melding of Marjorie and Fred. Emily only resembles Marjorie. You figure it out," spat Gary.

"Are you suggesting that Emily was not Fred's daughter?"

"You're not as dumb as you look."

"Whose daughter is she?"

"How the fuck would I know? I was 14 when she was born. I don't know what my mother was up to, do I?"

"Does your father suspect this too?"

"I don't know. Honestly. If I figured it out, you'd think he would too. We've never talked about it as a family, if that's what you mean."

"And you never questioned your mother?"

Gary glowered at the state cop. "Yeah, I'll get right on that," he said sarcastically. "Can't you imagine that conversation? 'Hey, mom, who'd you fuck today?' Gimme a break."

"Calm down, Gary," said Ed, moving his palm-down hands in an up-and-down motion over the dining room table. "Relax. I know this is awkward for you, but it might be important. Did you ever have an inkling who Emily's biological father might be? Is there anyone in town she looks like?"

"I never gave it much thought. Figured if dad didn't care, neither did I. And I didn't want to hurt Em. She was always such a happy, smiley girl. So, no, I don't know and I don't really care. Especially now. She's gone and it doesn't matter—she was my sister in every sense of the word." Gary looked despondent, and all traces of his belligerent behavior disappeared.

"Why do you think this happened while you were home visiting?" Ed continued. "It seems like a strange coincidence to me."

"Yeah, I've been wondering that too," he said morosely. "I can't answer that question, Lieutenant."

"Any ideas who might have done this? What do you think happened to Emily?"

Gary looked at Ed. "I don't have a fucking clue. We're not the closest family on the planet, but I have a hard time believing that my brother or sister or one of my parents stuck a knife in Em's belly and twisted it. It has to be some other weird shit. A random break-in or robbery, or something we don't know anything about. It's fucked up, for sure."

"For sure," Ed agreed. "When were you planning to go back to Eugene?"

"In about a week. Next term starts on January 15."

"Good. We'll need you to stay put for now while our investigation continues."

This is an angry, hurt young man, who feels betrayed by life and his family, but he didn't kill his beloved baby sister. Ed was certain. *Did Fred or Marjorie kill Emily to protect an explosive family secret?*

CHAPTER 18

Ed went into the kitchen and indicated to Matt he had what he needed from Gary. The forensics team wrapped up their work, and Matt instructed them to go to City Hall and wait for him.

Ed and Gary took seats around the table with Fred and Jack, and the five guys talked quietly while they waited for Jay and Fern to terminate their questioning.

With instructions from Matt to the family to stay home, and Fern checking with the parents whether they needed anything, food, medicine, and so forth, the four took their leave. Matt corralled them beyond the Bushnell's yard gate, and whispered to them what Ted Frolick had said about Marjorie and Craig Kenton.

"Oh, for God's sake," said a disgusted Jay.

"Hold on there, quick draw," admonished Matt. "We don't know yet if it's true. But we're sure as hell going to find out. This is the first lead we've got."

"We may have another motive—might even tie to what Patty learned," big Ed said, trying to whisper, but not quite pulling it off. "Gary thinks that little Emily had a different father than the other three kids. Says she didn't look anything like the other siblings, or like Fred. Says she only looked like Marjorie. Also said Emily had a different disposition than his brother and older sister…sweeter, not as quick to anger as the rest of them."

"Now that you mention it," said Jay, "Emily did look different from the rest of them. She's the only blonde in the family."

"You know, I'm not comfortable talking about this any further here," Matt said, glancing back at the front door. "Too open. Let's regroup at City Hall."

Turning his squad car out of Cranberry Drive, Matt asked Fern if she knew Craig Kenton.

"Yes, I know him."

"What color hair does he have?"

"Blonde. Fair skin."

"And? What do you make of this news about him being Marjorie's boyfriend?"

"I don't know," said Fern slowly. "There's no question it would be drop-dead ill-advised of her. But . . ."

"But what?"

"Honestly, I wouldn't put it past her. She's a complicated woman, in my view. And Craig Kenton is tempting."

"Oh?"

Fern's cheeks reddened and she looked out the window in an attempt to hide the blush. Matt thought it looked nice on her.

"He's quite the stud," Fern stammered.

Matt laughed at her use of the word 'stud'; it was hilarious coming out of her mouth.

"Well, he is," she said defensively.

"Did you ever date him?"

"No. I just met him last month when my Fitbit battery died. He was working at the hardware store and helped me with it. I planned to go back in soon with another hardware need, if you must know."

"That good-looking, huh?"

Fern ignored Matt's teasing. "He's a little young for Marjorie, I would think."

"Wonder how they met, if it's true?"

"Well, the volunteer firemen have a community-wide picnic every August. It's their big fundraiser, and the mayor always gives a speech and hands out awards. Or, she could have wandered into the hardware store like me."

"Did he make a move on you?"

"What kind of question is that?" Fern barked, and then, "He was friendly."

"Sorry, just trying to get a bead on this guy. So, did he?"

She hesitated. "Not really. What's Marjorie got that I haven't got?"

"Beats me," Matt laughed, and Fern, in spite of herself, smiled with him.

"Guess I'll be crossing him off my list," she said.

"We'll see where the Marjorie/Craig story takes us. And, if it wasn't Fred, who the hell was Emily's father? Finally, some possible motives to pursue."

"Finally?" said Fern sarcastically. "It's only been a little over twenty-four hours. I think you're doing great."

"If a homicide is going to be solved, it usually unfolds fairly quickly after the investigation starts. We're behind," Matt scowled.

* * *

Kill chief! Bite! Shark in tree! Eat arm! Too close. Touching! Stop touching! Kill cops! Kill Tex! Too pretty! Stop touching! Knife in eye! Eat!

CHAPTER 19

Sunday, Noon

"Goddammit!" Patty Perkins said aloud, although she thought she only said it to herself. But Sylvia Hofstetter, on the telephone at her desk in the police department's squad room next to where Patty was working, said "Shhh" to her, giving her the international finger-over-the-mouth shushing gesture.

"Sorry," Patty mouthed back to her.

The cause of Patty's swearing was an archival piece from the *Port Stirling Beacon*, dated six years earlier. Ted Frolick had appeared in Chinook County court on an assault charge, after slapping a sixth-grade boy in his home-room class at Port Stirling Middle School. The boy's parents filed suit against Frolick, and the district attorney brought charges. Frolick pleaded guilty, and was given a suspended sentence, as he had no prior record.

But it did get him fired from his teaching position. As far as Patty could tell, he'd not gotten another teaching job, and retired after the incident.

Great. Hitting a child. Is Ted a suspect after all? Maybe he doesn't like kids. There was nothing else about Frolick that stood out when Patty researched his past, but this incident didn't help her theory.

She closed out of the department's computer she'd been using, and with a wave to Sylvia, grabbed her purse. *Back to Frolick's house I go.*

Patty was happy to see that the blue sky and fluffy white clouds of this morning were still overhead, but the wind had picked up. And, there were some distinctly non-fluffy clouds out to sea that appeared to be barreling towards Port Stirling. But for now, she enjoyed what was sure to be the short-lived warmth of the sun.

Frolick welcomed her in and made tea for them. A fire burned, and the approaching storm's advance wind occasionally came rushing down the fireplace and ruffled the newspaper on his footstool. Why people liked living on the beach was beyond Patty.

"Can you tell me about Jason Wilbert and what happened the day you hit him in school?" began Patty.

To his credit, Frolick didn't get all huffy or petulant when confronted with this past transgression. "He was a snot-nosed bully," said Ted calmly. "And, he had a touch of ADD, although we didn't know it back then. He was pulling a girl's hair at the desk in front of him, and he wouldn't stop after repeated requests from me to do so. He also kept jumping up and down and was perilously close to being out of control. I slapped him to get his attention and get him to calm down. It worked. However, his parents weren't thrilled at my technique."

"Obviously," Patty had to smile. "Were you fired?"

"Yes. Too much pressure on the superintendent."

"Did you resent it?"

Ted sipped his tea and thought about her question. "No, I can't really say I did. I'd been considering retirement anyway, and this was the push I needed. My PERS account was substantial after 30 years of teaching, and—you may have noticed—I'm a man of modest means. I was rather happy to walk off into the sunset."

"Do you like children, Mr. Frolick?"

"I used to. My wife and I didn't have any of our own, and teaching—we were both teachers—seemed to make up for that in the early days. But after a few years, one realizes that children are as annoying as adults, they just come in smaller packages."

"Are you still married?"

"My wife died 15 years ago. Car wreck."

"Oh, I'm sorry." Patty paused. "Can we talk about Marjorie Bushnell? The police department is checking on your story about her and Craig Kenton, and I'd like to know if you can add anything to it."

"Only that I've seen Kenton at that A-frame several times, coming and going. And, usually with a different woman. He seems to do better with women than I do," he smiled. As if to ensure that Patty knew he'd made a joke, he over-dramatically ran a hand through his silver hair, which was now combed and much tidier than earlier this morning.

"But you're sure you saw him with Marjorie Bushnell?"

"Yes. I'm sure. Has she denied it?"

"I'm afraid I can't comment on that, Ted."

Patty and Ted chatted for a while longer over their tea in front of the crackling fire. He was forthcoming, she was relaxed, and it all felt quite cozy.

* * *

Sunday, 1:30 p.m.

Back in the War Room, Matt added to his list of case questions on the big board: 'Are MB and CK having an affair?', and 'Did Emily see something she shouldn't have?' He started to write 'Who is Emily's real father?', but then erased it. Couldn't risk anyone seeing that question. Patty joined the Chief, Jay, Ed and Fern. "Let's start with Marjorie and Kenton," said Matt.

Patty walked the team through her conversation with Ted Frolick and his revelation about Marjorie.

Jay said, ""Not sure I believe it. Old man Frolick is nuts, and I'd need another source before I'd be convinced."

"He's not that old, Jay," interrupted Patty. "Probably about my age, maybe a few years older."

"OK, but why would Marjorie risk it?"

"If I had a dollar for every ludicrous extra-marital affair I've encountered in this business, I could retire today," said Ed. "Plus, Patty's instincts are A+, and if she thinks there is the slightest possibility that Frolick saw what he says he saw, it's a motive, folks."

"I agree with you, Ed," said Matt. "Our first lead."

"There's one more teensy little thing," Patty said. Reluctantly, she explained what her research on Frolick unearthed, and related her second conversation with him.

"I remember that!" exclaimed Jay. "It was right after I started working in Port Stirling. I'm not a big fan of Ted Frolick's, but that was a bum deal. The kid's parents were classic helicopter parents, and they completely overreacted."

"Oh, dear," said Fern. "Mr. Frolick's explanation is certainly logical and believable, but it was still an act of violence toward a child. I don't like it."

"Neither do I," agreed Matt. "I need to meet this gentleman before we go any further."

"Just because Frolick slapped a kid once, doesn't mean he's lying about Marjorie and Kenton," argued Ed. "Finding out if his info is correct is still job No. 1 in my book."

"I'll talk to Frolick first and then we'll proceed with our potential adulterers," Matt responded. "Here's how it's gonna go down. Ed, Kenton might be working at the hardware store today, so I want you to go there and confront him. Take him by surprise. We have solid intel that he might be working near the battery section."

Fern looked down at the table to hide her smile.

"Simultaneously, I'll go back to the Bushnells and make small talk until you send me a text. If Kenton admits it to you, give me a thumbs up. If he denies it, thumbs down. Then I'll know what tack to take with Marjorie. Fern, I want you to come with me and pay attention to her body language. She will deny the hell out of this unless I can inform her that Kenton has admitted it. Jay, you will keep Fred busy while I confront Marjorie. I don't want to tell him until we're sure Frolick's got the story right. If Frolick is mistaken, so be it. If Frolick is right and Marjorie is having an affair, then she moves to the top of our list. To that end, I'm going to visit Mr. Frolick next. While I'm gone, you guys keep following up on the siblings' alibis. It would be great to rule out the three kids, or rule in one of them if the evidence goes that way. Fern, this would be a good time for you to start doing research on psychological traits of family killers. I'd like you to get a profile together on which of the Bushnells might fit. I ought to be gone about an hour."

"A mother would kill her baby to protect her secret?" said Fern, raising her eyebrows and looking grim. "Or, a father would kill his own child to cover up for his wife? Struggling with this."

"You'd be surprised," said Matt. "I've seen it all, and much of it is hard to believe. Some people are missing the compassion gene. Some get so strung out on drugs that they lose sight of the difference between right and wrong. Some are evil at heart, or narcissistic, and only care about themselves. Mental illness is a whole other story, and it's a lot more standard than people think. Bottom line is that somebody killed that little girl, and when we find out who it is, I'll bet you my first paycheck the people who know the killer will say 'We can't believe it'.

"Now, tell me what you think, Jay, about Fred possibly not being Emily's father." Matt paused and looked around the table, stopping at each individual for a split second. "It's important that this not leave this room because it may not be true, and could be extremely damaging to the family. Agreed?"

Vigorous nods.

"Well, I have no proof," Jay started, "other than the fact that Emily did look decidedly different from her three siblings. They're all dark, she's blonde. They all have Fred's long, narrow face, Emily's was more apple-like."

"But lots of siblings look different from each other," Matt insisted. "DNA is the only real test."

"True," agreed Ed. "Like I said, Gary has no proof either, but he told me that Emily was always different than the rest of the family, different temperament somehow. And she did come along ten years later."

"That's all circumstantial," Matt said.

"Yep. But Gary and, he says, Susan, are convinced that Marjorie was double-dipping, and Emily was the result. Also, Gary doesn't seem to have a lot of love for mommy."

"Did he ever confront Fred or Marjorie with his suspicions?" asked Patty.

"No. Said it didn't matter to him, that he loved Emily regardless. But he also hinted that it might have given his mother a motive to kill Emily. What if the real father was about to blow the whistle, and Marjorie panicked?"

"But you could also make a case that Fred somehow got wind of it, and decided that Emily needed to be erased," said Jay.

"Exactly," said Matt. "Fred is definitely on our list. We can't verify his alibi, and now there is doubt that Emily was his child. We may have to ask Fred to take a paternity test."

"Jesus Christ," said Ed. "Let's don't go there unless we absolutely have to, please."

"Agreed. I would guess that not one of you sitting around this table wants to make that phone call, including me. Especially me," Matt amended. "But a child is dead; we may have to."

CHAPTER 20

Sunday, 2:30 p.m.

It was remarkable to Matt how the weather changed what this place looked and felt like. Yesterday's driving rain and last night's soupy fog imparted a bleak, foreboding quality that touched on everything and everyone. Except for the white boats bobbing in the blue harbor along the shore in downtown, Port Stirling wasn't much to look it. Nondescript, squatty buildings, most built unimaginatively in the 1940s, lined the four or five streets that made up the commercial center. But on this Sunday afternoon, with the sun out, the town felt more benign and congenial. It was a glossy jewel of a day—sky, river, lighthouse, sea, all sparkling in the glow of the sun, and Matt rolled down the window of his squad car as he drove. If he hadn't seen Emily's body for himself, Matt never would have believed that brutal murder could take place in such an agreeable hamlet.

Driving from City Hall to Ted Frolick's place on Ocean Bend Road, just down from his new home, the road looped around a bluff, and showcased the first view of the ocean. This afternoon, the sun reflected off the sparkling water, and the waves wore reticent little white tops. Tons of water in the waves still pounded as they hit the shoreline, but now, it was a gentler sound.

Cries emanating from the seagulls seemed softer, not as urgent. The shimmering sand looked as though no human had ever tread on it. The little wind there was caressed Matt's skin instead of abusing it as yesterday's gale had done.

Heading south, the virgin coastline stretched on as far as Matt's eye could see. He wondered, not for the first time since he'd laid eyes on Oregon last month, why nobody knew about this part of the world. An incredible land of ocean, forests, rivers, lakes, and unblemished beauty, with hardly any people. No matter how this case turned out, Matt was grateful for this discovery of Port Stirling and of Oregon—it was possible he belonged here. In only one day, he felt more valued here than he ever did in Plano. *And no psychopath is going to steal my future, or get away with butchering this little girl.*

Pulling up in front of Frolick's house, Matt saw a man—who must be him—coming out the front door. He was dressed in gray sweat pants, sneakers, and an old paint-splattered sweatshirt that had seen better days. A floppy hat tied under his chin. His skin beneath his silver hair was fair, and Matt figured the hat was skin-cancer protection.

Matt got out of his car and approached, ready to flash his ID, which was his Texas driver's license.

"Hi. Are you Ted Frolick?"

"I am. And who might you be?"

Matt noted an intelligent face, and sharp, deep brown eyes. He held up his ID so that Frolick could clearly see it, and said "I'm Matt Horning. I'm the new police chief, just arrived yesterday, and this is the only official ID I have. I'd like a few minutes of your time. Is this a good time for you to talk?"

"Mr. Horning, it's nice to meet you," said Frolick, extending his hand to shake. "Welcome to our small burg. Please let the record show that I am cooperating with the police on this dreadful business, however, if you want to talk now, you must accompany me on my walk on the beach. We have a saying in Oregon: "When the sun comes out, go out.""

"That sounds like a smart saying, based on yesterday's weather," Matt laughed. "Let's go." He wasn't dressed for a stroll on the beach, especially with his dress shoes on, but he decided to improvise. They headed off to the staircase across the road that led down to the beach. At the bottom of the stairs, Matt removed his shoes and socks, carrying one shoe in each hand.

"North or south?" Matt asked, letting Frolick decide on their direction.

"I'm not afraid of the crime scene, Mr. Horning, let's go south." Frolick looked at Matt, and Matt nodded in agreement. He was secretly glad that Frolick picked this direction because he wanted to see his reaction as they neared the taped-off tunnel. Facial tics and body language could tell a story, plus, it would have been somewhat telling if Frolick elected to go in the other direction, away from Emily's tunnel. *Emily's tunnel*, thought Matt. *We can't call that awful place by that name.*

Frolick set a brisk pace and started the conversation. "Are you an educated man, Mr. Horning?"

"University of Texas, sir. Does that count?"

Frolick smiled. "It's a fine institution of higher learning. I thought I detected a bit of a Texas drawl."

"Where did you go to school, Mr. Frolick?"

"Oh, I'm one of those obnoxious eastern elite liberals," he chuckled. "I went to Dartmouth, up in New Hampshire. Why haven't you been properly announced to our fair citizenry as George's replacement? We knew he was retiring, but we don't know about you yet. I heard about you from Ms. Perkins."

"That's because I wasn't officially supposed to start work until Tuesday," Matt said. "But I arrived here yesterday morning, and, well, we have this murder to deal with. We didn't have time for a big public ceremony, and it didn't feel right anyway under the circumstances.

Especially considering it's the mayor's daughter. I started working on the case yesterday morning immediately after Emily's body was discovered. And that's why I want to talk to you." Matt looked sideways at Frolick, but there was no change in the older man's expression.

"I've already told Ms. Perkins everything I know, which is, essentially, nothing that can help you," Frolick said.

"Oh, that's not true, Mr. Frolick."

Frolick's head snapped around to look at Matt.

"You may have helped us big-time," Matt continued. "Your heads-up on Marjorie Bushnell's affair with Craig Kenton may end up being a huge clue. Thank you for sharing that bit of information with Patty— it's important."

"It is intriguing, considering what's happened, isn't it?"

"Yes, I can't get into specifics with you, but you did the right thing telling us. I've got a few questions. Let's shift gears, if you don't mind. Can you tell me where you were and what you were doing between the hours of 6:00 p.m. and midnight on Friday?"

"I've given a statement. Did you read it?" No sarcasm, just matter-of-fact.

"I've read it, and now I want to hear it in your own words."

Frolick hesitated, and bent over to examine a dead starfish. It was a reddish-brown color with white spots, and cracked in a couple of places. After a pause of several seconds, he said "I went to the store's deli and bought my dinner, came home, ate it while I listened to some music. Vivaldi, I think. Read a book until about 9:30 p.m., at which time I turned in for the night."

"Did you see or talk to anyone Friday night?"

"No, I did not. Only the clerk at the deli."

"Didn't talk to anyone on the phone?"

"No. I rarely use my phone as it is."

"What book are you reading?"

"*A Farewell to Arms.* Hemingway."

"I know the book," Matt said. "Did you go down to the beach at all Friday night?"

"No, I did not."

"Why would Lydia Campbell think you might have?"

Frolick smiled. "Lydia worries about me. She knows I tend to wander off occasionally."

"What do you mean 'wander off'?"

"Sometimes when I'm out walking or beachcombing for treasures, I forget how long I've been gone, or I end up far from my starting point. It's one of the joys of getting old, young man. You'll see," he smiled. No malice. Friendly.

"Do you like Mayor Bushnell?" Matt asked. "Did you vote for him?"

"Yes and yes."

"Do you know where he lives?"

"If you keep going down Ocean Bend Road, you turn left on Cranberry Drive opposite the Whale Rock Wayside," Frolick said, as if he was giving driving directions to Matt. "The Bushnell home is at the end of the cul-de-sac. Pretty, two-story house with a nicely-done garden. I believe they hire Jose Flores to take care of it."

"Do you know which window is Emily's room?"

Frolick stopped walking and turned to face Matt. "No, I do not. I've never been in the house, and I've had little interaction with the Bushnells. I have absolutely no motive whatsoever to kill that child, and I don't have the slightest clue who might have done such a reprehensible thing."

"But the deli workers can only confirm the early part of your story, and no one can fully verify your alibi, Mr. Frolick."

"I live a quiet, peaceful life, by design. If people think I'm weird because I collect things from the sea, or because I wander off on occasion, I can't help that. I also can't help you if you don't have any suspects. I wish I could, if for no other reason than it's unsettling to have a killer on the loose, but I didn't do it, and I don't know who did."

The two walkers reached the crime-scene tape that cordoned off the tunnel. Matt watched as Ted walked up to the tape and peered into the tunnel. The tide was low, about the same height as it would have been on Friday evening. His face and body language didn't reveal anything except curiosity.

"She must have been very afraid," Frolick said softly. "A dark, foggy night in this menacing tunnel with someone intent on doing her harm." He shook his head.

"The coroner thinks she died quickly, and probably didn't realize what was happening. I'm holding onto that, and you should too. That is, if you weren't the one who stabbed her."

Ignoring Matt's remark, Frolick asked "How old was she?"

"Four."

He shook his head again, inhaled and exhaled deeply, and said "Shall we turn around now, Chief?"

"Yes, my feet are getting cold," Matt said. "But what a beautiful day, so different from yesterday."

"We have another saying in Oregon, Chief: 'If you don't like the weather, wait five minutes'. Especially at the beach."

"It did change quickly, didn't it?" remarked Matt. They resumed their walk back the way they came. Matt took a moment to enjoy the beauty, and then said, "Did you see anything on the beach Friday night?"

"It was too foggy to see anything. Foggy and cold. That's why I built a fire and stayed inside where it was cozy. I may be crazy, but I'm not crazy enough to go wandering on a night like that. I can't really see the beach from my house anyway. I can see the water, but I'm too far back to see the beach itself."

"On your rambles last week, did you encounter any strangers? Anyone who stood out for any reason?"

"It's been pretty quiet around here since New Year's. The beach is full of strangers during that week between Christmas and New Year's, but then it drops off, and this year was no exception. I don't recall noticing anyone who looked capable of doing something like this."

"Do you see the Bushnells walking on the beach much? Would you know Emily's siblings if you see them?"

"I taught both Gary and Susan Bushnell, so, yes, I would know them for sure. In fact, I did see Gary last week and talked to him briefly."

"Where did you see him and what did you talk about?"

"I ran into him on the beach south of Whale Rock Wayside. We talked for a couple of minutes, mostly about the University of Oregon and how he was doing so far. He seems to like it."

"Was he alone?"

"Yes. Said his mother was feeding him too much food and he needed to walk off breakfast."

"Was Gary a good student when you taught him?"

"Not really. Stupid as a post, actually. It surprised me that he even got into Oregon. But he was an accomplished athlete so that probably helped his application. Susan isn't very bright either."

"Do you know Jack?" Matt asked.

"I know who he is and would recognize him if I saw him. I've seen him and his father around town—in some of the shops. I was retired, however, before he got to my grade."

"Did you see either Jack or Susan on the beach last week?"

"No, I don't believe so. The whole family was down there on

Christmas Eve. Had a bonfire going. That was probably the last time I saw Jack, Susan, or the mayor."

"But you saw Marjorie and Emily last week, correct?"

"Did Ms. Perkins put that in her report?" Frolick wanted to know.

"Yes, everything you told Patty is there; she's thorough. Why did you slap that boy in school six years ago?" Matt asked, abruptly changing direction.

"Because I hate children and I want them all dead. Look, Chief Horning—is that the proper salutation?—I've explained everything to Ms. Perkins, and it's all in my statement. If she's as thorough as you say she is, and I suspect you are correct in that assessment, you have everything I'm going to say on this matter. I'm not your man."

"We will look into your background, Mr. Frolick. In the meantime, I have to ask you, are you absolutely sure it was Marjorie Bushnell kissing Craig Kenton? No doubt whatsoever in your mind?"

"No doubt at all. It was her, and it was Kenton, and it was more than friendly. Between us men, Kenton had a very proprietary hold on Marjorie, if you know what I mean. They're an item alright."

"You're so sure that you will be comfortable with us confronting both of them?"

"Yes, I am. Wouldn't mind being a fly on the wall when you talk to the two paramours."

"This isn't a game, Mr. Frolick."

"Of course it's not. But if her mother's affair had any bearing on that child's murder, I expect you to prove it."

"I will," Matt said, looking him in the eye. "With your sighting of Marjorie and Kenton earlier, this second encounter with Emily in the car is also an important nugget of information. Do you remember if Emily was awake when you saw them in the supermarket's parking lot?"

"Oh, she was awake all right. She waved to me as I drove by them, big grin on her face. Sweet child. I waved back." Frolick looked down at the sand, clearly upset and not wanting Matt to see it.

Ted Frolick is either completely innocent of Emily's murder, or he's the scariest psychopath I've ever come up against, and, currently, I've got zero evidence either way, thought Matt.

CHAPTER 21

Sunday, 3:00 p.m.

The Port Stirling PD officers, under the direction of Ed and Jay, had been busy checking the alibis of the three siblings, Jay reported to Matt.

"Susan's alibi is watertight. She was at the slumber party with her friends from a little after 6:30 p.m. Friday until Saturday morning. There were multiple witnesses, and everyone's story jives." Jay said. "She was definitely at that slumber party all night after she dropped off Jack at the movies."

"What if she snuck out after the other girls went to bed?" suggested Matt.

"They were up until 2:00 a.m., according to the hostess," Jay said. "I personally checked with Chloe's mother."

"That puts Susan's opportunity out of the question then, according to the ME's time of death," said Matt. "Could Susan and Jack have taken Emily down to that tunnel when they left the house together, killed her together, and then gone about their separate ways?" he posed.

"The timing doesn't add up," said Jay, shaking his head. "According to both Marjorie's and Fred's statements, Emily was still up when Jack and Susan left. I think Susan is out of the picture. Her alibi and the timing make it virtually impossible."

"Do me a favor, Jay, and call Chloe's mother again and ask her if Susan was clean and tidy when she arrived. Any sand or blood, etc.

on her? If she showed no signs of the beach and she arrived when everyone said she did, I agree that Susan is off our list of suspects. The only thing holding me back from completely dismissing her is I detected some uneasiness in Susan when we got her statement," Matt said. "Did either of you feel it?"

"Yes, I thought she was a little squirmy," agreed Fern. "I felt she was telling us the truth, but I also thought she was hiding something. Maybe she knows about her mother and Kenton and was afraid we would find out and rock the boat?"

"Possible," mused Matt.

"Squirmy is a good word, Fern," said Ed. "But I often have that effect on teenagers. I could be a little gentler during interrogations, but I want them to understand and impress upon them that murder is no time to fool around with the truth. I believe that Susan was nervous because of the gravity of the situation and because of my approach."

"Plus," Matt added, "Susan doesn't strike me as the type of girl who has enough gumption to do something like this. She seems kind of lazy, if you know what I mean."

"Like it would be too much trouble to kill your little sister," agreed Ed.

"Exactly," said Matt. "Sort of like a whiny 'it's too hard'. Even if her alibi weren't firm, I'd have trouble believing Susan was our killer. Is she acting the way a sibling should react to her sister's death?"

Fern nodded. "Yes. I don't know if she and Emily were close, but she's teary-eyed and is upset and sad. She's also acting like a typical teenage girl. She's hysterical about Emily's death, but also concerned about its impact on her own life. It's teenage processing at its normal progression, in my view."

Matt walked to the big board and drew a black line through Susan's name. He turned to Jay. "What about Jack's alibi? What did we find out about his Friday night?"

"I talked to Joey Hawthorne's mother and she confirmed that he and Jack were meeting at the movie theater. She said she dropped Joey off in front of the theater a little after 6:30 p.m., and Jack was out front waiting for him."

"OK, so Jack went to the movies . . . we already knew that," Matt said. "But did he stay there until he says he did? That's the question. Did you talk to Joey?" There was a hint of irritation in the Chief's voice.

"Not yet. He and his dad went over to Buck Bay this morning and aren't home yet. I asked her to have Joey call me as soon as they get home. I'm sorry, I know it's important, but Mrs. Hawthorne said neither Joey nor his dad carry a cell phone. Not everyone here does."

"Not your fault. But keep on Joey; we need to know he was with Jack. I'm not convinced that Jack was at the cinema the entire evening. He was vague on how the movie ended, and the hair on the back of my neck told me that he might be dodging my questions. Do any of you know what the 'Rogue One' part of the title means?"

"It's the Imperial ship that the Rebels steal, of course," said Jay dryly.

"Have you seen the movie?"

"Yeah, I drove to Eugene to see it the first day because it takes forever for movies to get down here."

"How old are you?" Fern teased.

"What? It's a great movie," Jay defended. "I never miss a Star Wars."

"Wouldn't every kid know where 'Rogue One' in the title came from?" Matt asked.

"If you watched the movie you would know."

"So maybe young Jack didn't watch the movie after all. He told me that he and Joey jumped around some," Matt reported.

"Kids don't really pay attention to movies," Ed said. "At Jack's age, it's only an excuse to get away from their parents, and to eat lots of crap. Or, to make out with their girlfriends. It would be more likely if Jack and Joey met girls there and weren't paying attention to the flick for that reason."

"Dammit," Matt growled. "I didn't think to ask him if he has a girlfriend. Gary either. We'll have to get on that, but first things first. Ted Frolick is telling the truth about Marjorie and Kenton, I'm convinced. Or, at least his version of what he believes to be the truth. I'm going to prioritize getting a statement from Kenton, and then confronting Marjorie."

"Are you 100 percent sure Frolick's got this right?" asked a dubious Jay. "If we're wrong on this, it could come back and bite us big-time."

"Now you sound like the DA talking," Matt said. "Until the killer confesses, I'm not sure about anything. But Frolick is certain, he's a lot sharper than people give him credit for, and Patty and I both believed him. We have to take the next step. No choice."

* * *

Sunday, 3:30 p.m.

Craig Kenton caved almost the minute he saw OSP Lieutenant Sonders walk into the hardware store. According to the blonde, well-muscled Kenton who wore his jeans tight, he'd been having an affair with Marjorie Bushnell for five months.

Kenton had a bad Sunday, ever since Marjorie phoned him about Emily's murder. He told Sonders he didn't believe Marjorie had anything to do with her daughter's death, but he knew their affair was bound to come out.

And so it had. Kenton revealed to Sonders that an exploration of his computer would expose email exchanges between them, going back to last September.

"You're telling me this?" said Ed.

"I know how you cops work," said a defeated Kenton. "It's going to be obvious once you start checking into it. Might as well tell you the truth now and get it over with."

"That's an adult attitude, Kenton, I appreciate it."

"I didn't have anything to do with Emily's death. I want you to write that down, OK? I mean it," he said, pointing at Ed's notebook. "I might have been fooling around with her mother, but I don't know anything about this. I swear."

Ed made notes in his notebook, even though his tape recorder was running. "How did you learn about Emily's murder?"

"Marj called me this morning to give me a heads up."

"What time?"

"About 8:00 a.m. Said they found her body yesterday on the beach."

"Where were you Friday night between the hours of 6:00 p.m. and midnight?"

"I was in Twisty River Friday night."

"Doing what?"

"I had a date."

"And it wasn't with Marjorie, I'm guessing," Ed said.

"No."

"Do you want to tell me who you were with, or do I have to pull out your fingernails?" asked Ed, maybe kidding.

Craig Kenton filled in all of the details of his Friday night alibi for Ed, agreed to turn over his computer to him, and signed his statement.

Ed texted three 'thumbs up' emoji, followed by the word '*big!*' to Chief Horning.

CHAPTER 22

Sitting in the squad car at the end of Cranberry Drive with Jay and Fern, Matt's phone buzzed: new text arriving. He quickly saw the thumbs up from Ed, and said to his colleagues: "Affirmative. Let's go. Jay, you are to keep Fred in the other room while Fern and I take on Marjorie. Be direct in your questioning on if and/or what he might have known about a possible affair between his wife and Craig Kenton. Keep it calm, civil, and don't lead him—let him tell you whatever he does or, I suspect, does not know."

"Should I name Kenton when I start, or should I see if the mayor comes up with his name?" Jay asked.

"I wouldn't say his name unless Bushnell asks first," said Matt. "But he will ask. Wouldn't you?"

"I sure would," Jay agreed. "So, if he asks who it is, I tell him, right?"

"Yes. See how he reacts to the name."

"He'll also probably want to know who told us. How do I handle that?"

"I don't think it serves our purposes to have Frolick brought into this yet . . . not until Patty can get a better bead on him," Matt said. "Let's just tell the mayor and Marjorie that we have a witness who saw her coming out of the A-frame cabin at the Pacific View Motel with Kenton, and leave it at that. The pressure is on them, particularly

Marjorie. Fern, I want you to pay close attention to her body language, and be prepared to jot down your observations, OK?"

"Yes, I understand."

"This is going to be tense," Matt warned. "Stay cool like the cool cats you are. We're here to get the truth, not to judge. We're doing a job, and it's not our fault if the mayor and his wife have marital issues. Got it?"

"What if Marjorie really killed that child to cover up an affair?" Fern asked no one in particular. "It's unbelievable."

"If she did, we will uncover the truth." Matt's voice and demeanor were hard-boiled.

Matt knocked on the front door of the Bushnell house. He noticed that Fern tossed a penny in the wishing well along the front sidewalk as they approached the door.

"Couldn't hurt," Fern said when Matt caught her eye. She looked very, very nervous, as did Jay.

"We need to clear up a couple of details from this morning," Matt started somewhat brusquely, stepping into the foyer when Fred opened the door.

"Is there anything new?" Fred asked.

"Nothing concrete yet, but we are following some leads today. Please rest assured that we will let you know the minute we have any information. For now," Matt continued, "Jay will go with you, Fred, into the kitchen and, if you could call Mrs. Bushnell, Fern and I would like to talk to her. Is she available?"

"Marjorie is resting. I'll get her." He went to the end of the hallway, cupped his hand around his mouth, and said up the stairs: "They're here, Marjorie." If she responded, Matt couldn't hear her, but she soon appeared, looking more ashen than she had this morning. Both parents had calmed down since their earlier reaction to the search of their home. Probably worn out from the stress.

"Marjorie, Fern and I would like you to come with us into the living room. Is that OK with everyone?" Matt didn't care if it was OK with them or not, that's what was going to happen.

Matt closed the French doors between the dining and living rooms to block noise into the kitchen. Marjorie immediately had her hackles up, probably because she was outnumbered. Fern took her seat on the sofa next to Matt across from Marjorie, and subtly reached into her tote bag for her journal.

Marjorie, cool as a cucumber, said, "How can I help you this afternoon, Chief?"

"I want to ask you about Craig Kenton. Do you know him?" Matt asked.

Marjorie twisted the gold earring in her right ear, first one way and then the other.

"He's a volunteer fireman, and he also works at the hardware store," Matt prompted.

"I know of him," Marjorie finally said, "but I wouldn't say I know him."

"So, it's not true that he and you are having an affair?" Matt said, lowering his voice.

Marjorie smoothed her skirt and leaned toward Matt, staring at him hard. She did not utter a sound, but her eyes grew wider, and her whole body seemed to quiver.

"Let me repeat the question, Mrs. Bushnell," Matt said. "Are you having a romantic affair with Craig Kenton?" He leaned back against the sofa and looked at her. He was twirling his pen, which Fern thought was an excellent touch.

"How dare you come into my house after my daughter has been murdered and ask me a question like that," Marjorie said. There was pure rage in her voice.

"So, it's not true?"

"Of course it's not true. Who told you this?" she demanded.

"We have a witness who claims to have seen the two of you together in compromising circumstances."

"Where?" she spat out.

"At the A-frame cabin below the Pacific View Motel, and in the parking lot behind Goodie's Market. To name two occasions."

Any existing color in Marjorie's face drained out, but she remained belligerent. "That's ridiculous," she said, looking first at Matt and then at Fern. "You don't believe this, do you?"

"We need to know the truth, Marjorie," Fern said sympathetically, glancing at Matt who gave her a go-ahead nod. "It would be helpful if you told it to us first."

"Fern is right," Matt informed her in his tough-guy voice. "We'd rather not have to go into phone and computer records to confirm if you and Kenton were in contact." He let that statement hang in the air.

"Who told you this?"

"We'd rather not say at this point in time."

Marjorie looked defeated, but she wasn't about to admit it.

"I am not having an affair with this person, and whoever told you I was is mistaken," Marjorie said, sticking her chin out. "Why would I do something like that? I'm a married woman and a mother. And, a prominent member of this community, in case you've forgotten that fact. I strongly suggest you let go of this line of questioning."

"So, Emily saw the two of you together, and you were worried about her telling Fred?" Matt said, ignoring her threat, and going in for the kill. "Or your boyfriend was afraid the little girl would talk?"

The stark reality of what the police chief was saying hit her hard. Marjorie began to panic a little.

"You can't really think that," she said nervously. "Even if I was involved with another man, I would take care to not let my family know. And you can't be suggesting that I had anything to do with Emily's murder. She's my daughter."

"Someone killed Emily," said Matt. "There can't be too many reasons why someone would do a horrific thing like that, and it's my job to explore all possibilities. I'm going to ask you one more time, Marjorie. Are you having an affair with Craig Kenton?"

"No, I am not."

"It's my judgment that you are not being candid with us. Lying to the police in a murder investigation is a serious offense. Would you like to take a moment to think about your answer?"

"Marjorie," cajoled Fern. "It would really be better for you if you told the Chief the truth."

"Shut up!" she hissed in Fern's direction. "Are you going to share this ridiculous story with Fred?" she asked. She was tapping the index finger of her left hand on the sofa cushion.

"Jay is questioning your husband now to see if he has any knowledge of your activities."

"I can't believe you are doing this," Marjorie cried. "We've just lost a child, Chief. How can you be so cruel?"

"My job is to get to the truth, whatever that truth is, ma'am. I'm sorry if you are hurt further, but we have to chase down every lead. If the mother of the victim has something to hide, it could be important to my case."

"It's not your case," she screamed. "It's my daughter's life. Badgering me about some man is not going to find my Emily's killer. You should be ashamed of yourself."

"I'm not the one who slept with Craig Kenton." As Matt said that matter-of-factly to Marjorie, Ed Sonders came in through the front door, and handed a single page of paper to Matt.

"Last chance, Marjorie. What's it going to be?" he said after scanning the document.

"I told you the truth." Stiff, upright, formal.

"No, I'm afraid that you have not. In the interest of saving us all time, I have proof." On the coffee table between them, Matt slapped down Kenton's statement, and turned it to face Marjorie so that she could clearly see Kenton's signature on the document.

He let the paper lay there for a quiet moment while she scrutinized it. Marjorie looked down, crossed her legs at the ankles, and said nothing.

"And, in addition to Craig Kenton's admission, we have several email messages—both from your computer and from his—that passed between you over the last few weeks. A couple of them leave no doubt as to your relationship." Matt was bluffing here, as they hadn't yet analyzed either of the lovebirds' computers. But he was now certain what they would find.

Matt leaned forward toward Marjorie, his elbows resting on this knees and his hands clasped, and waited.

Fern was afraid to even blink.

"That cheap, no good prick," Marjorie snarled. The glacial chill in her voice brought goose bumps to Matt's arms. "We had a deal. How dare he do this to me? You're all alike, aren't you?" She looked directly at Matt.

Matt figured it was a rhetorical question. He also figured that the red-hot love affair between Marjorie and Craig was now pretty much over.

"Did Emily see the two of you together?" Matt demanded. "Did you kill her because you were afraid she was going to reveal your secret?"

"You mean my 'dirty little secret', right? That's what you wanted to say, isn't it?"

"I don't judge, ma'am. I'm only here to get to the truth. Did you kill Emily to keep her from spilling the beans? Did she see the two of you together and say she was going to tell daddy?"

"I did not kill my daughter!" Marjorie screamed, and moved within inches of Matt's face. Fern leapt up and grabbed Marjorie by the arm. She pulled her back toward her sofa. "Sit down!" Fern ordered.

"Leave me alone," Marjorie yelled at Fern, pushing her away. "The two of you make me sick. So righteous." Her face was contorted, and she lost whatever filter she'd had. "Harassing me when you should be out there finding whoever really killed Emily. How can you possibly think I could do such a thing? She was my baby." She was now sobbing, and buckets of tears ran down her splotchy face.

"You lied to us, Marjorie," Matt said calmly, trying to defuse the situation. "That makes us wonder what else you've lied about."

She started to rise up again, but Fern firmly placed her hand on Marjorie's shoulder, causing her to slump back on the sofa.

"Of course I lied about Craig. Anyone would under the circumstances. That doesn't mean I stabbed Emily."

"Did Emily ever see the two of you together?" Matt continued.

"No. Oh, wait. Maybe one time. We ran into each other at Goodie's Market, and Emily was with me. We talked briefly in the parking lot, but it was very brief." Marjorie interlocked her fingers, leaned back, and then stretched her neck, trying to get comfortable.

"She didn't say something like '*Who's that man, mommy?*', or '*I'm going to tell daddy you talked to a man*'? Anything like that?"

Marjorie glared at Matt. "My daughter was a sweet little girl. She would never question or threaten her mother. You are way off base."

"Did Kenton like Emily?"

"He didn't know her."

"Not at all? Never met?"

"Never. Emily was asleep in her car seat that time at Goodie's."

Ted Frolick said Emily was wide awake, remembered Matt.

"Is Kenton capable of murder, Mrs. Bushnell?"

"How would I know?" she grunted. "Obviously, I don't know him at all. Except for how big his penis is."

A faint blush crept across Fern's cheeks.

"Does he seem like the kind of man who could kill a child if he felt threatened?"

"Maybe," Marjorie said. It appeared that if Marjorie was going down, Kenton was going with her.

"We'll need to update your original statement," Matt said, officially. "You'll have to come with us now to City Hall. We're through with this interrogation." Matt strode out of the living room, and went into the kitchen.

Things weren't going any better in there. Fred's face was red with emotion, and his body language was aggressive.

"The mayor doesn't know anything about his wife's possible relationship with Craig Kenton," Jay reported as Matt came in.

"Your wife admitted to us that she and Kenton are having an affair. Kenton admitted it to Lieutenant Sonders just now as well. I'm sorry, sir."

"This is crazy, Horning," Fred said loudly. "Marjorie wouldn't do anything like this, and I would know if she did. You are browbeating my wife. You're barking up the wrong tree, and I won't hear any more of it. Have you upset her?"

"Yes, I'm afraid I have," said Matt. "Did you not hear what I said, Fred? Both parties have admitted it. It's possible that your wife might be hiding even more from us, and we need to understand what that might be. I'm taking her down to City Hall now to sign an amended statement."

"But I'm telling you this isn't possible. Marjorie can't have anything to do with this awful thing. She's the girl's mother, for God's sake. Please focus elsewhere, Chief," the mayor pleaded. "We don't even know this Kenton guy."

Jesus, get a clue, thought Matt. "A check of Marjorie's laptop will confirm that she does know him, sir," replied Matt, trying to soften the blow as best he could. "If our witness is wrong, and I've made an error, we'll know soon enough."

"I already asked Jay who it was that told you this malicious lie, but he won't tell me—will you tell me where you heard this?"

"It came up in the questioning of a potential suspect. Because that individual is still a possible suspect, we can't divulge the name. The witness's account of seeing your wife with Kenton was credible, and we checked it out. Again, I'm sorry to have to do this, but we are dealing with a child's murder, Fred, and the family has to be investigated. Please try to understand."

"I understand," Fred said. "I just think you're wasting valuable time to find out who did this."

"We are following all leads," Matt said. "The county crime team has met, and everyone has their assignments. We're having our second meeting later this afternoon to update any progress. Our police department is deploying all of our resources to investigate the local Ocean Bend Road area, and any and all potential suspects. Plus, the Buck Bay PD and the Oregon State Police are pulling in what officers they can spare to help us. We've got the forensics reports from both the tunnel where Emily's body was discovered, and from her bedroom, and I will personally go through those later today. I want to assure you that we are being completely thorough, and we won't miss anything."

"OK. I have to trust you . . . no choice. I hope to hell you know what you're doing. Maybe you should bring in George Simonson to help you."

Matt tried not to be insulted by that suggestion because he knew Fred was grasping at straws. But, still, it rankled.

"You don't really know me yet, Mr. Mayor, but I can promise you that I do know what I'm doing. Solving a murder sometimes involves a little luck, but it's mostly done by diligent legwork. If it turns out that your wife is having an affair and that, somehow, Emily knew, it might be a crucial piece of information."

"I tell you, you're wrong, and . . ."

"If I'm wrong," Matt interrupted Fred mid-sentence, "then I'll apologize, and it will go no further than this room. But if Marjorie is hiding something, don't you want to know?"

Fred tugged on the collar of his shirt. "Yes, of course. But it's not possible, I tell you."

As they left the house with Marjorie in tow, Fern turned her head to look back, and saw Fred standing in the doorway, watching.

CHAPTER 23

Hideki Ikeda had been in charge of Port Stirling's IT department for two months, and in that time the most exciting thing he'd done was order new software for the department heads. But he'd gotten a phone call from city manager Bill Abbott early Sunday morning, asking him if he could come into work ASAP. A murder investigation!

Ikeda took charge of all five of the Bushnell family computers seized in this morning's search of their home, and started, as instructed by the new police chief, on Marjorie's computer. Horning specifically wanted Ikeda to do a keyword search on "Craig".

Boom! Ninety-two messages between Craig Kenton and Marjorie Bushnell dating back to the previous September popped up immediately—all in her "Trash" bucket. Some were relatively innocuous, but others painted a clear picture of blooming romance, or more bluntly, blooming sex. When Kenton's laptop was brought in later, only the last four or five messages between them were saved; apparently, he wasn't as much of a romantic as Marjorie.

Marjorie, having a few more little grey cells than Kenton, had, on Saturday evening at 11:23 p.m., deleted all of her messages between them. But, Ikeda noted in his report to the Chief, she didn't empty her "Trash" bucket. Perhaps Marjorie and Craig were made for each other after all.

* * *

Sunday, 4:00 p.m.

Nine of the crime team members gathered back in the War Room; Dr. Ryder, having nothing further to share since her autopsy report, didn't attend.

Matt began the meeting by sharing Ikeda's report on Marjorie and Kenton's computers confirming that they were indeed having an affair.

"So Ted Frolick got it right?" said Patty.

"He got it all correct," Matt said. "Including seeing them talking in Goodie's parking lot with Emily in the back seat. Marjorie told us that Emily was asleep, but I tend to believe Frolick's version. And, Marjorie deleted all of the messages between her and Kenton last night, so she didn't want that info discovered."

"You identify your youngest child on a slab in the morgue, and you're on your computer later that night deleting email?" said Fern incredulously.

"Yeah, in my book," Matt said, "that's highly suspicious behavior. Marjorie is now suspect No. 1, and, until we can check out his Friday night alibi, Kenton is suspect No. 2. Good work on Kenton, Ed. What's your takeaway from your chat with him?"

"Kenton is a ladies man of the first degree. Pretty face," said Ed. "But, in my estimation, he's not a killer. He doesn't have the balls for it."

"I understand he's a volunteer fireman—doesn't that take a degree of bravery?" Matt asked.

"S'pose so, but manning a hose with a team is different than stabbing a little girl in the abdomen, even if her mother asked you to do it. Kenton cracked like a vase on a marble floor the minute I mentioned Marjorie Bushnell's name. He fessed up to being intimate with her on several occasions over the past few months, but he wanted nothing to do with her daughter's death."

Matt thought if he was interrogated by the 6'4", muscular Sonders, he'd probably crack too.

"You'll read in his statement, though, that he thinks Mrs. Bushnell is, in his words, 'a little whacked,'" Sonders continued.

"What does that mean?"

"I got the distinct feeling from Kenton that he thinks she's a little off her rocker. But he screwed her anyway. Sorry, ladies. Nice work if you can get it, I guess."

"What a charmer," Matt said.

"Yeah, not my cup of tea," agreed Ed, "but, hey, it takes all kinds."

Matt said, "Patty, I haven't ruled out Frolick yet, but I do agree with your characterization of him—he's not crazy, and he has no motive to kill Emily. He may have had the opportunity, however, and we need to keep working to verify his alibi."

Patty shifted in her chair. "Did you ask him about the slapping incident?"

"I interrogated him about it, and he didn't have much to say on the topic," said Matt. "Keep on him about his alibi and dig a little further on the incident. I don't believe it proves a pattern with Frolick, but I don't want to leave any stone unturned. Sheriff, can you fill in the group on Fergus Dunbar?"

"Wait a minute, Chief," inserted the district attorney. "Don't you think you're skimming over Ted Frolick a bit too quickly? He was arrested for assault on a child, and you can't verify his alibi?"

"Patty and I have both questioned him, and unless he's a practiced psychopath, all of his answers add up," Matt answered.

"I agree," Patty said.

"I don't agree," said Dalrymple. "Frolick fits the pattern of a child abuser, and the two of you just rule him out because you like him? That's unprofessional and sloppy police work."

"Look, Dalrymple," said Matt, "I didn't say anything about liking Frolick. As a matter of fact, I do like him, but that's not the reason I don't believe he's our guy. We have a record of one isolated incident in which he hit a child in full view of others. A pretty obvious heat-of-the-moment type thing, and a very far cry from what happened to Emily. That does not constitute a pattern of child abuse. Furthermore, he has no motive to kill Emily— none whatsoever. And he was right about Marjorie and Kenton. He's not off my suspect list yet, he's just not as high on it as Marjorie. Frolick told us the truth, Marjorie lied. Can we please move on now?" Matt stared at the DA.

"I want Jay to take another statement from Frolick," Dalrymple said, not letting it drop. "There's too much reason to suspect him, and you are glossing over him."

Patty sat straighter in her chair. "You suddenly have a problem with the way I question suspects? Because –"

Matt lifted a hand to Patty to stop, then turned his focus back to Dalrymple. "I have no problem with Jay talking to Frolick if that will satisfy you. But Patty and I aren't done with him, I can assure you," Matt said, his voice stony.

"He didn't do it, David," said Patty, and she stared him down. "I would stake my reputation on it, and I'm right more than I'm wrong. And I'm also right more often than you are. Wouldn't you agree?"

Dalrymple had to laugh. "Yes, I suppose you are. But it doesn't mean you're right this time. I think you and the Chief have this one wrong, and we can't afford to fuck it up."

"We won't," Matt said. "Can we move on now?" He didn't wait for an answer. "Sheriff, can you talk about Fergus Dunbar, please?"

The sheriff explained why Dunbar was a potential suspect, and the plan to get a statement from him as soon as he left here. After he finished, Buck Bay's chief told the group about a suspicious guy at Port Stirling Links, and Matt, jotting down the name, said he would talk to him first thing tomorrow.

He added, "Also, it will likely be tomorrow morning before we get anything from our PSPD guys on their local checks."

"So, there's still a chance we'll have other suspects?" Jay said.

"Of course there's a chance," replied Matt. "But the one fact we have so far is that the mother of the victim lied to us and tried to cover up her cheating."

"And, she's not exhibiting typical motherly reactions to her child's death," added Fern. "This afternoon, she seemed almost detached. Cold. Yes, she was sobbing, but, in my view, the tears were more about getting caught as a cheating wife than Emily's death. Could be a defense mechanism, but I think Marjorie warrants our close attention."

There was a rap at the door, and Sylvia Hofstetter poked her head into the room. "You're not going to like this, Chief."

"What?" Matt replied.

"There's a TV crew from KVAL in Eugene in the lobby. They want to talk to you about Emily's murder."

CHAPTER 24

Sunday, 5:00 p.m.

"Who is the reporter?" the DA asked Sylvia.

"It's that woman, Tammy something," replied Sylvia. "The blonde fluff-head."

Fern turned to Matt and said, "She's not so bad. She's friendly and won't ask the tough questions. I did a studio panel show with her last month on domestic violence, and she kept it clean and unobtrusive."

"I think I'd better handle this interview," Dalrymple said, looking at Matt. "You aren't familiar yet with the nuances of life around here or the relationships involved."

"Uh-uh," said Sylvia before Matt could open his mouth. "The fluff-head specifically asked for Matt. She knows we have a new police chief, and she wants her viewers to meet him."

"I appreciate the offer, David, but it's my responsibility," said Matt. "I'd rather be introduced to the community under different circumstances, but it is what it is. Jay, you and Fern come with me; I want there to be a team component and a couple of familiar faces. It will be important to reassure our town that they're safe."

"With all due respect, Chief, the town isn't safe," the DA said. "We've got an unknown killer on the loose. You will have to choose your words carefully, or you risk sparking widespread panic."

"Agreed. I've been in this situation before, and I know how to calm people down," Matt said with more confidence than he felt. "Carry on here as you need to. Fern, Jay, let's go."

* * *

Fern felt a butterfly doing the jig in her belly, but, *Yeah, let's say I'm OK appearing on live TV.* The show she did in Eugene in the studio was taped, and that felt much more comfortable. But it was important to support Matt, and she had every confidence in his ability to handle Tammy.

"I will alert the family about your interview once we're finished here," Fern told Matt. "They shouldn't be blindsided by the fact that word is out."

"Good point. I'm thinking we should arrange for a guard detail at the Bushnell house, too, at least for tonight and tomorrow. Just a car in the driveway. Jay, can you make that happen when we're done with the TV folks?"

Jay said, "Sure. Also, you should know that I'm an old hand at media interviews." He grinned to make sure that his new boss knew he was bluffing. Hell, they were all bluffing.

Matt patted him on the back as they walked down the hallway toward the City Hall lobby.

Matt greeted Tammy whatever, and introduced Fern and Jay even though they all remembered each other. He gave the reporter an extra firm handshake to indicate he couldn't be trifled with.

"I thought we would do this with the Pacific as a backdrop, but I'm afraid we'd blow away if we went outside," Tammy smiled at Matt. "Do you have a good place in the building we could film?"

Matt turned to Jay. "Do we?"

"There's the atrium between the two wings with that fountain."

"Oh, that's perfect," enthused Tammy. "It's covered with glass, right? I think I've been there before. Let's go there." She motioned to her cameraman.

So glad we found a scenic location to talk about the homicide of a little girl, thought Matt.

The cameraman mic'd up the three of them, and Tammy sidled up close to Matt. Fern gave her a look, but then put on her serious face, as did Jay.

"We're in Port Stirling talking to the city's new police chief, Matt Horning, who just arrived yesterday from his home in Texas," Tammy began. "Welcome to Oregon, Chief."

"Thank you, Tammy. I wish I'd met you and your viewers under different circumstances." He looked directly at the reporter and ignored the camera, as if they were having a personal conversation.

"Chief, is it true that Mayor Bushnell's daughter was found murdered on the Port Stirling beach yesterday morning?" started Tammy.

"Yes, I'm afraid it is true. Emily Bushnell's body, aged four, was found yesterday in a rock tunnel outcropping on the beach. We are treating her death as a homicide."

"How did she die?"

"Because this is an ongoing investigation, we'd rather not divulge those details yet. I'm sure you understand." He looked into Tammy's eyes.

"Is the public at risk?"

Matt had, of course, considered this question in the middle of the night when he lay awake, but he had come to the conclusion that it was unlikely Port Stirling had a serial killer on its hands.

To Tammy, and for the viewing audience, Matt said "We believe this is an isolated case and there is no risk to the public at large," trying to sound as calm and reassuring as he could.

"Do you have any suspects?" Tammy asked.

"It's far too early in the process for that," Matt answered. He was firm, yet pleasant. "The county's major crime team is meeting. We began our investigation immediately after the body was found, and we will continue around the clock until we apprehend whoever did this awful thing. Port Stirling and area residents should feel assured that it's only a matter of time until this case is solved, and they should go about their business."

"Our viewers don't know you, Chief Horning," Tammy said, moving in even closer to Matt, and turning up her face toward him. "Can you tell us how long you've been a policeman?"

"I'd rather keep the focus on the case than on me, but I have over a decade of experience investigating homicides as a police officer. We also have an excellent county team. We'll get our killer."

"Ms. Byrne, you've seen some nasty domestic violence cases in your job as the Chinook County Advocate. Is that what you're dealing with here? Is the Bushnell family involved?"

Matt visibly paled at that question, but the cameraman was focused on Fern.

"As Chief Horning said, it's far too early to know exactly what we're dealing with," Fern said calmly. "The Bushnell family has been through a terrible ordeal and it's an unimaginable loss for them. We plead with the community to allow them time and space to work through their grief."

Matt stepped up closer to Tammy and the mic. "I would also like the community's help. If anyone saw anything suspicious—anything at all out of the ordinary—on Friday night in the vicinity of Ocean Bend Road and the Whale Rock Wayside, please contact the Port Stirling Police Department right away. We'd really appreciate it. That's all we can offer today," Matt said, his voice commanding. Tammy took the hint.

"This is Tammy Parsons reporting live from Port Stirling, where the mayor's daughter has been found murdered on the beach. Keep it tuned here for ongoing updates in this terrible, frightening case."

* * *

Sunday, 8:00 p.m.

Fresh from a fragrant bath and wrapped in her favorite pearl pink terry robe, Fern curled up on her sofa with her laptop. As much as she had come to like and respect Matt in the past 36 hours, she realized during the TV interview that they were all putting their trust in this man about whom no one really knew much.

She went to Google and typed "Matt Horning". The first result that caught her eye was a *Dallas Morning News* item headlined "Plano Detective Suspended after Teenage Shooting".

She clicked on the article and was startled to see a one-third-page photo of Detective Matthew Michael Horning, identified as 41 years old and a 12-year veteran of the Plano Police Department. Staring at Matt's photo dated last September, Fern thought his body looked even more ripped than it did now. There was no question the new police chief was a hunk. Chiseled body. Cheekbones and startling blue eyes. Curly hair a smidge too long for police regulations. Handsome smile that unfolded slowly, and needed to be earned. She hadn't seen many smiles on his face yet, but the few that had come her way were worth the wait.

Fern, mesmerized, read that he and his partner, Sergeant Jessica Hernandez, responded to a call from the campus police of Collin College, Plano location. A party at an off-campus apartment building spilled out into the courtyard of the complex. The reporter said it had been a "welcome back to school" party. Fern thought it must have been a hot, sticky September night—another photo in the upper right of the article showed fifty or so young partygoers, all dressed in shorts and tees.

According to the police report, Matt Horning and Jessica Hernandez never saw 19-year-old Alicia Johnson come out of the crowd behind them, and jump Matt's back. Hernandez tried to pull Alicia off her partner, but she continued to flail and punch at both officers.

In their testimony to the Grand Jury, all Matt and Jessica remembered was the flash of Horning's pistol as Alicia lunged at his gun. The bullet caught her in the middle of her forehead, and she died instantly. Horning and Hernandez were suspended pending a review of the incident and the Grand Jury's verdict.

Whoa, thought Fern, and she clicked on the next article published ten days later, and featuring a photo of Alicia Johnson, along with photos of her parents. Alicia was the only child of Horton and Claire Johnson. The girl's father, a distinguished African-American scholar, was also the U.S. House of Representatives' most prominent congressman from the great state of Texas. Her mother was a U.S. Court of Appeals judge.

Skimming through another few articles, Fern pieced together that even though several of the partygoers testified that Alicia Johnson had a knife in her hand, tried repeatedly to stab Horning and Hernandez, and was "completely coked out", the Johnsons fought a public battle against Matt. The *Dallas Morning News* helped them wage the war, keeping their daughter's death at the hands of the Plano police front and center for several weeks.

While the Grand Jury exonerated Matt and Jessica, deciding that there was not enough probable cause to indict Detective Matthew Michael Horning in the shooting death of Alicia Johnson, and that

Horning and Hernandez acted within the limits of the lethal-force law because the victim had a knife in her hand, the Johnsons didn't let it go. They filed a civil suit against Matt.

Fern closed her laptop and stared at herself in the mirror over her fireplace. *No wonder Matt is so upset that Emily was the daughter of our mayor. Another daughter of a politician dead.* Even though the circumstances were completely different, Matt's motivation to solve this crime was abundantly clear to Fern now. And, she could only imagine the emotional pain this case was bringing to him. *How unfortunate this happened on the day the poor guy arrived!*

Well, she was a crime victim's advocate, and Matt was a victim himself in this case. She would do whatever she could to help their new police chief weather this storm, both professionally and personally.

* * *

Sunday, 8:00 p.m.

"Whadda ya got, Sheriff?" Matt said into his ringing cell phone. "Did you find Fergus Dunbar?"

"Yep, and this dude is a piece of work," Chinook County Sheriff Earl Johnson said. "He's a farmer, single, about 35, and appears to live alone. I caught up with him at his farm."

"Where is that?" Matt asked.

"He lives north of town, off of Old Van Dorn Road close to where it meets High Creek Road. In other words, the middle of nowhere."

"You talked to him?"

"Yes, sir, I did. Dunbar wasn't eager to talk to me, and I didn't find him particularly cooperative," said Sheriff Johnson. "He's a classic hippie left over from the 60's. We have a lot of them around here.

Shoulder-length hair that could use a shampoo, and tie-dyed tee shirt. He didn't smell all that great either. Get the picture?" Johnson asked Matt.

"Yes, I do have a vivid picture," said Matt, and smiled into his phone. He recalled from yesterday's team meeting that Sheriff Earl had a crewcut that Mike Ditka would have been proud of, and his uniform, straining to cover his belly, was starched to the max. His ruddy complexion looked like it had been scrubbed within an inch of its life. Matt doubted that the sheriff had much in common with Fergus Dunbar.

"Fergus doesn't much care for the mayor, I'll tell you that," continued Johnson. "'Typical useless politician', he called him. And he didn't seem particularly upset when I told him about the little girl's death. I explained that I was there investigating Emily's death, and he said 'shit happens'. Not exactly sympathetic. I wrote up my report and can bring it in now if you like."

"Yeah, I'm in my office for a little while longer, and I'd like to read it tonight. In your view, Sheriff, is Fergus Dunbar a killer?"

"He might be. I haven't ruled him out. He hates the mayor, doesn't seem to place a high value on human life, and he's likely a stoner. I'd like to see an aerial view of his farm—he's probably growing pot along with his vegetables and chickens. And if he has a grower's permit, I'm Lady Gaga."

"OK, so he's not fond of our mayor. Just a couple more questions then I'll let you go. Does he have an alibi for Friday night?" asked Matt.

"He says he was home alone, chillin and watching the tube. Says he never goes out on Friday night because it's 'amateur hour' in the bars. I concur with him on that front," the sheriff added.

"Did he talk to anyone on the phone? Send any emails? Can anyone verify he was home?"

"He said he didn't make or receive any phone calls, and no one stopped by. That I believe. His farm is a destination—you have to be going there on purpose, no one would just stop by. I didn't think to ask him about sending email." The sheriff's voice lowered a fraction; he was clearly embarrassed to admit this last part.

"Did you ask him about his beef with Fred Bushnell?" asked Matt.

"Yes. Dunbar's been agitating to get the city council to declare one week in July as "Community Supported Agriculture" week. His idea is that if people have more awareness of buying local, seasonal food from farmers—such as himself, of course—everybody will prosper. He's essentially trying to promote his CSA business, and he got ticked off when Fred told him that the city wasn't interested in promoting one for-profit business over another. Fergus got all riled up just talking about it to me."

"This doesn't feel like a big enough issue to kill a child over to me," Matt said. "And aren't hippies supposed to be all about love and peace, not violence? But I will want to talk to him and check out his alibi further. It sounds like Fergus Dunbar has a motive, however weak it might be, to harm the mayor; I'd like to know for sure whether or not he had the opportunity. Let's get a warrant tomorrow morning and go back out there and bring in his computer. That may tell us whether or not he was really at home Friday night. I'd also like to know if he had any email correspondence with the mayor."

"Sure thing, Chief. Dunbar was mad as hell at Fred, and if he's a druggie, which I suspect, there's no telling what he might do. I'll get a warrant from Judge Hedges first thing."

"Good. Make sure his address is on your report. I'll want to personally meet Mr. Dunbar. Thanks, Sheriff. Appreciate the leg work."

Matt made a mental note to always stay on the good side of rough, tough Earl Johnson.

CHAPTER 25

Sunday, 9:00 p.m.

Matt turned off Ocean Bend Road onto what he hoped was his driveway. The mist was swirling, and it was raining so hard, for the second
night in a row he wasn't sure he was in the right place.
He cracked open his window an inch, and heard the familiar sound
of gravel crunching under his tires. Home.

It was dark as hell, and he couldn't see any lights on even at
his closest neighbor, one driveway north. Matt hadn't thought
to turn on his porch light when he left that morning, and the darkness
enveloped him.

He grabbed his briefcase and slid it under his jacket to protect it
from the rain as he ran to his door. The rain, wetter than anything he'd
ever seen or felt, appeared to be coming straight down and sideways
simultaneously. The wind wailed, and blew his jacket's hood off his
head within seconds of exiting his car. Matt tried to locate the correct
key on his keychain with the wicked rain pelting his face.

"Christ Almighty!" he yelled to the wind and the rain. "Give me
a fucking break, will you?"

*Wonderful. I'm here two whole days, and I'm already swearing at
the weather.*

He unlocked his door, stepped into the dark warmth, and put his
weight against the wind-lashed door to shut it against the elements.

He felt like someone in a horror movie trying to shut the door against the Zombies. With rain dripping off his nose, and wet creeping down his neck and back, he shook out his jacket and took off his shoes in the little vestibule.

Actually, vestibule might be too fancy a word for what was in reality a tiny enclosed porch between the front door and the living room. Matt now understood why the area had a stone floor before the oatmeal carpet of the "great" room began. He reached for the light switch, and continued dropping wet clothes.

This was the second time today he'd been drenched to his skin. When they'd left the Bushnell residence, he, Fern, and his two colleagues had to walk down the longish driveway to reach their vehicles, and had been pummeled by the sudden deluge when the clouds burst. "We have this new invention here called an umbrella," Fern said, "but I left mine in the trunk of my car. Brilliant."

She was a corker, thought Matt. Jay, Ed, Patty, and the sheriff had all been rocks, too. Frankly, he was a bit surprised that his team was as strong as they were. Their reactions, along with Bernice Ryder's, on the fly had been exemplary. They'd all really stepped up in the face of adversity. What he would have done without them today, he had no idea. Until he got to know his own department better, it was reassuring to know he had help at the county level.

Matt stepped around four boxes from Texas that were piled in the middle of his living room, and found a blissfully dry sweatshirt and pair of sweat pants on top of his as-yet-unpacked suitcase. It seemed like months ago that he'd planned to unpack his stuff and settle into his new home. In reality, it had only been 36 hours. The longest 36 hours of his life.

He turned on a lamp in the living room, the one on the end table next to the sofa. Then he moved purposefully toward the fireplace. It seemed important to light a fire immediately and bring some cheer-fulness to his space. The mindful act of crumpling up newspaper and piling on kindling from the bin on the hearth was restorative. He lit a match to his pyramid and watched the flames catch, squatting in front of the substantial opening. The image of Emily's body appeared before his eyes, dancing in the blaze. He pushed it away, and headed to his kitchen.

He opened a beer from his fridge, and drank it from the bottle. It might never have tasted better. Damn good beer in Oregon, he had to acknowledge.

Before he'd flown from DFW yesterday morning, Matt had origi-nally planned to cook himself a nice pot roast tonight with a salad while he unpacked and watched *Sunday Night Football,* but after the brutal day, that plan was dead. Instead, he reached for a loaf of bread and a can of tuna fish, along with a bag of chips. It would have to do. He'd make an effort to get to a grocery store tomorrow for some fresh food.

Matt laid out his gourmet meal on the heavy wood coffee table in front of the fireplace, which was now really putting out the heat, and switched on his TV. He watched the late news on KVAL with an objective eye while he ate, and thought he and his colleagues had done an OK job. The camera loved Fern, he noted; she looked beautiful, and appeared poised and at ease.

After the news, he surfed the channels—his football game had ended; Cowboys won!—finished his beer, and dried out from the fire's warmth, not finding anything that interested him. It was no use; his brain would not veg out, even though he willed it to.

He was struggling with whether or not he believed the mayor and his family. All were distraught, of course, but something felt off to Matt. Experience told him to look hardest at Fred—and he would continue that line of investigation—but after today's developments,

Marjorie had to be Suspect No. 1. Based on the facts he had presently, she was the only Bushnell with a motive to want Emily dead. It might turn out that Fred knew he wasn't Emily's father, and/or that he knew his wife was cheating on him, but Matt felt strongly that today was the first inkling Fred had about Marjorie's boyfriend. His reaction to the news was too pure to be faked.

In a funny way, Matt had weirder feelings about Fred's two sons than he did about Fred himself. Both boys seemed a little peculiar, and it felt as if they were holding back in some way. He had a handle on where Gary and Jack had spent Friday night, at least on the surface. He was a little ticked off that they were unable to verify today that both boys had been where they said they were, but they would tie up that loose end tomorrow. It should be easily confirmed by witnesses at the tavern and at the cinema. And, now that the news was out, it would become easier to nail down potential witnesses.

He hunkered down with a notebook and a second brewski in front of his fireplace, stretched his legs out and warmed his bare feet, and began to write down everything he knew so far about Emily's murder. Thinking back to the interviews with Jack and Gary, Matt also made a list of statements the kids had made that needed following up. He did the same with Ted Frolick, although his heart wasn't in it. He knew it defied logic, but Matt was sure that Frolick was not his killer.

Matt occasionally thought about what kind of man he'd be when he hit his 70s, and it wasn't much of a stretch to imagine he might be just like Ted Frolick . . . alone, daily hikes, a great reader, a quiet life. He would keep a neater front yard, for sure, and he genuinely hoped the right woman and kids would come along, but Matt knew he wouldn't seek the big-city high life—he had already burned out on Dallas—and he didn't feel he needed tons of money to be happy. He wanted professional success, yes, but it was more about respect than anything else. He wanted to be known for being good at his job, and he wanted a lifetime of learning. Which is, he suspected, exactly what Ted Frolick wanted. Matt liked him, and if Frolick ended up being a sicko psychopath, it would be sad.

On every case he'd ever worked, Matt kept private notes for his own use. That kept his perspective on the investigation in focus, not swayed by anyone else's viewpoint. By the time he finished his beer, he had a short list of the facts, along with the players so far. He had a much longer list of the unanswered questions that would have to wait until tomorrow's light of day.

How could this have happened the first day I'm here? Matt thought, staring into his now-roaring fire. Gusts of wind hurling down the chimney from the gale outside were making the flames dance. His big picture windows were stable, but, on occasion, the paned windows in the panel next to his front door would rattle. The little cabin felt mostly solid, though, and tonight it offered up the coziness that Matt knew it would when he'd first laid eyes on it last December.

I just want a fresh start in a quiet place. Did I ask for a career-defining child-murder case? Did I?? No, I did not. But it was the cards he was dealt, so he had no choice but to fold or play his hand. And Matt Horning didn't fold. Ever. No how. No way.

In addition to his specific action items for tomorrow to move the case forward, he also added some logistical things to a new list: the "Things-to-do-after-I-catch-Emily's-killer" list. The War Room set-up was working nicely as a command center, but he needed a key for the door to keep out any curious City Hall employees. And he needed Mary Lou's assistance setting up his office and the department's squad room in a more user-friendly, professional manner. So far, Matt only knew where these three rooms and the men's room were located, and he didn't have a clue where supplies, extra furniture, etc. were kept.

He could operate in the short term, but to perform day-to-day operations, and to ensure that his leadership and order were maintained, the police department's digs and, he suspected, policies would need some fine-tuning. His predecessor, George, had run a loose ship.

Matt turned out the lamp next to his sofa, and stared, in the dark, at the dying embers of his fire, listening to the wind howl around his cottage, as the rain ran in rivers down his ocean-front windows. After midnight, he walked down the short hallway to his bedroom, dropped his sweats at the foot of his bed, and climbed in.

Laying there naked and exhausted for thirty seconds, Matt realized he hadn't brushed his teeth. *Hell with it.*

* * *

Sunday, 10:00 p.m.

Very dark out tonight. House is crazy. Garbage pickup yesterday right on schedule. Walking on top of truck and smelling real life.

I told Emily the truth and she understood. Should have eaten all of her. Is she walking in the water? How can I kill myself? Death is living!

CHAPTER 26

Monday, 6:30 a.m.

Last night's squall had moved on, and Matt stood in front of his cottage's big picture window looking out on a tranquil sea, clutching his coffee mug, and searching the waves for his new pet, Roger the seal. The ever-present misty fog over the water was lifting. Patches of blue sky appeared intermittently between the fast-moving downy white clouds coming in from the southwest.

The sun was just peeking over the Twisty River Valley hills behind him, and its first hit on the water was turning yesterday's angry, gray ocean into a placid blue. Soft, frothy waves broke gently. There was still some leftover brown foam from last night's tempest clinging to the upper reaches of the beach, but it would soon be washed away by this morning's friendlier breakers.

Even though it was a harsh time of year, Matt could see signs of the spring beauty to come. His little garden enclosed within the picket fence was showing tiny white snowdrops peeking out of the mossy cover at the far end closest to the ocean. Along the south side of his fence was a stunning yellow witch hazel in all its glory, especially with this morning's sunshine hitting it full-on.

No time for a run on the beach this morning, Matt decided. Shame, as it was shaping up to be a beautiful day. Weather-wise, that is, certainly not activity-wise.

Matt cracked open a side window to let in the early morning. Aside from the waves, all he could hear were the calls of the seagulls.

There he was! Roger, bobbing along about fifty yards out. It cracked up Matt how it truly did look like the seal was grinning at him. He lifted his coffee cup toward the window in a salute to him.

How goes it today, Chief?

Hey, Rog, thanks for asking. It could be better. How are you?

Oh, you know, same old, same old. Did you catch the girl's killer yet?

No, maybe today. Got any tips for me?

It's always someone in the family.

Right. I'll remember that. Know who you're named after, Roger?

Haven't a clue.

Roger Staubach, the Cowboys quarterback, and one of my idols.

Oh, yeah?

Yep. Staubach was steadfast and loyal, and that's what I see in you.

Well, I am here every day. There's that. And I seem to like you.

OK then, Roger it is.

I hate to break this up, Chief, but shouldn't you be on your way?

Roger that.

He quickly showered. The bathroom in his cottage was the one room that had been modernized. The former bathtub and pedestal sink had been replaced in favor of a walk-in porcelain-tiled shower with a rain showerhead, for which Matt was grateful this morning. His shaving kit still sat unpacked on the antique blue vanity between the two white sinks. He recognized the Home Depot vanity, and briefly wondered if he'd ever have anyone to share a second sink with again.

No time for that thinking today either.

* * *

Matt swiped his key card in the side door of City Hall, and made his way in semi-darkness to his office. In the peace of the early morning, he turned on his computer, and found the sticky note on his desk that Mary Lou had given him yesterday with his new City of Port Stirling email address. He logged on and found two emails, one from Dr. Ryder with the formal autopsy report on Emily's body, and one from Bill Abbott, his boss. The 'subject' line of Abbott's message read 'I'm giving you an order'. The body of the message read:

"Matt, I have one request. Actually, it's…more like an order. I want you to keep charge of this investigation. Don't let that asshole Dalrymple take over. Or the state police fucks either. Got it? This is our territory and our investigation. Just because you're new on the job, don't let them railroad you. You've got what it takes to get the job done—both the smarts and the experience. I hired you for this situation, just didn't expect it to ever come. See you Monday."

Matt understood all too well. A crime like this can really do damage to a community. He, and he alone, needed to control the outcome if he hoped to stay in Port Stirling. He so appreciated Abbott's support, and had told him so when they met briefly yesterday morning in Matt's office.

"Nasty business, this," Abbott said to Matt in greeting, extending his right hand in handshake mode. Matt grabbed it, and nodded his agreement.

"Maybe trouble followed me, Bill," Matt said. Somber, he had let down his guard.

"Bullshit, nothing of the sort," Abbott huffed. "Some creep killed this little girl in our town—got nothing to do with your arrival. We'll get him, and you will make me look like a genius for hiring you. Read me?"

"Yes, boss." The older man made Matt smile, and he would make him look like a genius when this thing was resolved. He would have eventually made his former boss, Plano Police Chief Billy Bob Grant, look good, too, but Grant couldn't wait out Horton and Clare Johnson, who badgered the Plano PD on a daily basis after their daughter's death. About two months after the incident, on one Friday morning in late November, Grant called Matt into his office and said "I'm sorry, but we're done here, Matt."

He wasn't telling Matt anything he already didn't know. He was done. In more ways than one. The horror and shock of taking a young woman's life, even under the circumstances, had been almost more than Matt could emotionally bear. He had joined the police force to protect and serve, not to kill unstable young women.

Alicia might have killed him if his gun hadn't gone off when she lunged at him. But still. She was only 19 years old, and had the promise of a bright life ahead of her. Maybe she was a druggie, but she could have been helped with that illness.

Instead, because of him, Alicia Johnson was now another young, dead, African-American statistic. Matt didn't blame Billy Bob for showing him the door, but it did make him all the more thankful for Abbott's support now. He would gently explain to the older man why it wasn't such a terrific idea to call their DA an asshole on a city email account.

* * *

Monday, 7:30 a.m.

After a quick rap on Matt's door and without waiting for a response, the DA himself came bursting into the office.

"You're up early, Mr. Dalrymple," Matt said calmly.

"I'm here to save you from making any more mistakes." The DA was wearing a sharp black wool suit, crisp white shirt, and a patterned red tie. As he did at yesterday's crime team meeting, he seemed over-dressed for Port Stirling, but he made Matt feel a little too casual in his sweater and slacks.

"Oh? I wasn't aware I'd made any so soon."

"What were you thinking bringing Marjorie Bushnell's affair into this case? All it does is embarrass the mayor," said Dalrymple, his voice firm but without rancor.

"You don't think it might have bearing on Emily's death? What if Emily knew about her mother's secret and Marjorie worried she would spill the beans? There aren't many reasons why someone would kill a 4-year-old. I think we have to explore every possibility."

"Marjorie did not kill her daughter, neither did Fred," said Dalrymple.

"Then who did?"

"Obviously, I don't know the answer to that question yet. But putting Marjorie's affair into her official statement and, therefore, making it part of the record on this case is unnecessary and inflammatory. Frankly, Chief, it's not very smart of you."

Matt blanched at that remark but stayed outwardly composed. "Frankly, Mr. DA, it appears to me that you care more about not ruffling the mayor's feathers than you do about finding Emily's killer. A potential suspect in this horrific crime lied to me about her activities in the days before her child's murder. Her husband needed to be aware of that fact. I'm sorry if you don't feel it was the smart thing to do, but I stand by my actions."

"Are you sure you don't have a vendetta against politicians because of your last work in Plano?" Dalrymple countered. "It's my understanding that the parents of the girl you killed were politically important and got you fired. Is that correct?"

"Yes, you've got my story right," Matt admitted. "But that case has absolutely nothing to do with Emily's case."

"How can you be confident that what are surely bitter feelings toward Alicia Johnson's parents aren't being projected onto Marjorie and the mayor?"

Matt was shocked to hear Alicia's name coming out of the DA's mouth.

"You're certainly up to speed on my life," was all he could manage.

"I just want to make sure that you aren't acting irresponsibly here because of an emotional hangover."

"That's not the case, David. I can assure you that I am conducting this investigation by the book, and bringing to it my years of experience with violent crime. Whether you like it or not, Marjorie and Fred are prime suspects in their daughter's homicide. I will tread as carefully as I can on the mayor's family, but you need to know that I will stop at nothing to resolve this case."

"And you need to know that I am watching your every move, Chief. I will not—NOT—have this investigation blow up in our faces. Is that clear?"

"Clear. You have to do what you have to do, and I will continue leading this case as I see fit."

"Are we having another team meeting today?"

"Yes. I want to follow up on some alibis this morning, and check in with my local team. Then, we'll update everyone this afternoon. Regular time, 4:00 p.m. How does that sound?"

"I'm headed to my office in Twisty River shortly, but I'll be back here by 4 o'clock. I've got something to do first in Port Stirling, and then I'll be in my office if you need anything." The DA stood up to leave.

212

"You're not going to the Bushnell house, are you?" asked Matt, pushing back his chair and also standing. "I'd rather you didn't until we verify the kids' alibis today."

"I don't think it's up to you to tell me where I can or cannot go, but, no, I'm not going to Fred's home." He turned his back to Matt and strode out of the room.

Alrighty then. Our erstwhile DA was living up to Abbott's nickname for him.

* * *

Matt found an old football on the shelf in his office's small coat closet when he hung up his jacket this morning. George Simonson must have overlooked it when he cleaned out his office, and Matt made a mental note to return it to him once things settled down. But for now, he tossed it back and forth as he looked out his window to the sea on this sparkling day.

Was there any truth to Dalrymple's assertion? Am I trying too hard to pin this on the mayor or his wife because I don't like politicians?

He put the football down on his desk and pulled out his phone, calling Sheriff Johnson.

"Anything turn up in your investigation yesterday? Anything I should know? I wanted to check in with you before our meeting later."

"Maybe, is my answer," replied the sheriff. "There were 14 golfers staying at Port Stirling Links on Friday night, and we're in the process of talking to them all. It looks like five of them checked out late yesterday afternoon before we had a chance to quiz them, and I'm currently in the process of tracking them down. I'm going to find the guys that left—and they're all guys—and then go out there to interrupt some golf games. As of this morning, there are only nine golfers registered at the resort. It's the slowest month, they tell me."

"I can't believe there's anyone playing golf in this weather," Matt said.

"You'd be surprised. I'm particularly focused on one oddball, a guest named Clay Sherwin."

"Oh?"

"Yeah. He arrived at Port Stirling Links last Wednesday and registered for a one week's stay. He arrived with no golf clubs, which rarely happens here. Most of the people who pay big money to come here want their own clubs, and think nothing of shelling out the bucks to ship them."

"Did you talk to him?"

"Yeah, and he's suspicious. He's from La Jolla. Says he's up here looking for peace and quiet, and to relax and think about his life. Wife just divorced him because she fell for another woman—get that!"

"Ooh, that's a rough one."

"Yeah. He's a good-looking guy, and probably never figured he'd be divorced because of something like that."

"Is he a suspect?"

"Maybe. He's not a golfer, and wouldn't tell me what he does for a living. His whereabouts since he's been here are vague. Says he was in the bar at the resort Friday night, and then went to eat at The Crab Shack. Then back to his cottage and to bed early. He's a reader, and there was a stack of books on his bedside table."

"Have you confirmed where Mr. Sherwin said he ate dinner Friday night?" asked Matt. "Was he at The Crab Shack—is that what you called it?"

"Yeah, it's a restaurant slash fish shop down by the wharf. We're going there today to verify he was there Friday night. I did talk to the bartender, and Sherwin was in the Links Bar early Friday evening like he said."

"He's still in town, right?"

"Yes. I told him to stick around, but he's booked until Wednesday anyway."

"Good. I'll want to talk to him," said Matt. *Maybe it was time he looked outside the family to make sure he wasn't overlooking anyone suspicious.* "Was he cooperative?"

"Somewhat. He wasn't belligerent or aggressive, but he was clearly not happy about being bothered."

"Well, you'll want to find out what Mr. Sherwin does in California, and if the story about his divorce checks out. If that happened to me, I'd probably want to escape to the boonies as well, but I will go chat him up."

"Yeah, it's not an implausible story. But there was something about him that didn't register with me."

CHAPTER 27

Monday, 7:00 a.m.

Fern awoke happy to see the sun coming up through the crack in her east-facing bedroom curtains, but with a sense of trepidation. To her surprise, she slept fairly soundly, and didn't dream about dead children. Growing up at the coast, she liked snuggling down into her bedcovers during a blustery storm, and found it comforting and not alarming in the least.

But still, pulling open her curtains, it was nice to see that the rain had stopped, and the sky was clearing. Fern's bungalow was inland from the Pacific—she couldn't afford those ocean-view prices—but she did have a bucolic view over a gorse-filled meadow to the Twisty River hills, where the sun was rising through the valley fog, producing a watery sunshine.

She wondered if Matt was up yet. She knew that he was a cop with years of experience and would obviously have a background, but for all that, she was shocked by what she'd read last night about his undoing in Texas. She wondered if he had killed anyone else during the line of duty. Deliberately, she'd stopped reading about him online after the few news articles detailing his last case. It seemed important to let Matt tell her his story in his own words.

Fern stood in front of her closet. She was determined to look professional and serious today. Although Emily's murder was frightful, she had a job to do and teammates to support. And, if she was honest with herself, deep down inside, Fern did feel something other than horror at her current situation. She felt needed. Maybe for the first time in years. Fern had strong, life-long ties to her community, and this child's murder would not stand. Her training and skills could truly help Chief Horning and the real detectives uncover the truth. In a way, she was a detective, too, and she wanted to do her part.

Let's say I'm not only a representative of Chinook County, but I'm also a skilled detective . . . what would I wear? she said to her closet. She chose a black blazer, black skinny nicely-fitting pants, and a lime green ribbed turtleneck. The pop of green next to her face was flattering, and contrasted nicely with her red hair which fell in gentle waves to her shoulders. She wore minimal makeup, which allowed her few freckles to show through. A small pair of pearl earrings her father brought her from a business trip to China years ago were a tasteful final touch, and, along with her watch, the only jewelry she wore.

* * *

Monday, 8:45 a.m.

When he and Sheriff Johnson rang off, and he had organized his thoughts, Matt moved to retrieve his jacket; it was time he hit the streets and started nailing down some details. He would spend some time with his department in the squad room first, and make sure everyone was clear on their assignments.

"Knock knock," said Fern, rapping on his open office door, and poking her head around the corner. The two almost collided.

"Come on in," Matt smiled at her, and held open the door, as she had her hands full.

"I went to Goodie's for coffee and I bought an extra one—do you want it?" she said.

"Yes, ma'am, I do." He took one of the fragrant coffees out of her hand.

She looked better than the last time he saw her, although she was still on the pale side this morning. But gone was the exhausted, haunted look in her eyes when they parted last night. He thought her bright sweater made her look cheerful, and it was welcome.

"Do all Texans call women 'ma'am'?" asked Fern. She genuinely wanted to know.

Matt laughed. "'Fraid so. It's considered respectful, and it's drummed into us from an early age. Why? Don't you like it?"

"It makes me feel like my mother," Fern smiled. "You know—old."

"Well, we can't have that. I will make an honest attempt to not call you 'ma'am' again. But you might have to cut me some slack."

"I can do that. You'll drop that Texas shtick and be an Oregonian any minute now. It will improve your quality of life. Can I have a word with you?"

"What's up?"

"I did a terrible thing when I got home last night," she started.

"What?"

"I Googled you."

"Oh."

"Don't you want to know what popped up?"

"Pretty sure I know."

"Do you want to talk about what happened with Alicia Johnson?"

Matt desperately wanted to tell Fern his side of the story, but wasn't sure she really needed to hear it right now.

"I'm not ducking what happened in Texas, but we have a job to do, Fern."

"Our killer can wait five minutes."

He stared at her, and realized that she had made herself comfortable in the chair across from his desk. She drank her coffee, and stared back at him, waiting.

Holding Fern's gaze, he said in a hushed voice, "The hardest part is having people who don't know me believe that I'm the kind of cop who kills black teenagers. I'm not that guy."

"No, I don't expect that you are. What happened that night?"

"It was a party of kids that was getting out of hand. Music too loud, spilling out into the street, open drinking and drug use, and using the sidewalk for a toilet. Standard Saturday night in Texas," Matt drawled, and that slow smile started unsurely on his face. "I told the crowd we needed them to tone it down, and think about dispersing before Jessica—my partner—and I started checking IDs."

"That was popular, no doubt."

"The next thing I knew there's this crazy woman jumping on my back. I heard her scream close to my ear—and I will never forget this as long as I live—'Leave us alone, you slimeball motherfucking cop motherfucker!' Sorry, but that's what I was dealing with. Along with her long fingernails gouging my neck and the side of my face. The force of her surprise attack made me stumble to the ground. I saw the glint of something that looked like a knife in her right hand."

"Oh!" Fern gasped.

"Yeah, I remember how the knife stood out against her blood-red fingernails. I wrestled with the woman, finally getting an upper hand. And I could feel that Jessica was fighting with her behind me. I thought we almost had her subdued, but Alicia wasn't quite finished with me. She somehow broke free of my grasp and lunged for my gun just as I was bringing it out of its harness. It went off."

Matt stopped his story and took a long drink of coffee.

"Was she the first person you've ever killed?"

"No. But she was the only accidental killing. Much worse."

"I'm so sorry this happened to you, Matt."

"Life's not always fair, right? And just when I thought it couldn't get any worse, it did. Turns out that Alicia wasn't only a cocaine-sniffing, vodka-drinking cop hater with anger management issues. She was also a leader of the African-American student union at Collin College. And her parents are a well-connected and high-profile couple in the Dallas area. They went after me big time."

"Did you try to talk to them and tell them how bad you felt? That it was an accident?"

"Oh, yeah," Matt snorted, "I tried. My encounter with her father didn't go so well. I quickly learned where Alicia got her cop hatred and her language skills. Let's leave it at that."

"And the police department didn't support you even though you were cleared by the Grand Jury? I find that difficult to believe."

"They tried to hang in, especially my boss, but the pressure from the Johnsons was too much. It was obvious they weren't going to drop it until they ran me out of town. Which is what happened. Irony is that before that night, I was headed for a promotion to Assistant Chief. And what nobody knows is that four years ago I was given a statewide medal for my work in community policing within the African-American community. I was stronger on race relations in Plano that anyone else in my department, and everyone in the department knew it. We had a lot of redneck boys who didn't like dealing with blacks, but I wasn't raised that way. I was just the wrong guy in the wrong place at the wrong time."

"That really sucks."

"Look on the bright side—I'm here, aren't I?"

Fern smiled. "It is most definitely the bright side for us. And, you'll think so too, soon, I promise."

"Thanks for saying that—it means a lot. And, really, thanks for listening. I probably do need to talk about it." He paused. "But right now, I have to see a non-golfer about why he happens to be staying at a golf resort."

CHAPTER 28

Monday, 10:00 a.m.

After asking one of his officers for directions to Port Stirling Links, Matt turned his car onto Hwy 101. The apparently world-class golf resort was a few minutes north of town.

He stopped first at registration, and asked the desk manager if he knew Clay Sherwin.

"Yes, I was on duty when he checked in."

"He's still here this morning, right?"

"Yes, he's staying until Wednesday."

"Can you tell me if Mr. Sherwin booked any tee times when he checked in or before he arrived?"

"He did not."

"So why is he here?"

"No idea. He has a rental car and takes off after breakfast, and we may or may not see him again during the day. Some nights he has dinner here, but some nights he goes elsewhere."

"Did he eat here Friday night?"

"As I told the sheriff, I'm not sure. I checked the books, and he wasn't in them. But that doesn't mean he didn't pop in to the restaurant. It's not like we're fully booked or anything."

"Did he give any clues what he's doing here?" Matt asked.

"He didn't say anything specifically, and we certainly don't ask our guests, but I got the idea he is some sort of creative type—writer, artist, something like that. He carries around some sort of big notebook, like a portfolio."

"How old a guy is he?"

"Again, I'm not sure, but I would say he's in his late 40's."

"Do you know where he is right now?"

"No, sir, I do not. You can drive around to his Lily Pond cottage and see if his car is there. It's a black BMW with California plates. He's in number 304. He didn't have anything to do with that little girl's death, did he?" Wide-eyed, he stared at Matt.

"Don't know yet. Can I count on your discretion . . ."—Matt peered at the manager's nametag—"James?"

"Of course. And we will count on yours."

As Matt drove around to Lily Pond cottage 304, a haunting vision of Emily's sad little body played on his psyche. *Goddamitt!*

He rapped on the cottage door with vigor. After a few seconds, a man who he assumed was Clay Sherwin opened the door. Matt's first thought was *"Ahh, the cliché stranger-in-town"*. Sherwin was tall, fit, handsome in a rugged sort of way, but with a cool, mysterious air about him

"Yes?" was all he said as he opened the door to his cottage.

"I'm Chief Matt Horning of the Port Stirling Police Department, and I'd like a few minutes of your time." He fished out his badge that had been laying on his desk when he arrived this morning, and held it up for Sherwin to inspect.

"I already told the sheriff everything I know about the child's murder, which is nothing."

"Can I come in?"

"I don't know anything," Sherwin repeated, not budging from his solid stance blocking the entrance.

"We're investigating a murder, and we're talking to all transient guests in town. That includes you, and I have some further questions of my own. We either talk here, or you will have to come down to City Hall with me."

That got Sherwin's attention and he stepped aside, motioning for Matt to come in. The suite was nice; beachy Oregon in tone, with high-end finishes and natural colors like forest green, sea blue, and sand. A nice fire was going in the corner fireplace, and it was comforting against this chilly morning.

Sherwin walked to a small table over by the glass doors that did, indeed, overlook a lily pond. He sat down in one of the chairs in front of a laptop, and Matt took the chair across the table, feeling the welcome warmth of the fire on his back.

"To confirm," started Matt, "you are Clay Sherwin, is that correct?"

"Yes."

"How long have you been in Port Stirling?"

"Since last Wednesday. I'm staying for one week." His tone was cordial, not overly-friendly, but polite enough.

"Why are you in town?"

Sherwin hesitated. "Why is that important to your investigation?"

"You don't appear to be playing golf, so it's curious that you're staying at a golf resort. We're trying to establish why any tourists are in town, especially since January isn't exactly our best month." Matt smiled, which got him a smile of sorts in return from Sherwin.

"It's a good month if you're trying to avoid crowds, and get some peace and quiet. That's what I'm trying to do."

"Why?"

"Because I'm overworked and underpaid, and I needed a break. Golf resorts are usually nice places, and offseason they can be tranquil."

"What is it you do for a living, Mr. Sherwin?"

"I'd rather not say."

"Why not?"

Sherwin looked out the window, and then back at Matt. "Unless you believe my line of employment is relevant to your case, I'd rather remain private."

Standoff.

"So, you're here for a little R & R, correct? Why Port Stirling Links? Why not a cabin on the beach if you wanted quiet?"

"Because the service in golf resorts is usually top notch, and this place has an excellent reputation. I didn't want to have to do anything myself."

"Are you married?"

Sherwin made a show of looking at his watch. "What time is it? My divorce should be final just about now." His face looked resigned, and not terribly upset.

"Sorry to hear that."

Sherwin shrugged. "It happens".

"Where were you Friday night between the hours of 6:00 p.m. and midnight?"

"Was that when your murder happened?"

"Yes. Where were you?"

"Let's see. Wednesday night I ate here at the resort because I arrived after dark and didn't know my way around. Thursday, too, I think. Friday night I recall going to that seafood shack down by the harbor. Yes, that's right. I had fish and chips, and coleslaw, and it was delicious."

"Are you talking about "The Crab Shack"? What time were you there, do you think?"

"Yes, that's it. I had a cocktail in the bar here first, and then went to dinner. I was probably in the bar about 6:30 p.m.—the bartender and I talked about the Kapalua golf tournament on his TV, so I'm sure he'll remember me. Then I went downtown and ate. I read a book at a corner table in the restaurant, and was probably there about an hour."

"What did you do after you left the restaurant?"

"Came back here and read until I went to bed. Exciting, huh?" Sherwin said, smiling.

"What time do you think you got back here?"

"Not sure. I probably got to the restaurant about 7:30 p.m., and left an hour or so later, so it must have been about 8:45 p.m.. Does that sound about right?"

"You tell me."

"See," said Sherwin, growing agitated, "part of the deal with being on vacation is that you're not married to the clock. I don't know what the hell time it was. I had a drink, I went out for dinner, I read my book—that's it."

"Where do you live? And, can I see your ID, please?" Matt agreed with the sheriff's assessment; something felt off here.

Sherwin walked across the room to a padded shoulder bag sitting on the floor near a closet. Reaching into a zippered pocket, he drew out his wallet.

"I live in La Jolla, California," he said formally, handing Matt his driver's license. The photo and description matched Sherwin, although he looked a little heavier than the 180 lbs. his license read. But the stated height of 6'2" fit the man before him.

Matt jotted down the license number, along with Sherwin's La Jolla address, and then asked "Do you know Fred Bushnell?"

"No," Sherwin answered immediately. "Who is he?"

"He's the mayor of Port Stirling. It was his daughter who was murdered Friday night."

"Wow."

"That's right. You're sure you don't know the mayor, or have any business with him on this trip?"

"No and no. I'm here to start getting over my divorce, and to think about my next steps in life. Is that so hard to understand?"

"Why are you getting divorced? Did your wife find out you're a pedophile, and she's bolting? Is that your secret?"

Clay Sherwin looked hard at Matt, and then spoke calmly. "I am not a pedophile. I did not kill the mayor's child. I am here to relax and think about my life. End of story."

"Why are you getting divorced? You didn't answer that question," Matt said, bulldog-like.

"My wife fell in love with her personal trainer. A woman." He looked out the window, and was suddenly intrigued by the lily pads floating on top of the pond's surface.

"I'm sorry, Mr. Sherwin. I'm sure that was a shock."

"Yes. Although it is a California thing," he said with a sardonic smile.

"So, you didn't take out your anger at the female sex by stabbing Emily Bushnell Friday night?" One more try.

"No. I don't know these people, and I don't know anything about your murder. Please talk to the bartender here and the restaurant people. They'll confirm I was where I said I was."

"Oh, we'll do that, you can count on it. But we don't know where you were the rest of Friday night, do we? I assume you had no guests in your room? No visitors?"

"I was alone, and I turned in early. I woke up at dawn Saturday, and walked the golf course before anyone was out there playing. You'll have to take my word for it."

"That's not how I roll, Mr. Sherwin," said Matt. "We'll be checking out every aspect of your alibi and your life. Things like, where do you go when you leave the resort and don't come back all day? We'll know if there is any link at all between you and the Bushnells. We'll learn why you're really here."

"Good God, man, I've told you the truth. What more can I do?"

"Where do you go when you drive out of the resort?"

"I drove to Buck Bay one day to buy a new battery for my computer. I went to their history museum—interesting collection. I wanted to see a cranberry bog, so drove out there one day. Just sightseeing and looking around. Takes my mind off my troubles." He stared at Matt, daring him to contradict him.

"Do you have any kids of your own?"

Sherwin stood up. "That's it, Mr. Horning. I'm finished answering your questions. I'd like you to leave now."

Matt stood up, too. "Please don't leave town until you hear from me that it's OK. I'll need a day or two to check out your story, and I want you to stay put until then. Understood?"

"Are you ordering me to stay? I just want to be clear."

"Yes, I am. Until we dismiss you as a suspect, you are not to leave Port Stirling."

"Do I need a lawyer?"

"That's your call, Mr. Sherwin."

"This is unbelievable," he said and appeared truly flabbergasted by this turn of events. "If I had killed this girl, wouldn't I have left town immediately afterward? And isn't it much more likely that it's someone the kid knew?"

"Both good points. But while we're gathering information in this investigative phase, I'd really appreciate you sticking around."

"I'll be here until Wednesday. After that, you're going to have to arrest me or let me go," Sherwin said. He walked to the door and opened it.

Matt walked through the door, turned to face Clay Sherwin, pointed his index finger at his face and said, "Stay put."

CHAPTER 29

Driving back to town, Matt's cell phone vibrated in the clip on his belt. It was his mother.

"I'm calling to check in on you," said Beverly Horning. "And to say we'll all be thinking about you this afternoon during your swearing-in ceremony."

Oh, shit, he hadn't called home since he'd arrived at the Buck Bay Airport Saturday morning. His family had no idea what was going on.

"Actually, mom, there was a change in the plan—I was sworn in Saturday. On the beach at the Pacific Ocean. In the rain. There's been quite a few changes since I spoke to you on Saturday."

"Changes? Already? What?"

"The mayor of Port Stirling's 4-year-old daughter was found murdered on the beach Saturday morning just before my plane landed. We don't know who did it yet, and we've launched a big investigation. I started my job Saturday morning instead, and it's all hands on deck. You can imagine."

"Oh my God," Beverly exclaimed. "Are you all right?"

"I'm fine, mom. But I'll be better when we figure out who did this. It's a bit of a tight spot, being it's the mayor's family and all. Just my luck, huh?"

"Is the family involved?"

"We don't know yet, and I really can't talk about the details."

Dead air on the phone.

"Mom, are you still there?"

"I'm here. What if you don't catch the killer? This couldn't be any worse for you, Matthew. You're going to be in the news again. I'm worried."

"It's gonna be OK. I'll solve this case, and I'll be a hero," Matt joked in an attempt to placate his mother. "Please don't worry, mom. Everyone here has been real nice to me, and it's starting to feel like home already. I'm going to get through this, you'll see. I do have some investigative skills, you know."

"Of course you do, dear. It's just . . . the mayor's daughter. So unfair."

"What's unfair is that a child was murdered. I'll try to keep you posted, but please understand that I'm up to my eyeballs right now.'"

"Do your job, Matthew, and don't worry about us. Everyone here is fine, but the drought is showing no signs of letting up."

"We've got plenty of water you can have," he laughed. "You would not believe the storm we had yesterday and last night. I bet it rained two inches."

"Have you met any nice women yet?"

"Lots of pretty women here, mom, the place is literally crawlin' with them. I can barely turn around without running into one."

"Now you're being sarcastic," Beverly chided. "No need to be a smarty-pants, I was just asking the question."

"There's no point in me even looking at a woman right now. If I don't figure out who killed the mayor's daughter, I won't be here long enough to have a date. Gotta run, mom. Give my love to dad."

He couldn't fail again. It wasn't an option. His mother didn't say that, but he knew she was thinking it, too.

* * *

Matt hit 'end call', and immediately punched in Fern's phone number.

"Hey, could you do me a favor? I need Joey Hawthorne pulled out of school this morning so I can talk to him, and I think it would be better for the kid if you did it instead of me. Could you call the principal and find out how we do this with the least amount of trouble?"

"I don't know," Fern said. "Everyone probably knows that he and Jack are buddies, and they certainly know why Jack is not in school today. I don't think it would be fair to have Joey tagged as having anything to do with the murder if he's innocent. Couldn't you wait until school gets out this afternoon?"

"I hate to be a bastard, but I don't really care if Joey gets teased. Our obligation is to Emily," Matt said. "Please call the school now."

Fern grasped the phone tightly in her hand and exhaled. "Look, buster, please don't act like you're the only one who cares about finding Emily's killer," she said angrily. "We're all in this together, and I don't need you ignoring my professional opinion and barking orders at me. If Jack did it, and Joey can help us, I'm all in on talking with him. I just believe we should have some compassion for a kid who might be scared about now."

"Buster?" Matt said. "Now I'm a 'buster'? I called you because I respect your professionalism and I think you're the right person for this job. But there's only one leader in this investigation, and that's me."

"I'm not questioning your leadership, Matt. I have to consider the child, too." He could tell she was tight-lipped on the other end of the line.

"OK, you're right," Matt conceded. "Let's do it this way. Please call Joey's parents and let them know we want to talk to him right away. Have them bring him home for lunch so I can talk to him then. He can tell his friends that he's going home for lunch."

"I like that," Fern said brusquely, still pissed off. "I can do that and still protect Joey's privacy."

"Listen," Matt started, reaching for the right words. "We're all wound tight. I forget that you didn't buy into this cop business like Jay and I did. If it's getting to you and you want out, say the word." Fern said crisply "It is getting to me, but I don't want out." She hung up.

* * *

While he waited for Fern's call, he turned off the highway on the road that he hoped led to Fergus Dunbar's farm. It wasn't marked, but it was the direction he'd gotten from Sheriff Johnson. When this was over, he vowed to drive every road in Chinook County until he knew where in the hell he was at all times!

After winding up two roads, the last one which ran adjacent to Twisty River, Matt found the farm, and sat in his patrol car in Fergus Dunbar's gravel driveway. He checked his notebook for the sheriff's notes on his first visit with the farmer. Although the farmhouse looked nice, Dunbar's place was as bleak and isolated as they come.

An aerial enforcement patrol conducted late yesterday confirmed Sheriff Johnson's suspicion that Dunbar had a healthy pot crop growing on his acreage, along with his vegetables and fruit. Unless Fergus was a licensed grower in the state's cannabis program, his crop far exceeded the legal limit of four immature plants per residence. The sheriff thought his crop canopy was so large, Fergus would be in the top tier of licensing, and Johnson seriously doubted that Fergus had paid that steep fee. The sheriff checked with the state, and he hadn't. *Doesn't anyone follow the law around here?*

Matt rapped loudly on Dunbar's door and waited.

No answer.

He tried again, and waited again. Still no answer.

He walked around the side of the house, and saw Fergus Dunbar, who was weeding between rows of what looked like potatoes. Dunbar saw Matt at the same time, stood up, and shaded his eyes with one hand in order to get a good look at who was there. John Fogerty and Credence Clearwater Revival's 'Lookin' Out My Back Door' was playing loudly on the transistor radio in Fergus' pocket.

"Ah, another cop, I'm guessing," said Fergus. "What do you want?"

"Mr. Dunbar, I'm the new Port Stirling Police Chief. My name is Matt Horning. How do you do?" he said, and reached to shake hands with the farmer.

"I do just fine, thank you," replied Dunbar as he shook the chief's hand. "Welcome to town."

"Thank you. This is a nice place you have here. Peaceful, and a real good view of the river."

Dunbar stared at him with his hands in his overall pockets.

"What crops do you grow here?" Matt asked, undeterred by Dunbar's silence.

"Just because I don't like her daddy doesn't mean I killed that girl," said Dunbar.

"I didn't say you did, did I?" responded Matt.

"The top guy wouldn't come all the way out here unless you thought I had something to do with this. Am I right?"

"This is routine, Mr. Dunbar. We're talking to everyone who may have had a beef with Mayor Bushnell. It's common knowledge that you had a squabble with him last week. I want to follow up on that."

"Ask away. Nothin's going to change from what I told Sheriff Johnson. I told him the truth. I always tell the truth. Life's too short to complicate it with lies, don't you think? Am I right?"

"I do think that, yes. Let's start with where you were Friday night between the hours of 6:00 p.m. and midnight."

Matt walked him through the same questions the sheriff had asked, and, to his credit, Dunbar answered in a straight-forward manner without attitude. He was mostly polite and seemed genuine, and nothing in his responses jumped out at Matt. One would never call Fergus Dunbar smooth, but there was nothing egregious in his demeanor. But, until Matt could definitely rule him out as a suspect, he ruled him in.

"Anything else?" Dunbar asked.

"There is one more thing, Fergus. I have reason to believe that you have a substantial, unlicensed pot-growing operation on this farm, probably out beyond that row of trees," said Matt, pointing towards the hills behind the farmhouse.

"I grow a little weed," Fergus admitted, wiping his hands on his overalls. "But I had nothing to do with the girl's death."

Matt suspected that Fergus just uttered two true statements, but aloud he said, "I'll be back. Stay home today, and that's an order."

CHAPTER 30

Monday, Noon

Matt picked up some chili and cornbread from Dolly's Café, a small restaurant he'd spotted in the older part of town, and took it back to his office. He took a few minutes to check out the view, looking out to the sea, deep in thought, while he ate alone.

Unbelievably, this morning's mild, benign weather was beginning to turn again. Matt was astonished at how the weather could turn on a dime. While it was still dry outside, scowling dark clouds were moving inland off the ocean, replacing this morning's extravagant blue sky, and the wind went from zero to twenty in what felt like seconds. It was clear that another pounder was headed their way. The wind gusts made his windows quake, and the howl was impossible to ignore. The suddenly enraged sea was throwing up monstrous waves, and the jetty had all but disappeared. It was fascinating in its violence.

Matt jotted notes while he finished his lunch, and made a mental note to give the café's cook his mother's chili recipe. Everyone in town would thank him.

After he wrote down his thoughts on Fergus Dunbar (jury is still out) and Ted Frolick (facts point to him telling the truth), Matt found he could not stop reflecting on Marjorie.

Would a mother actually kill her own daughter if she thought the child was going to rat on her love affair? Matt had been trained that all options were on the table when it came to murder, and not to discount those that he might find objectionable. But this. This was beyond. *What do I actually know is a fact where Marjorie is concerned?*

Marjorie and Emily home Friday evening

Fred slept soundly—can't confirm Marjorie there all night . . . alibi wishy-washy

None of kids saw mom Friday night—Saturday AM

Affair with Kenton

Marjorie/Kenton talking parking lot—Emily in car day before murder

What's missing?

Marjorie's clothes/shoes, where are they now?

Fred—Emily's father? If not, who?

Kenton search warrant

Anyone see Emily and?? Ocean Bend Road/Wayside Friday

Where two missing kitchen knives—Bushnell set?

Matt knew that it was a long way from an extra-marital romance to plunging a knife into your child's stomach. And how do those bite marks fit in? He would have to be careful in his next steps, and he needed to ensure that the crime team were all taking care of their tasks first, leaving no stone unturned. There was something uneven about Mrs. Bushnell, and on that point Fern, Jay, and Matt all agreed. But was she just an odd woman protecting her secret life, or was she truly unbalanced? One thing was for sure: If Marjorie was not the killer and Matt didn't pursue all other leads, the mayor would have his head on a platter.

And Matt already knew what that felt like.

237

* * *

Monday, 1:00 p.m.

Matt was grateful that his crime team seemed persistent on following up on their assignments, and as he had that thought, his phone rang. Ed Sonders.

"Hi, Ed. What's the latest?"

"Craig Kenton's alibi checks out," said Sonders. "He was with Barbara Allen in Twisty River Friday night. He got off work at the hardware store at 5:00 p.m., and was in Twisty River by about 5:45 p.m. He stopped to get gas at the Mobil station on the way into town. He and the attendant, Monte Wilson, know each other, and he confirmed the time. Wilson got off duty at 6:00 p.m., and he says that Kenton was the last customer on his shift. That's why he remembers."

"How far is that from Port Stirling?" Matt asked.

"It's about 25 minutes, depending on which road he took and how fast he drives," Sonders replied. "Barbara says Kenton was right on time for their 6:00 p.m. date. They went to the Twisty River Grill for dinner. Waitress said they had a couple of cocktails each and steaks. Says they were nice and polite, and looked like they were enjoying each other's company. She told me they left about 8:45 p.m."

"And then what?" Matt asked, although he thought he already knew the answer.

"What else with this guy? Barbara says they spent the night together at her house."

"Shocking!" Matt said sarcastically. "I need to learn this guy's technique."

"I'll pass that message along. Kenton's out, Chief. His alibi is nearly foolproof."

"What if Barbara is lying?" Matt persisted. "What if he really left after dinner, and she's trying to protect him? Women do seem to want to protect his ass."

"Yeah, I thought of that, too, so I talked to two of Barbara's neighbors who confirmed that Kenton's vehicle—a Ram cab truck—was parked out in front of her house. They both said it was parked in exactly the same spot all night. One of the neighbors saw him when he went out to get his newspaper. He said Kenton got in the truck and drove off alone about 7:00 a.m., and he identified Kenton to a tee. He was there all night, I'm sure."

"Did he work Saturday?"

"Yeah, the hardware store manager said he rolled in about 8:30 a.m. for a 9:00 a.m. opening. Said he looked tired all day."

"I'll bet. Well, shit, Ed, we're running out of suspects," Matt said, scratching his head.

"No, we're not, Chief, we have the Bushnell family. I'm perilously close to eliminating everyone but them, and I know you are, too. It stinks big-time."

"He's the mayor, Ed. Could this get any worse?"

"Rock bottom, agreed. But if he killed his little girl, I don't care if he's the fucking Pope, he's gonna fry."

"We have to discover the motive, it's the missing piece. The only person that we know of so far who had any reason to want Emily dead is Marjorie. The facts say it wasn't financial gain or a sexual motive, so why is she dead? Why is she dead?" Matt repeated quietly the second time.

"I don't know yet. But we'll get our man. Or woman. Count on it."

"I am counting on it. Thanks, Ed. Really appreciate your work on Kenton, even if it wasn't the outcome I was hoping for."

Matt liked the resolve in Ed's voice. Sonders was the real deal.

* * *

Monday, 3:00 p.m.

Matt added the latest known case facts on the left side of the white board, along with his follow-up questions on the right side. Once he finished writing, he sat in one of the faux leather chairs, and stared at the board while he waited for the crime team to arrive.

Jay was the first, about 15 minutes early.

"I'm glad you're here first," Matt said, rising to greet him and placing his hand on the young officer's shoulder. "Come on in. How're you doing today?"

"I would rather be fishing on the river, and I'm a little shell-shocked, but OK," Jay replied. "You?"

"The same. I'd like to unpack my boxes, but otherwise doing alright." Matt paused. "It's always unsettling, but know that the first dead body is always the worst one. I was exhausted and slept, but that howling wind woke me up once. Man, it was a real three-dog night."

"Yeah, that never happens around here," Jay smirked.

"I'm thinking about the tides, and have a couple of questions. Do people around here know tides?" Matt asked. "How they work, timing, etc?"

"Oh, yeah. You have to pay attention to the tides because you can't get around the promontories at high tide, and you can easily get cut off. The tide charts are published in the paper every day, and all the beach-front hotels have a printout they give to tourists so they don't get caught. It still happens, though. People are so pea-brained," Jay said, shaking his head.

"So a resident would know that the high tide floods that tunnel?"

"Yes, everyone who lives around here would know that. We're

taught it as kids by our parents, and anyone who's ever walked on this beach—even one time—would know it. It's real obvious."

"Our killer figured Mother Nature would dispose of the body."

"Yeah. In my estimation, it was a pretty good, well-thought-out plan. In a strong high tide that we can get this time of year, her body easily could have been swept out to sea. Should have been, actually."

"And then we would have just had a missing child," Matt mused. "Not a stabbed, dead body discovered by a barking dog."

"Correct-a-mundo."

"Hi, guys," said Fern. She came in and sat next to Jay.

"We're talking about the tides' impact on this case," Matt said to catch her up.

"The tides have come and gone, and that's all she wrote," Fern said.

"Yep," Matt replied. "It looks like the killer hoped the Pacific would take care of the evidence. And it nearly did."

Matt paused, and the three of them were thinking about that poor dead child in the dark, cold tunnel.

He cleared his throat. "Ed just called, and Craig Kenton has an alibi for Friday night, and it's strong. He was with a woman at a restaurant in Twisty River Friday night, and they stayed 'in' overnight," Matt informed them. "Ed's already verified it with a gaggle of people who saw him at various times during the evening and next morning."

"I presume it was not Marjorie?" asked Jay.

"No, it was not. Ed says her name is Barbara Allen, and she confirmed Kenton's story all down the line."

"Oh my God, I know Barbara Allen!" cried out Fern. "She's in my yoga class. Is that man sleeping with every woman in Chinook County?!?"

"If you know her, check in with Ed at the meeting, will you? He might want you to have a chat with her," Matt said.

"Will do."

"And please call Joey Hawthorne's parents and tell them we've been delayed. Sorry. Jay and I need to go back out to Fergus Dunbar's and do a search of his premises and computer right after this meeting. Tell them it will be about 5:30 p.m. at their house, OK? Are you still available then to go with me?"

"Yes, of course, I will go," Fern said briskly. "No matter what Joey has to say, this is liable to be an upsetting experience for both him and his parents. You're going to need me. Does Dunbar live alone, or is there a woman or any children at his place? Should I go with you guys while you search?"

"Not necessary. He's a loner, as far as we can tell. Jay and I will handle him."

* * *

"I took the liberty of following up on Ted Frolick," DA Dalrymple started the meeting. "Both of your statements from him were thorough . . . as far as they went. But I wanted to know more about his background, so I talked to the school administrator who fired him, and I had a phone call with the parents of the boy he slapped."

"I wish you'd checked with me first," Patty said. She raised both hands off the conference table and gestured toward Dalrymple. "I've scheduled a visit with the parents right after this meeting."

"That's no problem, Patty. I'd welcome your input on their story," the DA said, adjusting the knot on his gold tie.

"Of course it's a problem," she fumed. "It makes us look uncoordinated and like we don't know what we're doing."

"Well, I thought you and the chief ruled out Frolick, and I don't want him ruled out yet," the DA said defensively.

"Here's my phone number," Patty said, pushing her business card across the table in Dalrymple's direction. "A simple phone call, David, it's a simple phone call."

"And, I told you quite clearly that I haven't ruled out Frolick yet," added Matt. "He's just not No. 1 on our list currently. Marjorie is, because no one else on our radar has a known motive to want Emily dead, including Ted Frolick."

"What part of past child abuser don't you understand, Chief?" the DA said in an aggressive tone. "Frolick has a history in this area, while the Bushnells are squeaky clean. Your focus is off-center. I don't know how many times I can tell you this before I step in."

"You need to back off, David, and let us detectives do our jobs," Matt said. "Marjorie is not squeaky clean. She's having an affair with a man who's at least 15 years younger, and she lied about it. Repeatedly lied about it to my face. I'm sorry if you don't trust my judgment yet, but if you get in our way, it will only slow down this investigation. Is that what you want?"

"Of course not."

"Then get the hell out of my way," Patty said, her voice calm and unyielding. "The cops around this table know what we're doing, and we're making progress. Don't make the team look foolish by stepping on our toes."

"I'll stay out of your way only until I see you cops bungling this," said Dalrymple. "Am I clear?"

Matt understood that Patty knew he, being the new guy, shouldn't take on the DA publicly. He also understood that Patty owned enough credits with the law enforcement community and with the public that she didn't fear the DA's wrath whatsoever. She was a tough, smart cookie, and Matt appreciated her more each day.

In the dead silence that followed the DA's threat, Matt got up from his chair and walked over to the board. He went through the facts of the case as of the current hour, and his questions. He drew lines through the names of Craig Kenton and Susan Bushnell, and briefly explained to the team why their alibis were solid.

"Who does that leave us with, Chief?" asked Sheriff Johnson. "What did you think of Fergus?"

"Fergus is still on the list, Earl. Jay and I are going out there with a search warrant after this meeting to see if we can prove or disprove his alibi for Friday night. My gut tells me he's not our killer, but he definitely doesn't have the mayor on his Christmas card list. If I can prove he wasn't really home Friday night, he stays on the potential list of suspects.

"And," Matt continued, "We still have Clay Sherwin, the guy staying at Port Stirling Links. I talked to Sherwin this morning, and there is something off about him—his reason for being here is squishy. My department is running checks on him now, and I should have further info on him later."

Matt paused and turned to face the district attorney. "Even though Frolick told us the truth about Marjorie, and, in spite of how you think I'm handling him, David, he's still a suspect. If nothing else, he had the means and the opportunity because of his close proximity to the crime scene, and because his alibi is that he was home alone reading, and we can't prove or disprove it. And, while it's a jump from slapping an out-of-control student in a classroom to knifing a 4-year-old, we can't ignore Frolick's history."

The DA sat motionless and expressionless. *Flaming asshole.*

"So, that leaves us with Sherwin, Dunbar, and Frolick," said Sonders, "plus Fred, Marjorie, Jack, and Gary—correct?"

"That's right. Plus, my department is still running license plates from Ocean Bend residences and hotels, and Ken's guys are still following up with departed Port Stirling Links guests and checking Buck Bay hotels and motels for any fishy strangers. It's possible we could still get a lead. I've created a spreadsheet with these seven names across the top, plus blank windows for any other suspicious people that may yet crop up. But, discounting the family, these three guys are the only possible leads we have at this point. I was hoping that someone might come forward this morning after last night's TV interview, but not a single phone call so far."

"You did a nice job on that, by the way," said Sonders. "The OSP sent out a bulletin state-wide with your plea on it afterward. We thought there could have been some tourists in town for the weekend from Portland or other points around the state that might have seen something Friday night. No response at our place yet either."

"The silence from the public is deafening. In Texas, we would have had 10 crank calls by now."

"The public is afraid," said DA Dalrymple as he looked around the table. "And they're going to want to see progress on this investigation soon."

"You think I don't know that?" Matt said, slamming his fist on the table.

"Patty, I've worked with you for years now," said Sonders, quickly changing the subject, "and I don't think you've ever been wrong about a suspect. You seem to have a sixth sense about people, especially in regards to guilt or innocence. I'd take Frolick off our list based solely on the odds of you being wrong."

Patty smiled at the big state cop. "It's bugging me that we can't definitely prove his alibi. David and Matt are right; Frolick should stay on our list for now, but I will eat my laptop if he's our killer."

* * *

Driving the squad car north out of town, Jay said to Matt, "What are we looking for, beyond bloody clothes and a knife?"

"I need to verify his alibi somehow that he was home alone Friday night, and I want our IT guy to analyze his computer. I checked his phone records and he didn't make or receive any phone calls at home Friday, so that doesn't confirm he was home. If he sent any email that night, I would be more inclined to believe his story."

"You know," said Jay, "I was at that City Council meeting last week when Fergus went off on the mayor. He was pretty torqued. But then, one of the councilors told him to sit down, and he did. Didn't make another peep the rest of the meeting."

"Did he strike you as a guy who would hold a grudge?"

"Nope. As a matter of fact, when the meeting was over, Fergus stayed around for a while, drinking the punch and chatting with some other people who attended. I noticed him laughing with one group, and it seemed like he was already over it."

"Did he approach the mayor after the meeting?"

"No. Fred was off to one side of the council chamber talking to a guy who testified on a potential expansion of Port Stirling Links—they want to add a second golf course. Fergus left while Fred and the guy were still chatting."

They pulled up in Dunbar's driveway, and he grinned and waved to them from the front porch where he was drinking a beer. He was sitting in what looked like might have been a nice chintz-covered easy chair at one time, but had been ravaged by Oregon weather.

Matt patted the search warrant in his inside pocket, just to make sure it was there if Dunbar wanted to see it. This guy was so laid back, though, Matt thought he wouldn't care if they roamed all over his house. Unless he had something to hide, of course.

"You're baaaaack," said Fergus in a sing-song voice, as Matt and Jay headed up the stairs to the porch.

"Fergus Dunbar, you are a potential suspect in the murder of Emily Bushnell," Matt said in his best chief of police voice. "This is Officer Jay Finley, and we have a warrant here that gives us permission to search your premises."

"Hi, Jay. Always nice to see you. This is a waste of your time, Matt," said Dunbar in a friendly manner. "Is there anything in particular I can help you find?"

Matt ignored him and went on. "We want to take a look at your computer and your laundry, for starters. If you have a bloody knife, you could save us all trouble and turn it over now."

"I don't have a bloody knife, Matt. Is it alright if I call you Matt?"

"Cut the crap, Fergus. This is a serious matter, and it would go down better for you if you respect that we have a job to do."

"I do respect you, Chief, and I'm trying to help. I can't even kill my own chickens when it's time, much less harm a hair on that girl's head. I'm more the *'Imagine all the people living life in peace, you may say I'm a dreamer . . .'* he sang, in a voice that sounded remarkably like John Lennon's.

Matt cut him off. "OK, Dunbar, I get it. But your singing talents aren't hard evidence, and that's what I need."

"Knock yourself out then. Curious—why do you want my computer?"

"We need to know if you sent any email Friday night when you claim you were at home, among other things. Until we can verify your alibi, you're a suspect."

Fergus's eyes lit up, he slapped his thigh with the hand not holding his beer, and grinned broadly. "Well, officer, I believe I did send email

Friday night, now that you mention it. Probably about the time in question. I guess that gives me a gnarly alibi, huh?"

"It would support your statement, yes," Matt said, buttoned up. "Let's go have a look, shall we?"

"Door's open. Help yourself. Computer password is 'jerrygarcia', all one word, no caps. I need to get more work done out here today."

"You're sure you don't want to come in and observe what we do?" asked Matt. "You at least want to see the warrant?"

"Nope. I trust you fellas," smiling.

With that, he rose from his chair and headed out to his garden. They watched him go, and soon he was back to weeding his potatoes, unconcerned about the cops.

"I hate hippies," fumed Jay, as they entered Dunbar's house.

"Now, now, Officer Finley, we are open-minded policemen in search of the truth, and we serve all the public equally," admonished Matt with a smirk.

Sure enough, 'jerrygarcia' allowed Matt to view the inner workings of Fergus's PC, which they found on his kitchen table. He quickly scrolled down to Friday's messages in his 'sent' box—there were fourteen in all.

He started at the bottom and read up. The first message was sent at 8:36 a.m., and the last one at 11:42 p.m. There were six messages sent by Dunbar between 6:00 p.m.-midnight at various intervals. It looked as if he had been home all evening, as he stated. All six emails sent after 6:00 p.m. went to the same person, Buffy Dunbar, a woman who appeared to be his mother living in Honolulu. Fergus was helping her figure out how to load photos from her phone onto her computer, as there were detailed directions, followed by "Did that work?"

These messages did not seem to be written by the same person who had simultaneously brutally stabbed a child and left her to die. Dunbar had been home Friday night, just like he told them.

To be certain, they went through Dunbar's closet, laundry room, and garbage looking for any blood-stained clothes or shoes. Nothing.

Jay also checked all the knives in the kitchen. There was one plastic knife holder with six slots next to the cooktop, and all six knives were accounted for. He also had a drawer of silverware with some steak knives to the right of the divided tray, and, again, nothing looked out of order. In fact, the entire house looked tidier than one would expect a single male hippie to inhabit. All of Matt's training and instincts, added to the hard evidence on his computer, told him that this was not the home of a deranged killer.

Matt and Jay trudged back outside to where Dunbar was working. "Looks like we're done here for now," Matt said brusquely.

"My mom's great, isn't she?" said Fergus.

"Looks like she's as technologically challenged as my mother," Matt said. "Don't be a smartass, Dunbar; there's still that little matter of your unlicensed cannabis operation. We'll be sending a crew to dismantle it soon."

"Aw, c'mon man, can't you overlook it this one time?"

"Do I seem like the kind of guy who will overlook anything? Do I?"

CHAPTER 31

Monday, 4:30 p.m.

"I'm pretty good at talking to kids, you know," Matt said to Fern as he steered his car out of the City Hall parking lot.

"I never said you weren't."

"You've been acting like you're afraid I'm going to browbeat the kid."

"I am an advocate for victims, Matt, and Joey Hawthorne could be a kind of victim because of his association with the Bushnells. I'm here to protect him and his family."

"Joey could also be a perpetrator, or a co-perpetrator in this murder. You realize that, don't you?"

"I believe that to be unlikely," Fern said, scratching the side of her left nostril with a pale pink fingernail.

"Someone killed Emily."

"I'm just as aware of that awful reality as you are. But I'm with Ed—Marjorie is fitting the profile more than the kids."

"You know I agree with you, Fern, but we have to establish facts and collect whatever evidence we can. Some of it will eliminate suspects, and some of it will keep them on our list. As much as you don't want it to be true, teenagers do kill, and they have to be ruled out just like other suspects."

"I'm here by your side, aren't I?"

Matt nodded. "And I'm happy about that."

Joey's mom, Cheryl, was obviously upset and somewhat flighty, but welcomed them in.

"I was happy when school let out today," she said once they were all settled in the kitchen at their big square table. Something smelled good on the stovetop, and the room was warm and homey. "I want to keep Joey close to me," she said, rubbing her son's head.

""Mo-om," Joey protested, like every teenager throughout time, but didn't pull away from his mother's reach. "Is it alright if I stay here while you talk to Joey?" she asked Matt. "His dad's not home from work yet."

"Yes, of course," Matt allowed. "We have a few loose ends to clear up, and we think Joey can help us." He smiled broadly at the boy. "OK, Joey?"

"Sure thing, Mr. Horning."

Fern thought Joey sounded brave, but he sure didn't look it. His eyes were open wide, and he appeared to be frozen in his chair. His mother put her arm around his shoulders and said "Everything is fine, honey, just answer the Chief's questions."

Joey remained mute and waited for Matt to begin.

"We want to talk about Friday night, Joey. Do you remember what you did that night?"

"Yeah. I went to the movies with Jack." All three adults could tell the boy was nervous.

"What movie did you see?"

"We went to *Star Wars*. The new one."

"Did you like it?" smiled Matt.

"Yeah, it was cool."

"Oh, yeah? What you'd like about it?"

"The new droid was awesome," Joey said confidently, getting more comfortable.

"What was awesome about it?"

"He was funny and so big. I think he was seven feet tall. I also liked the combat walkers—huge!" At that, Joey threw his arms in the air above his head to demonstrate.

"What does Rogue One mean?" asked Matt. "What's it stand for? Do you know?"

"Well, duh, it's the spaceship that the Rebels take from the bad guys. It's nifty, too."

"Did you like how the movie ended?"

"Yeah. It was fun seeing Darth Vader again. He's so ridiculous."

"What did Jack think about it? Was he with you at the end of the movie? When Darth Vader comes on?"

"Uh, I can't remember," said Joey. Fern noted that he blinked quickly several times.

"Think hard, son, it's important," Matt urged. "Did he go to the snack bar or the bathroom? Did he miss the end of the movie?"

"We got popcorn and red sticks on the way in," Joey said and then clammed up.

"Did you talk about the ending on the way out?"

Pause.

"I don't think so. I can't remember."

"Did you go into the other movie, *Deadpool*?"

"Huh? What's that?" Joey, genuinely puzzled.

"There were two movies playing Friday night," Matt said. "Jack told us the two of you went back and forth to both movies. Is that right?"

"If he said that, it must be right," Joey, fidgeting.

"Joey, I need you to concentrate here, are you with me?" Matt asked gently.

"I can't remember," Joey whined.

"Did you leave *Star Wars* at any time and go see the other movie? Yes or no?"

"Uh, no. I didn't leave."

"Was Jack with you the whole time? Yes or no?"

Joey looked at his mom, pleading. "Tell Chief Horning the truth, Joey." She moved to put her arm around Joey's shoulder, and Fern quietly placed her hand over Cheryl's on the table.

Silence of the 'hear-a-pin-drop' variety.

"Jack left and I watched the movie alone."

"Did he come back?"

"No."

"Did he tell you to lie about him?"

"Yeah."

"Have you talked to Jack since Friday night?"

"Yeah. He called me Saturday afternoon and told me his little sister was dead." Joey looked queasy.

"What else did he say?"

"He told me he didn't do it, but if the cops knew he wasn't with me Friday night, it would be bad for him. Said I should say we were together."

"Did he tell you where he went after he left the movie?"

"Nope. He said he felt like being alone. I didn't ask."

"Was that normal behavior for Jack? To want to be alone?"

"Yeah. He doesn't like people all that much. 'Cept me."

"With everything that's happened, Joey, where do you now think Jack went Friday night?"

"Don't know. He wouldn't kill Emily, though. He wouldn't."

"Do you think Jack went to the other movie?"

"Maybe."

"Have you and Jack ever climbed out of his bedroom window?" said Matt, changing subjects.

"Yeah. Lots of times." Joey glanced at his mother. "Not to do anything bad—just to get out of the house."

"Was it easy to climb out?"

"There's one bush right outside his window, have to avoid it. But it's easy, close to the ground."

"Did you ever climb out of Emily's window?"

"Nope. No reason to. But it would be easy—her room is right next door to Jack's."

"Did Jack ever tell you anything bad about Emily?" Fern spoke for the first time.

"No. Well, sometimes he would say she was annoying him. But it wasn't bad."

"What did she do to annoy him?" Fern continued.

"He didn't like it when she touched his stuff, like his letterman's jacket or his backpack or his books—stuff like that."

"Did Jack ever say he wished Emily was dead?" asked Matt.

"Nope."

"Do you know if Jack ever bit Emily? Or anyone else?"

Joey's mother physically blanched, and stared at Matt. Fern patted her hand reassuringly.

"What do you mean?" Joey asked.

"Did Jack ever bite Emily on the neck or anything? Like maybe playing around?"

"No. I don't think so. That's kinda weird."

"You're sure, Joey?"

"Yeah, I'm sure. He didn't do it."

"How do you know for sure?"

"I just know. Jack's not like that. He's my best friend." He started to cry.

* * *

Matt and Fern were silent in the car until Matt pulled out of the Hawthorne's driveway. Fern broke the silence.

"So, Jack lied," she said. "He left the movies and went God knows where."

"Looks that way, yes. Are you OK?" He couldn't see her eyes to know what she was feeling, as she was turned away from him, staring out her window. Her usually pale skin was now white as a sheet.

"I may never sleep again at night, but I'm OK."

"We have to stay calm, Fern. All we know for sure is that Jack wasn't where he told us he was on Friday night. We still don't have any hard evidence, and he could have been anywhere. He might have gone home and gone to bed early. We don't know."

"Why would he lie?" Fern said quietly.

"He didn't totally lie—he did actually go to the movie. I admit he certainly didn't tell us the whole truth. But let's think for a minute: What was his motive? Marjorie has way more reason to want Emily dead. Having said that, Jack has seemed—how shall I say this?—a little off at times to me. Sometimes he's perfectly normal, and then other times he's a little nutty and creepy."

"You just described almost every 14-year-old boy on the planet," she said. "But I think I need to talk to Jack next. I've been so fixated on the parents that I haven't paid much attention to Jack or Gary. I guess, deep down, I couldn't believe one of the kids could do this. He's 14, Matt. Fourteen."

Matt changed direction in the car suddenly, and turned left on the road to the jetty.

Fern looked over at him. "Where are we going?"

"We are going to look at the ocean. Consider it your afternoon coffee break."

He pulled the car up to the front parking spot facing the ocean. The Twisty River was racing to join the sea on their right, and the jetty was standing strong, doing its job. There was only one other car in the parking lot—a Volvo with Idaho plates.

Matt and Fern didn't get out of the car, and, instead, sat comfortably together looking out to the ocean, with its combative white-topped waves and slate water. They could see four fishing boats just out past the bar. Way out near the horizon, what must be a very large, ocean-going ship was running parallel to the beach.

"I hope one of those guys is catching my dinner," Matt said.

Fern smiled. "That's what I always think, too, when I see fisherman out there. "It didn't take you long to get completely spoiled on having fresh seafood."

"Hey, there are worse vices. I don't smoke, I don't gamble."

"You left out 'drink,'" she noted.

"I don't drink," he added. "Too much, anyway."

"I didn't used to drink too much." Wistful.

"But you do now? This case is causing it?"

"I was a nervous wreck when I got home the last two nights," she admitted.

"Look, Fern, this case is as bad as it gets. As bad as any I've ever worked on."

"Good to know," she said weakly.

"I simultaneously kick myself and pat myself on the back for getting you involved. Honestly, your instincts are so solid, and you have been a rock since Saturday. I can't imagine how I would have coped without you and Jay. At the same time, I feel awful for dragging you into this hot mess. It's unfair of me, and I wanted to say that. No matter how it turns out. I wouldn't blame you if you called in sick tomorrow. And maybe you should."

"For heaven's sake, why do you feel guilty?" She turned to look at him. "It's my job!"

"Your job on the first day was to fight for the Bushnells and make sure they were OK. I didn't have to bring you in for the psychological profiling piece. I knew you didn't have any homicide experience, and I knew what a toll this case would take. It was unfair of me to grasp at everyone and everything that might help me. I should have relied on the crime team and my own department, and left you out of the down-in-the-weeds details."

She turned to confront him. "I resent that. My contribution is as important as anyone's, and, in fact, my work might be the catalyst that helps you solve this dumpster fire. Is this a Texas thing? Women are coddled and don't belong in a gritty workplace?"

"You know I don't think like that."

"I thought I did."

"It's not because you're a woman. It's because this is an evil, evil murder, and it's particularly tough on you and Jay who have not been down this road before. Ed and Patty and I have seen it all, and we've formed a shell of sorts. But you, you're raw, and I remember what that feels like. I'd like to be able to protect you from that."

"Well, you can't. I feel needed, and it would be harder on me if that went away than how the next shocking development will feel. Please don't take that away from me."

"I won't, if you're sure. I have every confidence in your skills; I just don't want you to be traumatized for life."

"I'll be much worse off if you don't ever solve this case, and I didn't do everything I could to help you. Don't protect me, dammit." She stuck out her hand, and said "Deal?"

Matt shook it and repeated, "Deal", but he did not smile at her.

CHAPTER 32

Monday, 5:20 p.m.

If Matt hadn't felt the pressure before, he sure felt it now. Mary Lou informed him that "everyone in Chinook County watched KVAL-TV last night, and they are all rooting for you." Plus, it was clear that the DA was waiting for the slightest misstep by Matt to swoop in and humiliate him by taking over his investigation.

Matt sent his team home just after 5:00 p.m. Everyone was exhausted, and he wanted to think about today's revelations. There were too many swirling thoughts in his head, several of them conflicting and confusing.

Even though sunset would soon come and nightfall would be upon him, he wanted to go for a run on the beach in the hopes of clearing his head. There was a streak of clear sky out on the horizon beyond the gloomy cloud cover, and he thought he might catch a break with the dwindling light, and could likely make a five-miler before it got too dark.

He pulled on the same sweats he'd worn last night and his Nikes, negotiated the bluff steps, and sprinted north from his cottage, that damnable tunnel pulling him inexorably toward it. When he ran up to it, thankfully there was no one around. He pulled up the police tape and ducked under it.

It was darker inside the tunnel, although he could see through it to the dimming light of the setting sun at the opposite end opening. He felt the side of the tunnel, and it was damp and cold. There appeared to be plant life growing on the walls—ferns, moss, and something like a star fish perhaps? The tide was coming in, but only a trickle of the surf reached his feet, barely enough to wet the soles of his running shoes.

Who could leave a fragile, small child alone in this tunnel? What kind of monster could do it? Who was he looking for? Matt closed his eyes for a moment, and listened to the waves breaking softly as he rubbed his hand over the ancient rock wall. Idly, he wondered how long this particular rock formation had been here. *Talk to me, doggone, tell me what you saw!* The rock maintained its centuries-old silence, mocking him. Only the shallow waters eddying about his feet whispered to him.

All the family's statements were technically in sync, and all their individual stories added up, with the exception of the Jack bombshell from Joey. But something about the Bushnells was funky.

He thought back, one at a time, to every homicide he'd been involved in over the past twelve years. Bottom line, there were no similarities between any of his past cases and Emily's death. None. Nothing he could call on at all.

It was over 48 hours since the discovery of Emily's body, and no one was cracking. The family was, for the most part, behaving as one would expect them to behave. They had a couple of potential leads on suspects, several loose ends to follow, and some serious pounding the pavement ahead of them, but usually by now, Matt had a theory, at least. So far, nothing made any sense. The facts were all seemingly unrelated pieces on a chess board. What was the connection?

Matt left the tunnel and continued his run. As he approached one of the deeper, wider streams feeding into the ocean, he paused to carefully pick his route across it, selecting the biggest, flattest rocks for his path.

His thoughts returned to the Bushnells, and although there was nothing overt in their reactions and behaviors, he couldn't shake how they didn't seem close-knit as a family. Instead, each of the three kids seemed distant from each other and from their parents. Marjorie and Fred said the right things, but they didn't touch each other much, and they didn't hold onto their three surviving children as hard as Matt would expect in the circumstances. If the same thing had happened in his own family, Matt knew his parents wouldn't loosen their grip on any of them, no matter what.

The mist was beginning to settle in above the sea as Matt judged he'd run about two-and-a-half miles. With not much daylight left, he turned around to head home. It felt so good to stretch his legs and fill his lungs with the crisp, fresh air. His stride was strong, and his gait was even and smooth. He couldn't think of any reason why he wouldn't take this run along this breathtaking stretch of land every single day for the rest of his life.

But he was not in denial; Matt understood that if he didn't solve Emily's murder, he might not have this job for long. *Whatta we got? I have two parents, two brothers, and one sister—and I've only ruled out Susan as the killer. Plus, I have one old man who some think is crazy and who just happens to live right above the murder scene. Throw in the weird stranger-in-town at Port Stirling Links who won't tell us why he's here. Also, they tell me the drug trade is active up and down the coast—have I fully explored that yet? No. Why did Jack lie? What's he hiding? What drove Marjorie to an affair with Craig Kenton? Is she unhappy in Port Stirling? In her marriage? Was Emily going to blow the whistle on her mother? Lots of questions still on Day 3. I need to get my shit together on Day 4.*

* * *

Guzzling water and starving after his run, Matt decided he'd grab a quick bite at the Inn at Whale Rock. Once Emily's killer was behind bars, he'd settle in to a routine and start cooking, but for now it was convenient to have a healthy alternative a few blocks down the road.

"Howdy, Tex," Vicki greeted him.

"I thought you might have tonight off," replied Matt. "Being Monday and all."

"I usually have Monday and Tuesday off, but there's a group checking into Port Stirling Links today, and they've got a reservation about an hour from now. Boss wants me here both nights, in case they come back tomorrow. It's low season, so I take what I can get."

"Makes sense," Matt said, and thought about the plight of a waitress dependent on tourism—can't be easy during the slow months. "What's good tonight?"

"We've got a homemade oyster stew that's to die for, if that's your thing."

"I think it might be my thing," he smiled. "Bring me whatever beer you think I should try tonight, a bowl of oyster stew, and your rib eye steak, medium-rare. Better throw a vegetable on the platter with the steak."

"I wouldn't let you not have your veggies," Vicki said, wagging her finger at him. "It comes with a baked potato and some spinach."

"Perfect. Make it so, Vicki."

When she brought his beer—today's tap was Ninkasi 'Pacific Rain', how totally appropriate—she stood silently by his table, fiddling with the tie on her apron. Matt waited. After a couple of beats, she said, "Have you made any headway yet on finding our killer?"

"We have some leads we're following, but no one behind bars as of tonight. I wish I had better news."

"I look hard at every customer who walks through our door and wonder if he's the murderer. It's gotta be a man, right?"

"We haven't ruled out anyone yet—male or female."

"Well, I'm keeping my eyes and ears open. We need to get this creep before it starts scaring off business."

Matt hadn't considered that a killer on the loose would hurt whatever tourism Port Stirling had in January, but, of course, Vicki was correct. "I can use all the help I can get, but I will get him. Or her. Take it to the bank, Vicki."

"I know you will, Tex. I know you will."

"Hey, while we're on the subject of business, I'll want to bring my department here for dinner once we catch our killer and things settle down. Can you set me up?"

"Sure thing. We'll make it a celebration. And, thanks." He knew that she knew that he was trying to throw some business her way, but that was OK.

* * *

Alone in his cottage at the end of this brutal Monday, feeling tired to the bone, drowsy, and mellow courtesy of Ninkasi, Matt relaxed in front of his fireplace, staring into the flames while hundreds of images and thoughts raced through his head.

Storm-tossed waves making the ocean the enemy. Marjorie the liar. Rain pummeling the windows. Jack picking crab off his sweater. A Farewell to Arms, thanks Papa. Oyster stew. Gary's first-term grades. The fragrance of his green tea steaming hot, mixed with oak wood smoke. Bernice pulling back the sheet covering Emily's body at the morgue. Fred and Marjorie calmly ID-ing her. This morning's dishes in the sink. Wash them. Where is the knife. How old is Sylvia Hofstetter. Not that it matters.

Wind sucking the life out of his walls. Fern's hair is nice. What about a funeral. Patty Perkins should be police chief. Golf resort but doesn't play golf. Flashlight—any missing. Bloody clothes. Lights flickering. Candles. Fern's hair is nice.

* * *

Matt woke up sprawled out on his sofa in front of the dying fire. One leg was half on and half off the sofa, and there were just a few doomed embers remaining in the grate. So, so weary.

Why is it so dark in here? What happened to my lamp and the light in the kitchen? He swung his feet onto the soft, warm carpet and stood up slowly while his eyes adjusted to the nearly pitch-black room. He was quite sure the lights were on when he dozed off. He looked out his north window, trying to see if the lights were on in the next house over, but it was still stormy, and he couldn't see anything through the weather. The fog, which seemed to roll in more nights than not, was also back. There were no signs of life outside his walls, and for a moment Matt considered that he'd been sucked up by an alien spacecraft and placed somewhere in a black hole. He stretched.

What was that sound? It came from the area of his entry foyer. Was someone knocking at his front door? Matt, barefoot, made his way silently toward the door. There it was again. *What the hell was that noise?* He took another step and banged his leg on something hard, forgetting about his sofa table in the dark abyss that his living room had become. *That'll be a nice bruise on my shin tomorrow.*

"Who's there?" Matt said, standing now in front of his closed door. The noise stopped.

"Is someone there?" he repeated. No answer.

He flipped the switch for his porch light, but nothing happened. *The power must be out. Great.*

Mary Lou warned him to keep flashlights handy; apparently the power went off at random times in Port Stirling, especially during winter storms. Matt felt around in the dark for his hall table; he remembered that he'd put a flashlight in the center drawer. Success!

He turned on the flashlight, which, much to his relief, came on instantly. Slowly, Matt unlocked his door and slid the dead bolt back. He opened his door a crack, and a gust of wind hit him flush in the face. He recovered, pulled the door open wide, and quickly scanned his front porch with the beam. Nothing and no one. Utter darkness, and buckets of rain. The wind threw the rain straight into Matt.

As he bent his head down to protect himself from the elements, he saw a branch that had clearly blown off a tree in his yard, and was brushing up against the side of his house. With every gust of the strong wind, it would bang against his wall and then fall back to the grass. *Mystery solved. If only they were all this easy,* thought a jumpy Matt. He picked up the tree limb and moved it out into his yard, where he would wait until daylight to deal with it.

Firmly grasping his flashlight, he made his way to the fuse box, where he flipped the switches. Nothing happened. So, it wasn't only his house; the whole town, or at least, Ocean Bend Road was out of power. Back inside, Matt threw a couple of logs on his almost-out fire and stoked it up to a nice blaze. The huge fireplace, strategically placed in the center of his cottage, would keep him warm tonight. He backed up to the fire and put his hands behind him to dry off. Life was pretty basic when one was faced with the fundamentals. A roof overhead, food in the pantry, and a warm fire. No killer with a knife at his door.

Matt hoped that Fern and Jay knew to securely lock their doors and windows. Surely, even small-town America has learned that it's not smart to leave houses and cars unlocked, especially when there is a killer on the loose. Might not hurt to reinforce that with the locals tomorrow. Matt and his trusty flashlight went around the corner to his bedroom.

CHAPTER 33

Tuesday, 6:00 a.m.

Matt woke up early, but felt surprisingly refreshed. Despite feeling uneasy when he'd gotten into bed, and with his cottage rockin' and rollin' from the shrieking, savage storm, Matt went immediately to sleep, and slept soundly for seven hours.

He quickly made coffee—power was back on, thankfully—and showered while it was brewing. Matt was determined to set a good example by being the first one in the police department to arrive for work every day. It had only been three days, but he was getting the distinct feeling that he would have to change the culture left by his predecessor, and to do that, he would behave in the manner that he wanted his staff to copy.

As he came around the corner into his living area just as the sun was coming up, Matt smiled when he glanced out his windows. Blue sky. Hallelujah. Not a cloud in sight, he could see for miles down the beach, and what a glorious sight it was. Gentle whitecaps. No wind. It was like last night's storm had never happened. Except for all the debris in his yard. That could wait, however, as he had plenty on his plate today.

He did a cursory search of the water for Roger and, sure enough, there he was bobbing along. Matt waved and said, "No time to talk this morning, Rog, I've got a killer to catch." He didn't feel the least bit silly talking to a seal. Roger was just like a dog if you thought about it; always there looking at you, friendly, loyal.

He quickly ate a bagel, gulped some coffee, and poured the rest of the pot into a small Starbucks travel thermos. He made sure his fire was completely out, and headed to his office.

On the quick, five-minute drive from his cottage to City Hall, Matt was amazed to see all the damage from the storm. There were branches and leaves blown everywhere, and a couple of trees uprooted. Thankfully, there were no problems with the road, other than some standing water in a few places.

He made his way down the hall to his office. The building was quiet, but there were a few lights on here and there. He set his briefcase on top of his desk and unlocked it, and was happy to note that he could see the lighthouse this morning—it hadn't been visible most of yesterday. Looking at it now, not really all that far away, it seemed impossible that it had completely disappeared from view during the worst of the storm.

"Clay Sherwin doesn't exist," said a gravelly voice behind him, and Matt nearly jumped out of his skin.

Sylvia Hofstetter.

"God, Sylvia, you scared me half to death," smiled Matt. "I didn't think anyone else was here."

"I'm an early bird." Apparently so. It was just after 7:00 a.m.

"What do you mean 'Clay Sherwin doesn't exist'?" he asked her.

"Somebody named Clay Sherwin lives at the La Jolla address on his driver's license, but there's no record of him ever having been issued that license," she said in a matter of fact way. "And he's never voted, or paid taxes, or had a mortgage, or been born, married, or divorced, at least not in the State of California, etc. etc. etc. He doesn't exist from a records standpoint. How do you explain that?" she demanded.

"Well, I can't. It's peculiar. We took a photo of Sherwin's driver's license. It looks real, doesn't it?"

"It does," Sylvia agreed. "But it can't be. It's all very fishy. What shall I do next? I'm stumped, to tell you the truth." She stood with one hand on her hip over today's outfit—a long, flowy, red cardigan over a white blouse and black pant. A vivid red and black geometric scarf was tied French-style at her neck.

Matt rubbed his chin. "Talk to someone in the La Jolla PD, and ask them to investigate on the ground for us. They should physically go to the address and see what they find. Ask them if they know Sherwin's name, and if he's on their radar at all."

"Sounds good, Chief." And, with that, Sylvia spun around and moved briskly down the hall to her desk. Clearly, the culture change would not have to include Sylvia Hofstetter.

Matt went into his 'suspects' spreadsheet and put a star next to Clay Sherwin's name. Matt knew he hadn't gotten the whole story from Sherwin; something shady was up with this guy.

Matt studied his spreadsheet and made a list of things to get done today. He waited until 7:45 a.m., and then called Patty Perkins.

"You're in the office bright and early," Matt said when Patty answered her phone with a sprightly 'Perkins here'.

"We're on a case, Chief. We can sleep after we catch our killer," she said.

"Ain't that the truth. You sound like me. Is this a good time to talk for a minute? I want to ask you about Frolick."

"Fire away. Are Dalrymple's doubts about him getting to you?"

"Not really. I share some of his doubts, and I want to make sure we don't overlook anything. I've read his statement twice, and have gone over my notes from my talk with him. You did a nice job trying to pin him down," Matt said, "but his non-alibi is bothering me. Can you think of any way we can confirm that he was home alone?"

"I've racked my brain, and the answer is 'no', I'm afraid. I even went back to his house again on the pretext of having left my favorite pen there so I could snoop around to find the book he said he was reading Friday night."

"Were you successful?"

"Yes, I was. 'A Farewell to Arms' sitting on an end table next to an overstuffed chair with a floor lamp behind it. Honestly, it wasn't hard to envision him sitting there reading that book Friday night, like he said he did. Plus, I got a warrant from Judge Hedges—or should I say, our lovely DA got a warrant—and two of my officers did a search last evening. No bloody clothes or shoes, no bloody knife, no little girl's clothes, no nothing, essentially. I was just about to call you."

"You believe him, don't you?"

"I do. I keep trying not to, because he would be an easy get—proximity to the crime scene, quirky personality, past issue with a child—but in my head and in my heart, I believe every word he said, and I don't think Ted Frolick killed that little girl."

"I don't think he did either, but I can't go on our gut instincts alone, Patty. We've got to make sure we've turned over every stone on this guy. Appreciate the search of his house. Frolick told me the same book—Hemingway. Did you quiz him further on the incident that got him fired? Hitting that student?"

"I did, and his explanation made sense. It wasn't the act of a violent man. He was trying to restore order to his classroom and calm down an ADD kid who was out of control. I'm not saying Frolick made the right choice, but it's understandable. I also don't believe that one incident in nearly 30 years of teaching makes him a child hater."

"What did the kid's parents tell you? Did it change your opinion of Frolick?"

"If anything, it made me believe him all the more. Their son is a sophomore in college now, and they're still hovering over him. They don't like Frolick—they made that clear—but the way they described what happened six years ago, it sounds like a classic overreaction on their part. The mother hounded the school administrator to fire Frolick, to the point where the district really had no choice and caved. I think he got screwed."

"Talk to the administrator again, will you? I want to be 100 percent positive there were no other incidents in Frolick's teaching past."

"OK. I also learned there are a couple of older teachers at the school, and I'll check in with them to see if there was anything else in Frolick's tenure that we should know about."

"Thanks so much, Patty. I don't think he's our killer, but we have to be certain."

After he hung up the phone, Matt walked down the hall to the squad room, where he was delighted to find his Sergeant, Walt Perret.

"Morning, Chief."

"Mornin', Walt. What do you have for me on this beautiful Tuesday morning?"

"We've gathered up all the car registrations from the Ocean Bend Road motels and private houses, and run them through the state's computer. There was nothing suspicious about any of the cars, no warrants out or anything like that. But one SUV at the Pacific View Motel had, according to the registration desk, come in on Friday afternoon, and left before dawn Saturday morning. The clerk said that was an unusually short stay, as most of their guests stay an average of two nights. Because of his long, straggling hair and beard and red

Pendleton flannel shirt, the clerk remembered him. He was "uncommunicative and unfriendly", according to the clerk.

"Did you dig deeper on that guy? Do we know where he ate dinner? What time? Where's he from? That kind of thing?"

"I went to the nearby restaurants and described him, but nobody remembered seeing him Friday night. Sylvia's looking into his registration now."

"She's pretty good at research, isn't she?" asked Matt.

"She relishes it," Walt smiled. "Although you might not guess it looking at her, she's a whiz on the computer. That woman can find anything. I'm not sure what we'll do when she retires."

"How long has she worked here?"

"Don't know for sure, but I think it's about 15 years now. She's spooky smart, and you should ask her about her early years sometime when you have some time to kill. She lived a fascinating life in New York before she 'retired' out here. Sylvia is a City Hall legend, and it wouldn't be the same without her. You will love her once you get to know her."

"I will make it a point once we catch our killer. I'm going back out to the Bushnell house this morning—got some follow-up to do with Jack, the youngest boy. I'd like you and Jay to see what you can find out about Port Stirling's garbage."

"Garbage," repeated Walt, more a statement than a question.

"Yes, garbage," smiled Matt. "We've searched the Bushnell house top to bottom, Fergus Dunbar's farmhouse, and Ted Frolick's house and we haven't found a hint of bloody clothes or a murder weapon."

"Did I hear my name and garbage in the same sentence?" asked Jay, putting his bag down on his desk and pulling off his jacket.

"Can't be the first time, Officer Finley," said Walt, and winked at him.

"Funny guy," Jay said to Matt, and jerked his thumb at Walt. "Why are we talking about garbage?"

"Because I need to know what day garbage gets picked up in this town, and what happens to it after it gets picked up. There has to be some physical evidence somewhere in Port Stirling unless it's all in the Pacific Ocean . . . there was too much blood at the scene for there not to be."

"My garbage gets picked up on Saturday morning," said Jay.

"Mine too," said Walt.

"Was it picked up last weekend?" asked Matt.

Both men nodded yes.

"OK, go forth and find out where it was taken on Saturday. And make sure the Bushnell house, the golf course, and Frolick's house had pick-ups that morning too. Call me the minute you get any information. Clear?"

"Garbage," said Jay. "On it."

* * *

Mary Lou came into the squad room and said to Matt, "Ah, there you are." She put up both hands straight out in front of her, palms facing Matt, in the classic 'stop' pose.

"What?" Matt asked her.

"There are two gentlemen waiting for you in your office," she said breathlessly. "I told them I didn't know when you'd be back, but they insisted on waiting. I'm sorry, but they wouldn't take 'no' for an answer."

"Who are they?"

"I don't have the foggiest. Suits."

"Suits, you say? Well, that can only be bad," Matt chuckled, and patted Mary Lou on the shoulder as he walked her down the hallway to his office. "Not to worry."

"Gentlemen," Matt greeted the two, who were, indeed, wearing suits. One navy, one grey, both white shirts, both royal blue ties. For some reason, Matt thought of clowns. "I'm Chief Horning. How can I help you?"

Both men rose from the two chairs in front of Matt's desk, and simultaneously stuck out their hands to shake.

"I'm Joe Phelps and this is Roderick McClellan," said the elder of the two men. "We'd like to speak to you alone, please," he said, glancing at Mary Lou.

"Just leaving," she said, and made a quick exit, closing Matt's door behind her.

"What's the big secret?" asked Matt.

"Rod and I work for the federal government, and we need to talk to you about Clay Sherwin. It's highly classified information and, therefore, completely confidential—for your ears only. Do you understand?"

"Yes, I guess so," Matt said, unsure. "May I see some identification, please?"

"Yes, certainly," said Phelps, and both men took out IDs from inside jacket pockets.

Matt carefully studied their proffered badges, both of which read 'Bureau of International Narcotics and Law Enforcement Affairs'. "You're narcs?", incredulous.

Phelps bristled. "We are employees of the United States Department of State. I'm Deputy Chief in charge of Narcotics Enforcement, and Rod is the lead investigator in my division."

"Okaaay," said Matt, drawing out the word. "How are you connected to Clay Sherwin, who, by the way, doesn't exist?"

"Clay doesn't exist because we don't want him to exist," said McClellan aggressively, speaking for the first time. "He is a special agent, working clandestinely for us. He's here on a covert mission, and he had nothing to do with your homicide. We're here to ask you to stop bothering him, and to explain why he's not your guy."

"What could the State Department be working on in this backwater town? I'm seriously curious," said Matt.

"Have you ever considered how all the cocaine and heroin gets into the U.S. from the countries who manufacture this stuff?" asked Phelps.

"I dealt with it every day in Texas," Matt replied. "Gulf cartel smugglers use the Rio Grande River like I-5. I would think you'd be hanging out in Texas border towns instead of here. What's Clay Sherwin got to do with this?"

"We believe there is a drug smuggling operation in Chinook and/ or Bell counties, and we are looking for evidence. Clay Sherwin is our agent, and his mission is to uncover any hidden coves or bays where international bad guys might be landing. We need you to stop calling attention to the fact that he's here. He's supposed to be undercover, for Chrissakes!" Phelps' face was starting to redden.

"Are you telling me that boats from abroad are coming into Chinook County harbors and unloading illegal drugs?"

"We don't think they're sailing into ports and chatting up the Coast Guard, no," said McClellan. "We believe that they are landing on isolated beaches on the Oregon coast, discharging their goods to American entrepreneurs, and then heading back out to international waters lickety-split. This part of Oregon has hundreds of isolated beaches with secret coves and inlets where they could land undetected. We think there could be a major narcotics pipeline somewhere between Buck Bay and the California border."

"Wow," said Matt.

"Yes, wow," agreed Phelps. "Clay Sherwin knows this part of the world very well, so when we got an anonymous tip recently, we sent him here to scope it out."

"So, when Sherwin leaves the Links every morning and doesn't come back until late, he's snooping around secret beaches?"

"Yes, and he thinks he's narrowing it down. It's absolutely imperative that he be allowed to remain incognito. He's just another tourist, here for some R & R. You could nuke his cover, and we'd have to start all over with someone new."

"And you don't want to do that," said Matt, poker-faced.

"And we don't want to do that," repeated McClellan.

"Clay Sherwin is not your killer, Chief," said Phelps. "He's one of the good guys who has devoted his life to helping our government. Leave him alone and move on. Understood?"

"Gotcha," Matt said, giving the two narcs a thumbs up. "I have one question."

"Shoot," said Phelps.

"Did his wife really leave him for another woman?"

Both men laughed. "That's his cover story," said McClellan. "I thought that one up. Pretty good, huh? I figured it would make people so uncomfortable, they'd quit asking questions. But you and your other guy powered right through it—kudos to you, I guess."

"What am I supposed to tell my sheriff? I'll have to give him a reason why Sherwin is off our list. We both suspected something about him wasn't quite right."

"It's your call," answered Phelps, "but I'd tell him you've verified his alibi. You checked it out, and it's true, so he's off your suspect list. That way, you're not really lying, but you're also not telling his real story. Sound good?"

"I think I can pull that off," Matt replied. "We had no way of knowing."

"Of course not. We're all square," Phelps said, standing. "We want to fill you in on our operation soon because we're going to need some local assistance. Catch your killer first, and then we'll bring you up to speed. Best of luck to you, Chief Horning. Vile case you've got."

And, with that, the two agents from the United States Department of State left the building.

* * *

Well, that was interesting, Matt thought, swinging his chair around to look out his window. He could see for miles up the coast today, with nary a cloud in sight. Two small craft were motoring down Twisty River, headed out over the bar. *They don't look like international drug smuggling boats.* He watched them, caring that they made it safely across the rough patch where the river met the ocean. *Catch me a fish for dinner, guys.*

Matt dialed Fern's number. "Where are you?" he asked.

"In your parking lot…just pulling in."

"Stay there. I'm coming out."

Matt opened the side entrance and waited for Fern to exit the powder blue VW. He noticed that the red rose was looking a little sad in its vase. Time for a replacement.

"Howdy," Matt greeted her, as she walked toward the building.

"Howdy back," she smiled. "What are you doing?"

"Talking to Jay and Walt about garbage. You?"

Fern looked quizzically at him, but replied "I've been in Twisty River. I went to talk to my buddy, Barbara. She confirmed that she went out with Craig Kenton Friday night. Then he spent the night at her place."

"Yeah, Kenton appears to get around. Unfortunately for us, his alibi for Friday night is airtight, according to Ed. Everybody saw them—gas station attendant who knows Kenton, waitress at the restaurant, your friend's neighbors. There's no way he could have been in Port Stirling to kill Emily."

"That's what Barbara said, too, and I believe her. She was shocked to hear about what happened, but she said she knows for a fact that Craig was with her all night. I don't even want to think about how she knows that," Fern said, grimacing.

"But you said he was cute, if I recall," Matt teased.

"That was before I knew he was sleeping with half the women in Chinook County," she replied, indignant. "Ugh."

"Did you tell your friend about Kenton and Marjorie?"

"Couldn't quite bring myself to do it," admitted Fern. "And, I also had doubts about whether we should be spreading that info around at this point in our investigation. So I kept my mouth shut."

"That's good. She'll probably find out anyway—Kenton himself might even tell her. I would if I were him. But until we either arrest Marjorie or cross her off our list, the fewer people who know about their affair the better."

"Why are we standing out here?" asked Fern.

"Before we go in, let's talk about how we're going to approach the family next. I don't know if these walls have ears or not," Matt said. He gestured at the building.

"Getting paranoid, are we?" Fern said.

"Maybe. Can you call the house and tell the mayor we'll be there about 1:00 p.m.? Tell him we want to talk to Jack just to tie up some loose ends. The rest of them can go for a walk or something, but we need Jack at the house when we get there. If you call and he knows you're coming, he might be more relaxed about me talking to Jack again."

"I'll do it, but he probably won't like it."

"Tough," Matt responded. "I don't like it that his daughter was murdered." He held open the door for Fern.

CHAPTER 34

Tuesday, 11:00 a.m.

Jay looked up the phone number for the local garbage transfer station, and, ashamed, realized he hadn't once called it before today. It had never occurred to him on previous cases that a contact at the dump might be important. Leave it to his new chief to grasp that it might be an evidence goldmine.

Jay was patched through to the Port Stirling Transfer Station manager Russell Throckmorton. He explained who he was.

"What can I do you for, Officer Finley?" said Throckmorton in friendly fashion.

"We need to know if the Saturday morning garbage pick-up in town includes everyone in Port Stirling. Is it all residences, including local farms, and businesses like the golf course?"

"Yes, it is. Anyone with a garbage can within six miles of Port Stirling gets pick-up on Saturday between 7:00 a.m.-4:00 p.m."

"And what happens to it after it's picked up?"

"It's brought here to the Transfer Station, about 20 miles up the highway from Port Stirling. And then, twice a week it gets loaded onto the transfer trailers that haul it to the Dry Creek Landfill in White City, down in southern Oregon by Medford."

"Has the Saturday pick-up left your place yet?" Jay asked and held his breath, primarily because he didn't want to drive the three hours to Medford.

"No, it will go out tomorrow morning. The transfer station is always closed on Sundays, and it usually leaves here on Monday. But because yesterday was the MLK holiday, we were closed two days."

"Yes! I'm going to bring some officers and come up there," Jay told Throckmorton. "Please leave everything as it is right now, OK? I'll explain what we're looking for when I get there. I've got to do a couple of things here first. Will you be there about 12:30 p.m?"

"I'll be here, and I'll help you in any way I can. Bring boots you don't care too much about."

* * *

Tuesday, 1:00 p.m.

Fred Bushnell answered the door with an extremely grim look plastered to his face. "Do you have any leads?" he asked Matt once he and Fern were inside.

"No, sir. In fact, we have eliminated several potential suspects during questioning and following up on alibis over the past 24 hours or so. I'm sorry," said Matt.

"It feels like you're spending more time on us than out there looking for the real killer," Fred said with some defiance.

"Our investigation is ongoing, sir. We've got the county crime team and all of the area police departments focused on Emily's murder. But you need to understand that much of our work is plodding in nature, following up on even the smallest leads and details."

"Who have you talked to?" Fred demanded.

"At this point it's inappropriate to name suspects," Matt stood his ground. "We have looked at people who may have a grudge against you, local ne'er-do-wells, and transients in the area last Friday. We have already ruled out some people who were potential suspects because they have airtight alibis, so you can see that it's pointless to name them until we have fully investigated."

"I suppose that's true," said Fred, glumly. "Is there anything I can do to help you? Sitting around here is getting old."

"The only thought I had is that you might want to start planning Emily's funeral," Matt said. A hush fell over the room. "The medical examiner has completed her investigation, and has released the body."

Fern moved closer to Fred and said, "Do you know what your family wants to do?"

"We talked about it this morning, and we'll have a service. Emily will be buried in the family plot at the Port Cemetery in Mohegan. Always thought I'd be the first one in this generation to make it there." Fred teared up, and withdrew a ready handkerchief from his pocket.

Matt put his hand on Fred's shoulder. "Perhaps you, Gary, and Susan might go for a drive and a walk on the jetty on this sunny afternoon, and discuss plans. Fern and I want to talk to Jack to clear up some loose ends, and Marjorie might want to stick around while we do that. Does that sound OK to you, sir?"

Fred nodded silently. Marjorie appeared behind him. "You again." It was a statement directed at Matt, not a question.

"Marjorie, we have some follow-up questions for you and Jack," Matt said. "OK with you?"

She frowned. "Yes, Jack is waiting for you in the living room, as Fern instructed." Snide tone.

"Thank you. Your husband, Gary, and Susan are going for a drive while we talk."

"Why? Is that necessary?" Marjorie was on alert.

"Just to get some fresh air, and they're going to talk about arrangements for Emily's body. I'm so sorry to trouble you with this," Matt said.

"It's alright, Marjorie," said Fred. "We'll clear out for a bit while you and Jack talk to Chief Horning." Matt detected a note of coolness in Fred's voice directed at his wife. Not surprising, really.

Matt broke the tension by heading off toward the living room, and saying "I'll go find Jack then." Fern trotted along behind him.

The three remaining Bushnell children were in varying degrees of slouch as Matt went into the room. Jack was laying on the floor, holding up a comic book in front of his face; Susan was curled up in a club chair with Vogue magazine; Gary was stretched out on the sofa, and looked to be asleep.

"Hi, Jack," Matt leaned over him and greeted him. "How're you doing today?"

"OK, I guess."

"Let's go in your room and talk for a while, shall we?"

Jack sat up quickly. "Why do we have to go in my room?"

"I'd like to see where you live, if that's alright with you," Matt smiled.

"I guess. Still don't see why," he grumbled, getting to his feet and moving into the hall. Matt followed behind the 14-year-old, while Fern said a few words to Susan. Gary didn't wake up.

Matt turned around in the hallway and said to Marjorie, "Do you want to come in Jack's room with us?"

"You go ahead. I've got some cleanup to do in the kitchen." She flapped one hand in the direction of the kitchen.

"I'll help you," Fern said to Marjorie, on her heels, and not giving her a chance to object.

Jack's room was fairly typical for a teenage boy, thought Matt. He had a nephew, Andrew, about Jack's age, and their bedrooms looked similar. Jack's room was a little neater than Andrew's, but they had some of the same stuff.

"Whadda you want?" Jack asked.

"I just want to get to know you a little better," Matt started slowly. "Why don't you tell me again about what you did Friday night? I'm not sure I've heard the whole story yet."

"Do you think I killed Emily?"

"I don't think anything yet, Jack," Matt answered the boy's question honestly. "But the only way we'll find out who did this to your sister is by asking questions. OK?"

"Makes sense."

"So, you ate dinner with your family Friday night, and then you went to the movies. Have I got that straight?"

"Yeah, me and Joey—he's my best friend—went to the movies."

"And you saw the new *Star Wars* and *Deadpool*, correct?"

"That's right." Not offering anything to Matt.

"Did you tell me the ending of *Star Wars* is good? I haven't seen it yet."

Jack looked puzzled for a minute. "You know, it just kinda ended. Like the other ones."

Matt leaned back into a small chair, trying to appear casual as he studied Jack. "You also snuck into *Deadpool*, right? How did it end?" Matt made it a point to keep smiling at the boy.

"Uh, I don't remember exactly what happened in that one. Oh, yeah, wait . . . we went back to *Star Wars*. That's why I don't remember much."

Matt scribbled a note in his notebook. Jack watched him, right leg bouncing up and down, and didn't say anything.

"What did you do after you left the movies?"

"I walked home and went to bed."

"What time was that, about?"

"Couldn't tell you."

"Didn't you look at a clock when you went to bed?"

"Nope."

"Was your sister's light off?"

"Yeah, her room was dark."

Matt got up from the side chair he'd been sitting in, and moved around the room. Jack eyed him.

He fingered a throw pillow at the foot of his bed and said "Did you like Emily?"

"She was OK, I guess," he said flatly. Not much emotion today.

"She wasn't a pain-in-the-you-know-what?" he smiled at him. "I have a sister, too, and growing up she used to annoy me all the time."

"Sometimes. But mostly, Em was OK."

"What were you wearing Friday night?"

"I dunno. Probably jeans and a sweater."

Matt moved to where Jack's letterman jacket was hanging on the back of his desk chair, and stroking it, he said "You weren't wearing this cool jacket?"

"Please stop touching my things!" Jack said, growing agitated.

Matt stopped. "I need you to think hard about Friday night and tell me what you had on. Imagine you're sitting in your seat at the movies—can you remember?"

"Jeans, and a red, no, black, sweater. That's it, a black sweater. I'm sure."

"What were you wearing on your feet?"

"My old Nikes."

"Can I see those clothes now?"

Jack moved to his closet and pulled out a pair of jeans and a black sweater. No signs of blood.

"You have several pairs of jeans. Are you sure these were the ones you were wearing Friday night?"

"I think so."

"I don't see a red sweater. Do you have one?"

"No. No red one."

"Then why did you start to say you had on a red one?"

"I used to have a red sweater and I wore it a lot, but I outgrew it. I guess that's why I thought of it."

Matt nodded as if in agreement. "Where are your Nikes?"

"Well, funny thing. Mom said I needed new shoes, they were getting too small. So I threw them in the garbage Friday night after I got home. We were going shopping on Saturday for new shoes. Until, you know, Em."

"What day is your garbage picked up, Jack?"

"Saturday, I think."

Shit, call Jay ASAP!

"Why did you walk home? I thought the plan was for Joey's parents to pick you up and bring you?"

"I felt like it. I like fog. It's cool, don't you think?"

Matt, who, so far, hated fog, smiled and nodded. "How long a walk is it from the movies to your house?"

"I ran most of the way—I'm pretty fast. Probably about ten minutes."

"I hear you're fast. On the track team, right? Is that how you got this letterman's jacket?" he asked, rubbing it again.

"Please leave that alone!" Jack said, and moved to take the jacket out of his hands.

"Oh, right, sorry. I forgot you don't want me to touch your stuff. Was Emily always touching your stuff?"

"No. She knew better. My room is off limits to everybody."

"Are you hiding anything in here?" Matt asked. "Something you don't want anyone to see?"

"No. It's my room and my stuff, and it's private. Are you done?" Jack looked at Matt with a blank, bored look on his face.

"Did you kill Emily, Jack? Did you?"

Jack's face was blank. "Why would I kill my little sister? Don't you need a reason to do something like that?"

"Maybe she made you really mad, and you lost it and stabbed her. Is that what happened? You can tell me, son."

Jack fidgeted, but looked directly at Matt and said "It wasn't me. She's my sister and I didn't hurt her."

"Did you ever walk on the beach with Emily? Have you been in the tunnel where we found her body?"

"Yeah, we all walk on the beach, and everybody goes in that tunnel. There's nobody in town that doesn't walk through that tunnel at low tide. Why do you think it's me?"

"I think that with Emily out of the way, you would be the baby of the family again. Maybe you liked that, and resented it when she came along. You weren't the baby anymore. Weren't special anymore."

"I'm no baby. That's crazy," Jack said. He was considerably calm and mature, especially under the circumstances, thought Matt.

"But you were the special child for almost ten years before Emily was born. Didn't it make you angry when she arrived and started getting all of the attention you used to get?" Matt persisted.

"No. I didn't give a shit."

"It would be normal if you reacted badly to a sister stealing your thunder. Are you sure you didn't hate Emily from the minute she was born?"

"I already told you. I didn't hate her. I didn't hurt her."

"You keep saying 'I didn't hurt her' not 'I didn't kill her'. Which is it?" Matt said in his toughest voice.

"I didn't kill her. There. Are you satisfied now? Leave me alone." He glared at Matt.

Ignoring his plea, Matt said, "Did you hide the knife, Jack, or did you throw it in the ocean?"

"There's no knife. There's no reason. I was at the movies. You need to find out who really killed my sister and stop bothering me. Now."

"OK, you win. If you say you didn't kill Emily, I believe you," Matt told the boy. He gave him a deliberate smile. "Someone killed her. Do you have any ideas on who might have wanted to harm your sister?"

Jack screwed up his face, and Matt could tell he was thinking hard. He waited.

"Do you know Em was sick?" Jack said finally.

"What do you mean?"

"I think she had something big wrong with her, like a brain tumor or something. Mom and Dad have been acting weird, like something bad was wrong."

Matt sat, stunned, and looked at Jack. "Have your mom or dad said anything to you about Emily being sick? Why would you think such a thing?"

"Nobody's told me anything. But mom has taken her to the doctor a lot lately. I just kinda figured it out. Maybe mom killed her because she knew she was going to die anyway, and she didn't want Em to suffer." Jack looked directly at Matt, unblinking.

"Don't you think your mom or dad would have mentioned this to us?"

"Probably not if they killed her. Don't you think?" Unblinking still.

Matt was completely flummoxed and couldn't think of a single thing to say to Jack. The two sat staring at each other.

"You've been helpful, Jack. I'll see you later," he managed. "Stay home today, OK?"

Matt hurriedly left Jack's room, found Fern in the kitchen, and tersely said, "Ready to go."

CHAPTER 35

Tuesday, 12:30 p.m.

On his way out, Jay stopped at Mary Lou's desk. Two other patrol officers trailed behind him. "Mary Lou, will you call Russell Throck-morton at the garbage transfer station and tell him we're leaving now? Here's his phone number." The three cops took off, leaving Mary Lou to imagine how things could get any more bizarre. She picked up the phone and dialed the dump.

Jay had rounded up officers Doug Lewis and Ralph Newman, who weren't currently engaged in Emily's casework, and they scrambled up the highway. He'd even put the siren on in the patrol car, which he'd done only once before.

The nice lady in the station's traffic booth directed them to the Commercial Truck Area, ahead on the right side of the facility. He screeched the car to a stop and got out to talk to the two attendants who waved them down.

"How can we help you, officer?" said Russell Throckmorton, who had worked at the transfer station since the day it opened in 1981. He had retired early last year, but when his youthful replacement turned out to be a complete dud, the Chinook County administrator had talked Russell into coming back for "a couple of months" until they hired another site supervisor. That was eleven months ago, and Russell's wife, Janis, had cancelled their retirement trip to Scandinavia twice now.

"Are you Mr. Throckmorton? Did I talk to you on the phone a while ago?" asked Jay.

"Yes, sir, that's me. You're trying to find out who killed the mayor's little girl, huh? Terrible thing, that," he said, shaking his head. "What can we do to help you?"

* * *

Tuesday, 1:50 p.m.

"Jay, where are you, man? I need you to drop everything and listen!" Matt said.

"I've reached the pinnacle of my career, boss. I'm at the dump looking through garbage."

"Perfect!" replied Matt. "I can now tell you precisely what I think you're looking for. A pair of boys' silver-and-black Nikes, probably about size eight. I think they will have a great deal of blood on them."

"What?"

"You heard me. They belong to Jack, and he threw them in the garbage Friday night. Unless I'm really wrong, I think they got picked up Saturday morning, and they will have Emily's blood on them."

"Better to be lucky than good, my grandmother used to say," said Jay, shaking his head through the phone. "Mr. Throckmorton here tells me that Port Stirling's garbage usually leaves here for southern Oregon on Mondays, but everything is still here because of yesterday's holiday."

"That's a good break, Jay. I think you're also looking for a boys' red sweater. There might a black one with blood on it, but I think you're looking for a red sweater. And, of course, a knife. Do you have guys helping you?"

"Yeah, Doug and Ralph are with me."

"This is a priority, Officer Finley. Perhaps the most important work you'll ever do. I've got some loose ends here, and then I'll come out and help you search."

"The transfer station manager and a couple of his guys are going to help us, so I think we're good. You do what you have to do, and leave the garbage to me. If there are bloody Nikes here, we'll find them."

"You'll call me?"

"I'll call you."

* * *

"We are looking for a pair of shoes," Jay explained to Russell Throckmorton, his crew, and his two police colleagues. "We believe they are silver and black Nikes, and that the size would be about eight, somewhere in that neighborhood. They may or may not have blood on them."

"Oh, my," said Mr. Throckmorton.

"Yeah," Jay agreed. "They could be a very important piece of evidence for us, so if any of you find these shoes, don't touch them—just yell at me. We're also looking for a boys' red sweater that may also have blood on it, and a boys' black sweater, same deal. Plus, we're looking for the murder weapon, which we believe to be a kitchen-style knife, probably eight-to-ten inches long and serrated. Any questions about what we're hunting for?"

"A young boy did this horrible thing?" Throckmorton asked in pure disbelief.

"We don't know that yet," Jay said quickly. "But it's possible, and we have to pursue every suspicion and every lead. You're not to discuss this with anyone, gentlemen, is that clear? We could be barking up the wrong tree here, and there's no use alarming any of our fellow citizens until we know for sure what we're dealing with. Got it?"

Nods around the circle.

Jay continued, "Can you point us to a logical starting place for us to look? The garbage in question was picked up by Port Stirling Disposal Saturday morning at a house off Ocean Bend Road. Would you have any idea what part of this area they might have dumped that truck in?"

"That driver would be Terry Hillstrom," said Throckmorton, "and he likes to unload in the far back right-hand corner. His truck is the biggest, and there's more room at that end. Terry's load would have been among the last ones brought in. Because of the holiday yesterday, there haven't been any new loads. There may have been one truck Saturday after his, but that's it. Terry's load should be close to the top of the pile. Did you bring gloves and boots?" Russell looked at the officers in their nice uniforms and dress shoes. He was dressed in a denim work shirt and jeans with more than a few years on them, along with sturdy boots and heavy-duty safety gloves. Otherwise, Russell Throckmorton, with his neatly-trimmed beard, rash of styled, wavy, dark hair, and lively brown eyes would look more at home in a fine liquor ad than he did at the dump.

"We've got gloves and boots in the car," Jay responded. "And, honestly, I don't care if my uniform gets trashed, as long as we find those shoes."

The six men divvied up the pile in sections and set to work. About an hour into their search, Jay later recalled to Matt and Fern, he laughed to himself that this is what he'd gone to college for—to dig in a pile at the dump. But he and the five others kept at it.

CHAPTER 25

Tuesday, 5:45 p.m.

"Nothing yet, Chief, and we ran out of daylight," Jay said into his cell phone.

"Dammit!" Matt swore. "I was so sure."

"You could still be right . . . we're not finished, we're going back at sunrise tomorrow. There's a shitload of garbage, and we've still got lots of places to look, according to the manager. Who's a good guy, by the way."

"Guess I was hoping those damnable Nikes would jump into your hands. Maybe Jack tossing his in the garbage Friday night is a coincidence."

"His shoes are there, Chief, or something diabolical is—I can feel it. I know that sounds a little woo-woo, but there is something there. You know how sometimes the hair on the back of your neck and arms stands up? Well, mine did today. Plus, you know you don't believe in coincidences."

"True, I don't. And I also don't discard woo-woo. Who am I but a speck on this earth, and how do I know the forces that could be at work? If you felt something, you felt something. Take a breather, clean up, and get yourself some good grub tonight."

"We don't have 'grub' in Oregon, sir, we have farm-to-table."

"Whatever. You've earned it."

* * *

Tuesday, 7:45 p.m.

Matt pulled his squad car into the restaurant parking lot, not even arguing with himself tonight that he ought to hit the market and cook for himself. Just too tired and spent.

Near the front door, he tripped over something, looked down, and saw that it was an elderly man wrapped in a filthy blanket.

"Hey, watch out," he yelled up at Matt.

"Sorry, man, I didn't see you. Here, let me help you up."

"Don't want up. Sleeping here tonight."

Matt took a hard look into the man's bloodshot eyes, and got close enough to smell the booze on his breath. "You can't sleep here. What's your name?"

"Robert."

"You can't sleep here, Robert. This is private property and, besides, it's cold and wet."

"So what else is new?" Robert said.

"Here, take my hand," said Matt, giving the old geezer a hand up. He walked him across the parking lot to the Pacific View Motel, where he registered at the front desk, and gave the clerk his credit card.

"Take this key, Robert, and go get a hot shower and a good night's sleep. I'll be back in the morning to pick you up."

Robert locked his red eyes onto Matt's and said, "Thanks." He took the key from Matt's hand, his own hand shaking but determined.

* * *

"Well, if I've ever seen a man more in need of a drink, I can't remember when," Vicki greeted him. Pointing at his chest, she said "You, I'm bringing a Deschutes Black Butte Porter tonight. Try to relax before I get back—your shoulders are touching your ears."

Yeah, I'll get a man right on that relaxing thing. How the hell can I relax when there's a killer out there outsmarting me, and my town has homeless old men sleeping outside in January? As if to drive home his point, rain was starting to splat hard against the restaurant's big windows, and Matt could see the wind bending the trees just beyond at a severe angle.

Not only am I being outsmarted, it's probably by a 14-year-old boy or by an unstable, cheating housewife. Matt sipped the excellent porter, and made an executive decision: *Then there were two. Time to focus.*

Fergus Dunbar is clean. He was home sending emails to his mom, and unless he plugged in his PC in Emily's tunnel, the timing makes him innocent. No opportunity to commit the crime. And, on a hunch, Matt had phoned the town's lone butcher this afternoon and asked him if he ever featured chickens from Dunbar's farm. Jim the butcher had said, "Oh, yeah, Fergus raises the best poultry in the county, and I buy them from him regularly." Then he had laughed. "Have to go out there and butcher them myself, though. Fergus is wimpy on the back end."

So, Dunbar hadn't been joking when he'd said he couldn't even kill a chicken.

Ted Frolick is no murderer either. *I hear a 'but' in there,* Matt said to himself. *But,* he does have a reputation for being a little crazy. But, he was the first person Lydia thought of. *But,* he lives directly above the murder scene. *But,* he slapped a child six years ago and got fired for it. And, but, his alibi is unprovable.

Were he and Patty being charmed by Frolick? People liked Ted Bundy, too.

"Word is you're runnin' out of suspects," Vicki said, sliding a plate full of razor clams in front of Matt.

"That might have been mentioned once or twice today," Matt said drolly.

"Are we gunna be votin' for a new mayor soon?"

"That's pure speculation, Vicki, and you know I can't comment."

"Oh, I know. Truth is we're all gettin' nervous." She played with the strings of her apron. "You want another beer?"

"No thanks, not tonight. I hear you, and I still have work to do."

CHAPTER 36

Wednesday, 6:15 a.m.

Matt woke up on this gloomy, wet Wednesday morning unable to stop thinking about yesterday's interrogation of Jack. He dressed quickly, pulling on old jeans and a Cowboys sweatshirt, in case he was needed at the dump later. Coffee in hand, he stopped at his window to check on his pet. Roger was nowhere to be seen, but Matt talked to him anyway.

What the hell happened in Jack's room yesterday? That kid is a piece of work.

Jack got rid of his shoes because they were covered in blood.

When I asked him what he was wearing Friday night, I'm sure he lied to me. He was wearing jeans, a red sweater, and Nikes. He doesn't have a red sweater in his closet, but he started to say he was wearing one, I know he was. Is it covered in blood, too, and at the dump with his shoes? Had Jack worn a red sweater on purpose because he planned to kill Emily and thought it wouldn't show any blood splatters?

Did Jack talk Emily out of her room Friday night, and walk her down there with the promise of some sort of adventure?

Did he really think his sister had a brain tumor? Did she, or did he deliberately make up this story to throw me off? Had Jack just tried to pin Emily's murder on his parents? Was he that diabolical?

Just then, Roger appeared in his usual spot, waggling along, and staring directly at Matt on the bluff above the water line. Matt smiled at the seal.

It could have been him, Roger. He's only a kid, but it could have been him. There's something in him, something beyond his years. Something scary. He thinks he's smarter than I am.

Roger nodded, as if in total agreement with Matt, and flipped over, floating belly-up. The look on Roger's face said, *"Organize your thoughts, don't waste a minute, Chief."* Roger called him 'Chief'.

Call Bernice and find out if she examined Emily's brain during the autopsy. Talk to Emily's physician. Check Jack's school records and see if he's had any behavioral problems. Don't tell Marjorie or Fred anything about Jack yet; all you know for sure is that he left the movies early, and he threw away some shoes. Don't overreact. Call Jay and make sure he's got enough manpower to help him this morning.

One chilling thought remained lodged deep inside Matt. Could Jack really be **that** demonic? What was he really dealing with here? What kind of monster?

* * *

Matt rapped on the door of room 121 of the Pacific View Motel. Robert answered dressed in the same clothes as last night, but smelling better and looking more robust.

"Let's go, friend," Matt said, and Robert followed, carefully closing the motel door behind him.

* * *

Wednesday, 7:30 a.m.

Matt pulled into the City Hall parking lot, which was empty except for one car. A powder blue VW beetle.

298

He found Fern in the War Room with five reports spread out around her. Each report had the name of a Bushnell family member on it. Susan's report had a big red X on the first page, denoting she was 'crossed out'. Fern was studying her report labeled 'Jack'.

"Don't you ever sleep?" asked Matt softly as he came into the room so as not to scare his colleague. Fern jumped anyway.

"Oh, sugar!" she exclaimed. "You scared the bejesus out of me!"

"Sorry. I tried not to. You were deep in thought."

"It's Jack or Marjorie," she said, looking up at Matt. "There is absolutely nothing in Fred's, Gary's, or Susan's psychological profiles that indicate they are capable of murder. But Jack and Marjorie have some troubling tendencies. And, what the heck are you wearing?"

Matt smiled and spread his arms out to present himself. "I'm going to the dump. Is this the right fashion?" He noted how sharp Fern looked in a green and black python print jacket, cream V-neck sweater, and black skirt.

"Ah. Yes, I suppose it is."

When Matt prioritized what needed to happen today, finding Jack's shoes ended up No. 1 on his list. He decided on the drive to his office that he would be too antsy to work on anything else while Jay and his buddies searched the dump.

"I made a quick run on the Port Stirling Tavern last night. I went there to check for minors, but I discovered something more important; the whole tavern is wired with surveillance cameras. The owner forgot they were there. I fast-forwarded through all of the tapes from Friday night, and Gary was there the entire time—from about 6:45 p.m. until well after midnight. No lengthy period of time when he was not there, and he had on the same clothes the entire night."

Fern drew a red X through Gary's report. "I was stuck on the coincidence of Emily being murdered while Gary was home from college, but there is nothing in his makeup that points to homicidal tendencies or mental illness," she said.

"He's out," Matt confirmed. "So, now we're down to three, and I'm choosing to focus on Jack today. Let's track down Bernice Ryder first," Matt instructed. "Stay here with me, and we'll put her on speaker phone."

Not for the first time since he'd moved to Oregon, Matt was relieved that officials seemed to answer their phones here more often than in Texas. Dr. Ryder picked up on the third ring.

"Bernice, it's Matt Horning. Fern is here with me, and we have a couple of questions for you regarding Emily. Do you have a minute to talk to us?"

"Of course, Matt. What's up?"

"It's been suggested that Emily may have had a brain tumor or some other life-threatening illness. Did you uncover anything of the sort in your autopsy that might not have made it into your report?"

Bernice laughed. Matt and Fern exchanged a quizzical look.

"You may be used to big-city ME's, Chief, but I can assure you that if Emily had anything life-threatening, I would have discovered it during my examination of her body."

"I didn't mean to offend you, Bernice," Matt said hastily. "I just wondered if your focus had been entirely on the wounds since we knew that was obviously the cause of her death."

"No offense taken. I'm having a bitch of a day so far, and I'm crankier than usual. But, no, I did a thorough exam of Emily, and there wasn't one other thing wrong with her. No evidence of natural disease."

"So she was a perfectly healthy child?" asked Fern.

"Yes. Everything completely normal. Who told you she was ill?"

"Jack, her brother," Matt answered. "He told me that Emily's parents had taken her to the doctor a lot lately, and he thought there was something bad wrong with her."

"They may have taken her to the doctor—I couldn't say. But that girl didn't even have a cold."

"It looks like Jack either has a wild imagination, or he was trying to throw us off the track," Matt said.

"You should talk to Emily's regular physician to be sure," said Bernice. "But I'm telling you that the only thing wrong with Emily was a knife in her abdomen."

"Thanks, Bernice," Matt said. "And I'm sorry if you thought I was questioning your judgment. I may have dropped the ball on Jack initially, and I need to be sure we don't miss something else. My bad."

"No hard feelings. This is a tense time for all of us. Keep me posted."

"Will do, Bernice. And thanks again."

Matt hung up the phone and looked over at Fern. "Do you suppose it's possible that you are the only person in Oregon who doesn't think I'm an idiot?" he smiled.

"Oh, I think you're an idiot, too," she deadpanned.

"Great. I'm on an island. Horning Island, where no one dares to be seen."

"Shall we call Emily's doctor next?" Fern suggested. "I think the family goes to Dr. Richards at the Port Stirling Clinic."

Matt jumped on his phone, looking up the clinic's number.

"This is Police Chief Matt Horning," he said to the clinic's receptionist. Pause. "He retired, and I'm the new guy. I'd like to talk to Dr. Richards if he's available." Pause. "Oh, OK, could you please get a message to him as soon as he gets there? Please tell him it's urgent. Can you do that?" Pause. "Great. Matt Horning." Matt gave her his number.

He moved to the wall board and studied the columns under Jack and Marjorie. While he would wait for a definitive statement on Emily's health from the Bushnell's doctor, Matt trusted Bernice's diagnosis. Which meant that Jack either erroneously believed she was gravely ill, or he was deliberately trying to divert attention from himself onto his parents. Diabolical, indeed, and Matt wrote "Lied about Emily's health—why?" in one of the squares under Jack's name. Under that note, he wrote "Where did he go after he left the movies?", and under that one "What happened to his sneakers?" And, last, "Why would Jack want Emily dead?" *Not because she threw a measly piece of crab at him, surely.*

The notes under Marjorie's name were more centered on motive, and, on the surface, she appeared to have more reason for wanting Emily out of the way. But Matt struggled with Marjorie's opportunity to commit the murder. Would Fred really sleep through his wife getting up out of their bed, getting dressed, sneaking out and sneaking back in? It seemed implausible. Did Fred know the truth, and was he covering up for his wife?

The one thing in this entire mess of a case that Matt was certain of was that Marjorie was not going to crack. She was either guilty of stabbing her own daughter, or she was protecting someone in her family whom she knew to be guilty, or she really didn't know what happened to Emily. She wasn't doing much to help the police, but Matt didn't know if that was because she was hiding something, or was pissed at them for outing her affair with Kenton.

Matt reluctantly made one note to Fred's column "Paternity test". Man, he hated to go there, but if Fred wasn't Emily's father, it was important to confirm that piece of information. What if, somehow, that truth was about to come out, Marjorie feared it, and took matters into her own hands? Or, what if Fred knew that Emily was not his child, and he didn't want that truth out there?

Matt knew that once he broached this topic to the mayor, there was no going back. It might be crucial evidence, and he knew he would have to go to the mayor—his boss's boss—and ask him to take a paternity test. *Sweet Jesus.*

CHAPTER 37

Wednesday, 8:00 a.m.

Fern walked over to the board, and drew big X's through Gary and Susan. Then, she added a note under Marjorie's name: 'Exhibits personality characteristics consistent with other mothers who've murdered their children, specifically narcissism and violent outbursts'.

He nodded and, together, they stared at the board.

"Do you want to hear what I think happened?" Fern asked.

"Yes."

"I think Emily saw her mother and Kenton together, and said she was going to tell daddy. Marjorie panicked, took Emily out of her bed after Fred fell asleep and the other kids were gone, walked with her down to the beach—with that flashlight that Mrs. Campbell saw—took her out of sight into that tunnel and killed her. She thought the tide would carry her body out to sea. She disposed of the knife and her bloody clothes somewhere, and went back to bed before Fred woke up."

"She's the child's mother. Doesn't that trump her fear of being discovered?"

"She looked you right in the eye and told you a bald-faced lie. Don't forget that, Matt."

"Yeah, I'll give you that one. But wouldn't you lie to keep your husband from finding out you had a lover?"

"I don't know what I'd do," Fern admitted.

"You wouldn't ever find yourself in that position," Matt said to her.

"Thanks, I hope I wouldn't," Fern said seriously. "Marjorie's psychological profile does match up with several women in the nation's files who have killed their children. Having an affair. Burdened with more than one child. Narcissistic. Even some prominent women in their communities."

"So, if Marjorie killed Emily, she wouldn't be all that unusual?"

"No, she would still be an anomaly. In the files I read, most of the mothers who murdered their children were economically disadvantaged or mentally ill. In my professional view, Marjorie is neither."

* * *

Matt's phone jangled. He flinched at the noise. It was Mary Lou.

"Two things, Chief," she said briskly. "First, everyone on the county team will be here at 4:00 p.m. for today's meeting."

"Great. What else is going on?"

"I've got the Clarksville police chief, Bryce Ellington, on the phone for you. Says it's important. Can you talk now?"

"Sure. But if Dr. Richards returns my call, will you let me know? He's a priority. And, hey, thanks for coming in so early."

"Sure thing. Here comes Ellington when I hang up."

"Chief Ellington? Matt Horning. How can I help you?"

"Hi," responded Bryce Ellington. "We haven't had the pleasure of meeting yet, Chief, and I understand you are new on the job. I hadn't realized that George Simonson had retired. He was a good old guy."

"Yep, that's what I hear," said Matt. "I was supposed to meet him this week, but that got postponed for now. You may have heard we've had some excitement down here. Where exactly is Clarksville? Still trying to figure out all the local geography."

"We're up the coast from you. About 120 miles north. Is this a good time to talk? I think it might be worth your while," Ellington said mysteriously. Chief Ellington was driving his patrol car over the Clarks Bay Bridge on his way back to the office after meeting up with one of his officers at Stoppard State Park.

"Fire away."

"Have you found your murder weapon yet? The APB from the state police said it was a knife that was used to kill that little girl. Is that correct?"

"Yes, sir. Our ME says it was likely a medium-sized kitchen knife with a serrated edge, and, no, it hasn't turned up yet. My bet is that it's halfway to Japan by now."

"Actually, I think it's sitting here in the seat next to me," Chief Ellington said.

"Say what?"

"One of my patrol officers studied the ocean currents analysis you sent over the wire, and he figured you might be correct about our area being a likely possibility. He's off-duty today and was out for an early morning walk on the beach at our state park with his wife, and they found a knife in the surf, partially buried in the sand. The sun was glinting off it, and it caught his attention. It's got some residue on it. Good chance this is your murder weapon."

"You mean I was right?" asked a stunned Matt Horning.

Ellington laughed. "Currents around here are a funny thing. We might get part of a wharf from the Japan tsunami wash up on our beaches, or an old shoe from Brookings," explained Ellington. "You just never know."

"Does it look like a kitchen knife?"

"Yeah, it does. It's got about an eight-inch stainless steel blade and what looks like a Rosewood handle. There is a 'ChefsPlus' logo on the blade. It's what I would call a kitchen utility knife."

"I don't know what to say, Bryce. 'Thank you' seems too weak."

"There's a chance it's not what you're looking for, but it seems pretty coincidental. I'd say there's a strong probability."

"Shall I send one of my guys to pick it up? Obviously, we need to see it, and then take a second look around our suspects' kitchens." Matt's heart raced.

"That would be great. I'm a little short-handed today. If you could have someone on the Port Stirling force drive up and get it, you'd get it faster. Tell me who you're sending and when, and I'll make sure it's in good hands. We placed it in an evidence bag immediately, so it's OK for transport."

"I'll check with one of my officers, Rudy Huggins, and see if I can put him in a squad car right away. If it's someone other than him, I'll call you back."

"Sounds good. We'll plan a get-together when your case is over," Ellington said.

"I'll buy you dinner at your favorite place if this turns out to be my murder weapon!" exclaimed Matt. "Thanks again, Bryce. And please thank your officer for being so alert and heads up—I really appreciate this."

"You got it, Matt. Best of luck to you."

* * *

"What?" said Jay, who walked into the War Room just as Matt was hanging up the phone. The Chief and Fern were grinning from ear to ear.

"That was Clarksville's police chief," said Matt, beaming. "They found our knife."

"No shit! Where? How?" Jay asked.

Matt related the conversation to Jay and Fern, and then the three planned out their morning. Fern would head back to the Bushnell house to ostensibly help them with final plans for Emily's funeral tomorrow. She was really there to keep an eye on Marjorie and Jack, and to note any further suspicious behavior from the two.

Jay would head to the dump with Doug, Ralph, and Walt, while Matt got their remaining officer, Rudy, started on his way to Clarksville, and, hopefully, talked to Emily's physician. Matt would join them all at the dump a little later to continue the search for Jack's shoes, or any items with blood on them.

Were there any bloody items at the dump, or was this a wild goose chase?

* * *

Wednesday, 10:00 a.m.

While Matt, Jay, and their colleagues were digging at the dump, Rudy Huggins raced up Hwy. 101 to the Clarksville PD. Most days, even on a dismal day like today, he would enjoy the drive. But not today. His new boss had made it quite clear that he was to hustle his butt up to Clarksville and get back as fast as he could with the goods.

Rudy parked in front of the PD and met Chief Ellington in the lobby, who came out with the knife in an evidence bag. Huggins had been told by Matt what to expect, but he still felt a jolt looking at the knife. How was it possible that someone in his hometown had stuck that knife into the stomach of a little girl?

"Here you go, Officer. I speak on behalf of the Clarksville PD when I say we hope this is what you're looking for, and that it helps you catch this bastard, whoever he is. Be on your way, and safe travels," said Ellington.

"Can I use your bathroom?" asked Rudy.

* * *

Wednesday, 1:30 p.m.

Matt continued digging through a mountain of garbage, while his brain raced through hundreds of, mostly unpleasant, thoughts. *And where the hell is Rudy? Shouldn't he be back by now with the knife?* Matt stood up straight, stretched his back, and pulled out his cell phone.

"Rudy, where are you?"

"Almost there, Chief. A few miles north of Buck Bay. Be there in about half an hour."

Matt checked his watch—1:35 p.m. "Sounds good. You're on 101, right? Do you know where the Transfer Station is? Stop here and ask for me at the gate. She'll tell you where we are."

"Sure thing. Getting close."

"Thanks, Rudy. This could be our big break."

* * *

Wednesday, 2:15 p.m.

Matt left the dump and headed back to his office alone. Alone, that is, except for the bagged knife on the seat next to him. The bagged knife which matched the set in the Bushnell kitchen. The handle on this knife was exactly like the set sitting in the wood block in the Bushnell's kitchen on the counter next to the sink. It was quite distinctive, and Matt was sure.

Matt stopped at Mary Lou's desk. "Any word yet from Dr. Richards?"

"No, he hasn't called. Doctors," she said and rolled her eyes.

Matt, holding his briefcase close, passed his office and headed to the squad room. Rudy had come straight back after their meeting at the dump.

"Hey," Matt said to him. "I want you to stick around here. We have a county meeting soon, and I want the ME to see the knife. Once she's given an opinion on it, I'll want you to continue your journey today, and get it to the lab. It'll probably be about 4:30 p.m. OK?"

"You bet. I'll give them a call and let them know I'm coming."

* * *

Wednesday, 2:30 p.m.

Why? Why? Why? Why doesn't that dopey Fern leave us alone? Why am I stuck in these walls listening to her drone on? I have voices of my own to listen to, don't I? Well, don't I?

Funeral. Funeral! Tomorrow I'll be free. Eat! Shark!

Funeral! Freedom! Funeral! Fun! Goodbye, Emily! Bite! Funeral!

CHAPTER 38

Wednesday, 3:45 p.m.

Before he headed down the hall to the War Room, Matt called Jay one more time.

"Any luck yet?"

"Nope. Sorry. But we still have a lot of crap to wade through," Jay reported. "I'm not going to make it to the meeting. We'll keep going here until we lose the light."

"I hope this isn't a waste of your time," Matt said.

"It might be," Jay conceded. "But I still have that funny feeling, and something's telling me not to give up yet. Instincts are important in this biz, right? Didn't you say that?"

Matt laughed. "Yeah, I said that. Instincts are important. Catch up with me later, OK?"

Matt hung up and had a hangdog expression on his face. Shit. No bloody shoes. *A possible murder weapon that is the very definition of long shot. County crime team meeting No. 5. Are we any closer, or are we spinning our wheels?*

You're a good cop. Keep going.

And he did, down the hall where he sat quietly, alone, in the War Room staring at his big board.

Everyone else arrived promptly at 4:00 p.m., which continued to amaze Matt—it was so un-Texas like. The team was missing Jay, whose absence Matt said he would explain in a minute, but he'd made sure Dr. Ryder was back for this meeting. She, hopefully, could tell them if the washed-ashore knife was consistent with Emily's wounds.

Matt took the bagged knife out of his locked briefcase and placed it on the table in front of him. He filled in the team on Chief Ellington's discovery up north, and the news from Clarksville elicited shouts of jubilation.

Ed Sonders spoke for the group. "Thank you, ocean currents. Do you think it might really be our knife, Chief?"

"Yes, I believe it is."

Fern got up and walked over to Matt's chair, and leaned over the table to get a good look. "Oh my God," she exclaimed. "That's from the Bushnell's kitchen set."

"Yep," verified Matt. "I recognized it immediately, too. It's our knife, Ed. We're going to send it to the lab for tests. I just want Bernice to take a look at it first, and let us know if it's consistent with Emily's wounds. Bernice?"

Bernice got up and slowly walked to Matt's end of the table. She put on glasses that had been perched on top of her head, and took the bag from his hand, picking it up gingerly at one end. She studied it for about 30 seconds. "I'd want to look at my photos from the autopsy to be certain, but I would say that the size of this knife and the edge of this blade match up perfectly with Emily's entrance wounds. This is your murder weapon, people." Bernice handed the bag back to Matt and said, "Have the lab check for any blood remnants. If they can capture anything, I'm sure it will match Emily's." Quietly, she patted Matt on the shoulder.

"So, we are definitely down to the family, then, if this knife's edges match the wound, and the knife set in their home," said Patty, shaking her head. She looked sad.

"**If** it matches the set at the Bushnell's," emphasized Dalrymple, who had been silent while the knife drama unfolded. "I'd want to make sure that this particular knife is not common around here. What if Ted Frolick has the same knife set?"

"Point taken, David," Patty said. "We'll go back to his house and check."

"Alright, then, we're in business," Matt said taking charge. "Rudy is standing by to get this over to the lab immediately. We're looking for blood, hair or skin fragments—the usual; they'll know what to do."

"How can there still be meaningful traces of anything?" Dalrymple persisted. "Wouldn't the ocean have washed everything off?"

"You might be surprised," Bernice said."Blood evidence is harder to destroy than you think. If any got between the blade and the handle, for example, we might get a good sample. It's a longshot we'll get any-thing usable in a court of law, but it's worth having the lab take a look."

Matt stared down the DA and said, "I'll be right back."

* * *

"While we haven't ruled out Marjorie completely yet," Matt started, standing in front of his big board, "I've moved Jack to the top of our list, and I want to go through my reasoning with you and get your feedback." No one on the county team had moved a muscle in his absence.

"There are some inconsistencies with Jack's first statement to us that, on follow up, put him squarely in our crosshairs." He turned to his board and put a red star next to where he had noted 'Was not at the movie Friday night'. "Jack's best friend, Joey Hawthorne, on interrogation broke down and admitted that Jack had not stayed at the movies with him. Jack called Joey on Saturday morning and asked him to lie for him. Said he didn't kill his sister, but he needed an alibi for where he was. Joey believed him, and so he lied for him initially."

"That little shit," said Patty.

"They're best friends, Patty," sympathized Fern. "Joey doesn't believe Jack killed Emily, and he didn't want him to get in trouble."

"Still," said Sonders, "kids need to understand that lying to the police is not acceptable. Shall I put Joey in the hoosegow for a night to teach him a lesson?"

Matt couldn't tell if Ed was kidding or not.

"Let's deal with Joey later," Matt hurried on. "So, not only does Jack not have an alibi, he also told me when I asked about his clothing from Friday night, that he threw away his shoes."

"Kids don't ever throw away their clothes," interjected Patty.

"Exactly! That's what I said," Fern said.

"This is circumstantial," said the district attorney. "Kids lie for lots of reasons. This doesn't mean Jack is a killer. C'mon, Chief, you need to do better than this."

A knock at the conference room door spooked everyone.

In walked Mary Lou with a platter of food. "Just in case you're here for a while," she smiled. "We wouldn't want starvation to set in for Chinook County's finest."

"Thanks, Mary Lou," said Matt. "Very nice of you."

After Mary Lou set down the platter and left, Matt said to Dalrymple, "I understand what you're saying, David. My point is that Jack did lie, and while we don't know the reason, I have to pursue it."

Dalrymple asked "What possible motive could Jack have for wanting his sister dead?"

"That's the question of the day," answered Matt. "We don't know the 'why' yet, only that we now know Jack had the opportunity and the means to commit the crime. It's suspicious that he threw away his shoes on the night in question. And, asking his friend to lie for him at the least denotes that he is worried about something. If he didn't stay at the movies for long, where was he?"

"All good points," said Sonders. "It's natural to overlook a youngster in this kind of situation, but we should hone in on Jack, in my estimation. Fourteen-year-olds do commit murder. It's rare, but it does happen. What else did Jack say or do that creeped you out?"

"He suggested that Emily had a life-threatening illness, and that perhaps her parents had killed her so she wouldn't suffer. But it came off as self-serving, like he was trying to throw suspicion off himself and shade onto Marjorie and Fred. It felt like he was trying to trick me."

"Have you spoken to Emily's doctor yet?" asked Bernice.

"No, he's been with patients all day, and I'm waiting for him to call me back."

"I would swear on a stack of bibles that there wasn't one thing wrong with that girl," said Bernice. "We did a thorough autopsy, and there was absolutely nothing else that showed up. I'm anxious to hear from her physician, though. Who's spent the most time with Jack during this investigation?"

Fern and Matt looked at each other. "Both of us, I would say," said Matt. "Why?"

"Is there a chance that Jack is schizophrenic?" asked Bernice in a hushed tone.

"Abnormal social behavior. A disconnect from reality. Delusional," answered Fern. "Yes, there's a chance. You think so, Bernice?"

' "Yes," said Bernice. "And it can develop in the teen years, particularly between 14 and 18. Withdrawal from family and friends. Irritability and depression. Some teens even have visual hallucinations or hear voices. Hostility toward others and a lack of restraint—what we call 'no filter'. Tell me, does Jack make eye contact with you when you're speaking to him?"

"Not really, no," replied Fern. "He kind of looks at the wall behind me. Plus, he's weird and disturbing. That may not be politically correct to say, but that's the vibe I get."

"Same here," said Matt. "The first time we talked, he never focused on us, his eyes wandered around the room. Is that a symptom?"

"It can be," Bernice said. "It's tied to a lack of emotion, like an inappropriate emotional response to something."

"Such as you've just been informed that your sister is dead, and your first thought is that you want breakfast?" Matt said, and felt the hair on his arms stand up.

"Precisely. Did Jack do that?"

"Yes," Matt said.

Quiet.

"Schizophrenics can pose a danger to themselves or society," said Fern, mainly to break the silence.

"They can," agreed Bernice, "especially if they are undiagnosed. Treatment options have good results, but often, especially in teenagers, schizophrenia goes undiagnosed—parents think their kid is just being a typical teenager. But once we know what we're dealing with, the outlook for the disorder can improve. Meds and a loving support network can help keep the symptoms under control. Whether or not Jack killed Emily, he should be evaluated by a mental health provider. My opinion is that you might have it right, Matt."

"A delusional, paranoid, hostile kid hearing voices—that could make up for the lack of an obvious motive in this case," said Sonders. "Yikes."

"Yikes, indeed," echoed Bernice. "We need to make sure that Jack is kept at home until we get to the bottom of this. Absolutely no school until we can examine him."

"The family is having Emily's funeral tomorrow morning," said Matt. "Jack won't be going to school. And, we need to have a presence at the funeral to see if anyone strange shows up, and to observe the family. Bernice, could you come and keep your trained eye on Jack?"

"Yes, that's a good idea. Where and what time is it? I need to be there," Bernice said. Firm jaw, unblinking.

"It's at Port Cemetery in Mohegan. Starts at 10:00 a.m.," Matt said. "Do you know where…"

The War Room door suddenly opened and in walked Jay grinning broadly. In his hand was a large evidence bag and a pair of what looked like Nikes.

"Yee-haw!" yelled Matt in Jay's direction. "Are those what I think they are?"

"If you think they are a size 8.5 pair of silver and black, blood-soaked Nikes, then yes," Jay said.

Matt stood frozen in position, the dry-erase marker in his hand poised in mid-air. Fern started to quietly cry and shake, and Patty put her arm around her. She was shaking, too.

Sonders was the first to regain his equilibrium. "Jumpin' Jehoshaphat!" he exclaimed. "That's nice work, Officer Finley. I presume they match the description of Jack's shoes, Chief?"

Matt nodded, unable to speak for a moment.

"What's more," Jay piped in, "Russell Throckmorton, the transfer station manager who found these"—he held up the bag—"found them in with crab shells wrapped in newspaper, and mail and circulars with the Bushnell name on them. It's clearly their garbage. Oh, we also found a kids red sweater and a pair of jeans, also blood-spattered."

Fern buried her face in her hands and her shoulders shook. Even crusty Sheriff Johnson surreptitiously wiped a wayward tear off his chin.

"Marjorie told us the family had a crab feast Friday before the kids dispersed," Matt, regaining his composure, explained to the others. "So that would account for the crab remains. Please tell me you also preserved the pieces of mail with their name and the boy's clothes?"

"Naturally," said Jay. "I learned everything I know from you," he grinned.

"Don't be a smart ass," Matt grinned back at his officer. He'd never been prouder.

Bernice cleared her throat. She was also distressed at the violence, now obviously in front of them and impossible to ignore. "Jack Bushnell," she began to speak, "is suffering from undiagnosed schizophrenia, he takes a utility knife from their kitchen, talks Emily into climbing out her window and going to the beach with him, kills her in an acute schizophrenic episode, and leaves her to die, figuring the night's high tide will take her body out to sea, lost forever. He tosses the knife into the ocean. He then comes back to the house, throws his bloody shoes and clothes in the garbage, knowing it will be picked up Saturday morning, and goes to bed."

Silence around the table while everyone contemplated the truly heinous violence.

"You've got it right, Bernice," Matt said quietly. "The one thing that's always bothered me in this case was the bite marks on Emily's body. An acute schizophrenic episode often involves hearing voices. It makes some sense that Jack's voices told him to eat Emily." He paused and looked down at the floor, taking a deep breath. "We'll try to get a confession. I'd like to get the lab results on the knife and clothes, and get our evidence neatly tied up before we confront Jack. Are we all agreed on that?"

"Yes, that's proper procedure," said the DA. "I'm not sure you'll even need a confession if the knife can be proved to come from the Bushnell home, and if these shoes and clothes can be identified as belonging to Jack. It's strong physical evidence on its own. Especially with his alibi blown to smithereens by Joey."

Ed Sonders asked, "I'm wondering, Bernice, is there a chance that Jack might not remember killing Emily?"

"There's a chance," she nodded. "But the fact that he asked his friend Joey to lie for him likely means he remembered Saturday morning what he'd done, and was determined to cover it up. This poor kid is really sick. I mean, I guess that's obvious if Emily's death went down like we think it did, but this is an especially acute episode that's more closely associated with full-blown schizophrenia. Jack needs help and he needs it now."

"We'll make sure Jack gets the help he needs," Matt assured Bernice, "and I appreciate your legal take, David, but first I want to try for a confession. Once we're sure the knife came from the Bushnell set and not from Ted Frolick's – David, can you get us new warrants to check?"

Dalrymple nodded, and Matt continued, "Even if the lab can't give us much, it's a strong piece of evidence based solely on the fact that someone threw it in the ocean. I agree with David that coupled with Jack's shoes and clothing, I'd say we've got 'beyond a shadow of a doubt', but if we can get him to confess, it's a lock. I'll allow the family to get through Emily's funeral tomorrow morning before I confront Jack."

"My grandmother is buried at Port Cemetery," Sonders said. "I'll join you. You might need some extra hands."

"Ed's right," Patty said looking around the table and getting confirming nods. "We'll all be there, Chief." said Patty grimly.

Fern sat motionless.

"Thank you, ladies and gentlemen," Matt said. "While we wait for lab results and search warrants, let's go through everyone's tasks for tomorrow," Matt said.

CHAPTER 39

Wednesday, 8:30 p.m.

Matt pulled into his driveway, switched off the engine, and sat for a minute with his forehead resting on the steering wheel. Overhead, a billion stars glittered in a black sky that never ended. The full moon's reflection on the water appeared to reach all the way from the horizon to the shore. It produced enough light to clearly see the rocks and sand on the beach. In his worn-out state, Matt stopped to appreciate the glassy, calm sea lit up like fireworks on the 4th of July.

He knew it wasn't quite over yet, but Matt felt as calm as the vast Pacific in front of him. Lots of emotions were going through him on this night, the night after he was originally scheduled to begin his new job, his new life. Relief. Accomplishment. Gratitude. Mostly gratitude, because the rag-tag crime team that had been thrown together out of necessity had pulled off an amazing feat under adverse conditions. One of the big unknowns when Matt decided to take a new job in an entirely new place and situation had been 'would there be anyone he could count on?' Now, with no misgivings whatsoever, he could answer a resounding 'yes' to that question. He'd led the investigation—did his job—but his team did everything he told them to do, and their dogged persistence helped him get results.

Jay Finley was a rock: dedicated, smart, and hard-working. In just five days' time, under pressure-packed circumstances, Matt now knew in his heart that he and Jay would be a terrific team going forward. The quarterback and his top wide receiver; joined at the hip forever after this successful Hail Mary pass.

And Fern. She had kept him honest, and her skill set on profiling Jack and Marjorie had been indispensable. She'd done a great job on Day One uncovering the first hints of a dysfunctional family. Methodically, Fern had examined some of the weirdness which might turn out to be at the root of Jack's illness.

Beyond work, he enjoyed Fern's and Jay's company as well. When this was all over, he would also thank them for their friendship. He'd held back on doing that in the first few days, even though their immediate acceptance of him had meant so much when he first arrived; better to keep it all business during an investigation.

Patty, Ed, Bernice—they were all way better at their jobs than this remote part of the country had any right to hope for. Even David Dalrymple—while he would never be best friends with the district attorney—had done his job. Matt hoped they wouldn't be put to the test again anytime soon, but he knew where to turn if trouble struck Port Stirling.

Finally, Matt hauled himself and his briefcase out of the car, walked around the side of his cottage, and stood on the bluff staring out to sea on this tranquil night. The only sound was the gentle burst of the waves hitting the shore. There was not another human being in sight. He knew he wanted to be here in this quirky small town with its astounding natural beauty. Tonight, he was not afraid to look down the beach toward Emily's tunnel, just beyond the promontory. *I still don't know why your brother did this to you, Emily, but we're going to find out, and we'll try our best to let you rest in peace.*

As he entered his front door, the weight of the past five days pushed down hard on his shoulders. He dropped his briefcase inside the door and rubbed his bleary eyes. No more work tonight, Matt needed a good night's sleep.

He went to his frig and peered inside, and first popped the top off a Deschutes beer—his new go-to brand—chugging it while he looked over his potential dinner choices. It was after 8:30 p.m., so he didn't want to stuff himself, but the hunger pangs were real and he knew he wouldn't sleep with his stomach growling at him. When all else fails, cheese omelet. He pulled out three eggs, some Port Stirling cheddar cheese—made right here in town according to his market check-out girl—and some mushrooms. Matt didn't know it, but the delicious shrooms were also local, picked in the forest between Port Stirling and Hornbuckle River.

Sitting at his dining room table in what tonight was a soundless cottage, Matt thought about how to handle his two biggest problems tomorrow: how to wrangle a confession out of Jack, and how to tell Fred and Marjorie that they were about to lose a second child. As he ate his omelet and washed it down with the beer, he was, however, having trouble focusing on the task at hand.

Fern kept jumping into his mind. Smart and committed, yes, but she was fragile, as evidenced by her reaction to Jack's apparent violence and how close she had been to it. Natural, of course; it even gave Matt the shivers to recall his interaction with Jack in his room yesterday.

He knew that Fern had relished being part of his team, although that excitement might now be tempered by today's turn of events. He could use someone with her advocate's resume in his new department. Or, was he trying to find a way to justify the fact that maybe, deep down, he wanted Fern closer?

It's not that. People can become close at work during intense periods like this one, and that's all it is between Fern and me. That's all this is, the strain and immediacy of this case.

He walked his dirty dishes over to the sink and rinsed them off. Whether it was personal or professional, he wanted to protect Fern while she was in this delicate, breakable state—he didn't want her at the funeral tomorrow morning, even though her job called for it. He dried off his hands on a dishtowel with sea gulls on it, reached for the phone, and dialed Fern's cell.

"You OK?" he asked when she said 'hello'.

"I'm OK. I've stopped crying, that's something."

"Yeah. That's something alright."

"You don't have to check on me, Matt, I'm a grown woman."

"I'm not checking on you. I want to talk about tomorrow. I don't want you at Emily's funeral."

"Why not?"

"Look, Fern, you're not used to this level of violence, and it can bring down even hardened police officers—I've seen it happen more than once. I realize it's your job to be there for the family, but until you have a chance to catch your breath, it's not a good idea for you to see Jack."

"At this point, Chief Horning, I know Jack as well as you or anyone. I may not have known what full-blown schizophrenia looks like in a teen, but I recognized that Jack was off. And, yes, this case has scared the daylights out of me. But Bernice and I are the two people who should be observing him tomorrow at Emily's funeral. I will be there."

"I appreciate your viewpoint, Fern, but I'm telling you this straight up: it's not going to be good for your psyche and your own mental health to see this kid yet. And we don't really know how he…"

"Good night, Chief. Sleep well. See you in the morning." And she hung up.

CHAPTER 40

Thursday, 7:00 a.m.

Thursday morning, the day of Emily's funeral, dawned slate grey and appropriately gloomy. It was dry so far, but ominous clouds were forming out to the southwest sea, and the granite ocean waves were beginning to churn and grow in height. Matt watched the black clouds move toward the shoreline. He drank his strong coffee, and scanned the water for Roger.

Their eyes met, and not for the first time, he was sure that Roger was looking directly at him. Matt waved, and immediately felt like an idiot. "Hi, buddy. How are you doing today?" he said to the window in front of him.

Roger the seal dived down into the waves and popped back up a couple of yards closer in, as if to show Matt that he was doing fine. "Lucky you," Matt said aloud. "You don't have to go to a funeral today and ruin a kid's life."

Roger bobbed up and down, showing his friend that he understood. Matt finished his coffee and moved away from his window.

He stood under the hot shower as long as he could, and then dressed in his one black suit and slipped on his black dress shoes. He would later be shocked at how casually some people were dressed at the funeral; where Matt came from, it was important to show respect for the dead. Jeans and flannel shirts at a little girl's funeral? What the fuck was wrong with people?

He met Jay at City Hall at 8:00 a.m. as they had planned. The lab still had the knife, and they had heard nothing so far. But the knife was undeniably part of the kitchen set in the Bushnell house—Matt remembered the gap in the set's lineup where the murder weapon would fit. No question, they had the weapon that Jack stabbed Emily with. Nevertheless, he was relieved that the DA had come through with the new search warrants..

Matt was also relieved to see Jay in a nice charcoal grey suit, white shirt, and black tie. As he was driving in, he worried that Jay might wear his uniform today, and it wouldn't seem quite right to have uniformed cops at a child's funeral. Jay was still holding the bag with Jack's shoes, and Matt wondered for a fleeting moment if Jay had slept with them under his pillow. Normally, Matt would have sent the Nikes off to the lab, too, but he wanted them for effect later today, so he'd asked Jay to safeguard them overnight.

"I just retrieved these from the safe," Jay said. "I assume you want to take them with us?"

"I'm glad you didn't sleep with them," Matt smiled at his officer. "Yes, bring them along. We'll see how young Jack reacts. I suspect he thinks these are long gone. We'll escort the family to the funeral like there's nothing wrong. They deserve to bury their daughter in peace. Then, we'll come back to the house, and confront Jack."

"Sounds like a plan, boss."

"After sleeping on it, I've also asked Ed and the sheriff to follow us back to the house in case we have any unforeseen trouble with Jack or any of the Bushnells. The whole team will be at the funeral to keep an eye on things, but I'm not expecting any trouble there."

"Do you expect trouble at the house?"

"Jack stabbed his sister and left her body for the ocean to take away. No telling what he might do."

Jay stood silently.

* * *

Thursday, 9:00 a.m.

"Oh, no," said Matt, groaning, as he and Jay drove up in front of the Bushnell's house—a powder blue beetle with a dead red rose in its flower vase was parked in the driveway, minding its own business, its driver sipping coffee.

"This is not a good idea," Matt growled as he approached the open VW window. "You don't have to put yourself through this, Fern. I know you're tough. You don't have to prove it."

"This is not about you; it's about me," she said, unfolding her long legs out of the car. Her hair pulled back into a high ponytail, she looked more severe and drawn than usual, but it was right for a funeral. She was wearing a long, mid-calf black wool coat and black boots, over what Matt glimpsed as a royal blue turtleneck dress. "And, for your information, I'm tougher than I look."

For all her tough talk, she looked vulnerable to Matt, and he instinctively reached out and gave her a hug.

"Don't be nice," she said softly. "We have a job to do. What's our plan?"

Jay came up to the beetle and also gave Fern a hug. The three stood close together, and Matt explained the plan.

Gary opened the door, and walked them into the living room, where they would wait for the others to be ready to go. His eyes were red and his face was splotchy. Fred and Marjorie came in next, with

Fred a couple steps ahead of his wife, Trump-style. *Their marriage wasn't going to make it,* Matt thought. Marjorie still looked dry-eyed and calm—*had she cried at all yet?* Fred looked 80 years old, stooped and ashen-faced. His black suit looked too big for him.

Jack was sitting on the living room carpet, leaning up against the wall near the fireplace. He was looking out the window, and didn't acknowledge the cops when they came in.

While they waited for Susan to come out of her room, Fern said "Excuse me, but may I pop into your kitchen for a drink of water before we head out?"

"Help yourself, Fern," Marjorie said coolly.

Fern trotted off to the kitchen while Jay and Matt made uncomfortable small talk with the family. She took a glass out of the cupboard and turned on the sink faucet to complete the charade as she stared at the set of knives glaring at her from the countertop.

The Clarksville knife, as Fern now thought of it, matched the set exactly. Rosewood handle, 'ChefsPlus' logo, and an empty slot precisely where the utility knife should be.

"He really did it," whispered Fern to the wall.

* * *

Thursday, 10:05 a.m.

Port Cemetery was a bleak and windswept place. More than 150 years old, it looked every bit its age. The procession entered through a small gate with an overhead, weather-beaten, wooden banner that read 'Port Cemetery'. The banner had a hokey rendering of a fish surrounded by fir trees to the right of the wording, and an inexplicable drawing of a tractor also surrounded by fir trees to the left. *The gateway to fishing and farming in heaven,* Matt surmised.

The gravestones were placed far apart and randomly, and it appeared to Matt that there was plenty of available land. A few trees, all leaning inland from decades of tenacious ocean winds, sprinkled the grounds, but the overall effect was of a mostly flat, barren landscape.

The procession pulled up at the end of a dirt, rutted road, and Matt could see a tent with a small coffin placed on a pedestal and rows of chairs ahead about 100 yards in the distance. Behind it, a freshly-dug grave inside a stoned-in enclosure was covered with a tarp.

"Don't take a seat," Matt told his group, gathered inside the gate. "It looks like there aren't enough chairs for all the cars with us. Be discreet and keep your distance, but try to position yourself where you will have a good view of the family at all times. Patty, you be on the lookout for any funny-acting strangers. We think we've got our killer, but we want to remain alert. Bernice and Fern, you stick close to me; we're not going to take our eyes off Jack, OK? Jay, you keep Marjorie in your sights, and Ed, you've got Fred. Earl, I want you and your guys to position yourselves between the family and the exit . . . just in case." To Walt, Rudy and his patrol officers, their new boss said, "You guys keep your wits about you and survey the big picture for anything unusual. Everyone clear?"

Somber nods all around.

"I want to take this moment to thank all of you for your tireless work over the past five days. This is a tough one, and I couldn't be more grateful for all your support. Jay, Ed, Earl, and I are going back to the Bushnell residence after the funeral and confront Jack. We will let y'all know later today how it goes." Matt paused. "And, if you see my boss, Bill Abbott, be nice to him—I just realized I should have called him last night."

That brought a smile to most faces.

"We'll tell him that you're a nightmare to work with, and what the hell was he thinking when he hired you," Patty wisecracked.

"Thanks, Patty, I knew I could count on you," Matt countered. "This will be the worst day, folks, and then we'll have some sunny skies ahead together. Promise."

Just then, a mammoth, exclamation point gust of wind blew Matt's tie up over his shoulder, and the rain started pelting down on them.

* * *

The Bushnell family sat side-by-side in the front row with Emily's casket immediately in front of them. Jack was on the end of the row, seated next to his mother. Gary was on the other side of Marjorie, with Susan to his left, and Fred on the other end.

There were approximately 75 people in attendance. Matt was thankful for the relatively smallish, manageable crowd. As it was, they could all fit under the tarp, which was now rocking-and-rolling in the wind, with water streaming off the edges. Fingers crossed it held through the ceremony. Matt noticed that Jack's chair was half in and half out under the tarp, and the right side of his head and body were getting soaked. He appeared not to notice.

Matt watched as Bernice kept a watchful gaze on Jack. Her eyes seemed to follow his every movement, from the drumming of his fingers against his legs to the rise and fall of his chest as he breathed. Matt could almost see the mental note she was cataloging in her mind.

Fred, Gary, and Susan were openly crying, and Fred's shoulders were violently shaking from his sobbing. Marjorie dabbed at her eyes once or twice, but it looked more for show than anything. Jack stared at the casket, impassive. None of the family touched each other. Not once.

Thankfully, nothing out of the ordinary happened, and even more thankfully, it was a brief service. Only one friend of Fred's spoke about Emily, and it was touching. Bernice whispered to Matt that he was Fred's oldest friend and his regular fishing partner. None of the family spoke, which was also to Matt's great relief.

Marjorie placed a bouquet of white lilies on top of the casket, letting her hand rest briefly, and it was over quickly. After people paid their respects to Fred and Marjorie, a distinguished gentleman with a shock of black hair and dressed in a well-fitted navy suit approached Matt and Bernice, trying to control his umbrella.

"I'm Dr. Paul Richards, Emily's physician," he said reaching out his hand to shake Matt's, "and you're the new police chief, correct? I'm so sorry I didn't return your phone call yesterday, but I ended up with a first-time mother giving birth and I didn't get home until quite late."

"I guess the good Lord gives Port Stirling a new baby to help us with our grief over this," Bernice said, inclining her head toward Emily's casket.

"So true," agreed Dr. Richards. "How can I help you, Chief Horning? Why were you calling me?"

"Had you seen Emily professionally recently?"

"Yes, about two weeks ago. She had a case of the sniffles."

"Nothing seriously wrong with her?" Bernice asked.

"No. Common cold, and when I saw her she was on the tail end. It worked its way through most of the children in town around Christmas time. Much to the parents' chagrin," he added.

"Have you examined Emily in depth in the past few weeks or months?" asked Matt.

"No, not really. She was a healthy child for the most part."

"She didn't have a brain tumor or anything serious like that wrong with her?"

Dr. Richards gave Matt a funny look. "Why ever would you say a thing like that?"

"We heard it around, and wanted to confirm with you," Matt hedged.

"Emily most certainly did not have a brain or any other kind of tumor, or any serious illness. She was a happy, healthy 4-year-old girl, healthier than most children her age. She was also a beautiful little thing, cheerful and perfect. It's a terrible tragedy," Dr. Richards said, shaking his head. "Did you perform the autopsy, Bernice?"

"Yes, and my diagnosis completely agrees with yours, Paul. Emily was healthy at the time of her death. We just needed to be sure," she said, reaching out to pat his arm.

"Thanks, Dr. Richards, I appreciate hearing from you today," Matt said. "Is there anything else about Emily or her family that you think we should know?"

"I'm afraid I can't add anything else. It's a complete mystery to me."

"In that case, our day is not finished yet, so please excuse us. Thank you again."

"Of course. Good luck to you, Chief."

CHAPTER 41

Thursday, 11:15 a.m.

The procession of funeral cars back up Hwy 101 was slow, mainly because it was now raining so hard the drivers could barely see through their windshield wipers. Fern had left her car at the Bushnells and ridden with Matt and Jay. Matt asked her now: "What are you going to do when we get back to the house?"

"I'm going in with you boys to confront Jack," she said matter-of-factly.

"Not a good idea," was all Matt said in reply.

"I appreciate that you're worried about my mental health," she offered. "But don't you see? It's more important that I face up to my fears and see this through to the end. My fear of Jack is probably far worse than the reality of being in his presence will be. I can handle it, Chief."

Matt turned his eyes from the road and looked at her. "Alright, but this is liable to get nasty," he said. "If Jack took that knife from his kitchen, stabbed Emily and left her to die, and he still had the smarts to get rid of his bloody clothes, that's one fucked-up boy. I'm not implying you can't handle it, Fern, or that you're any more fragile than the rest of us. Hell, I'm scared, too. I'm just saying that you have a choice in this."

"Understood," she said.

Jay snorted from the back seat.

* * *

Matt's patrol car, with Ed and Earl in Ed's state police car following behind them, turned into the Bushnell driveway behind the family car. Gary was driving, and pulled their vehicle into the garage. The four officers, plus Fern, went into the house through the unlocked front door.

Fred was shuffling through the foyer into the living room. Matt approached him and said: "On behalf of all of us, Fred, we're so sorry for your loss." The compassion in his voice was real.

Fred croaked out a weak "Thank you", and he collapsed onto the living room sofa.

"Can I get you anything, Mr. Mayor?" Lieutenant Sonders asked Fred. "A glass of water? A shot of bourbon?"

Fred looked up as if he were seeing the others in the room for the first time. "Why are you all here?"

"We need to talk to Jack, sir," Matt said softly, as the other Bushnells came into the room.

"Why are you here bothering us?" Marjorie said in an icy tone. "Why aren't you out there catching whoever is responsible for me burying my baby today?"

Matt said to her, "I'm trying. I need to talk to Jack."

"What do you want?" Jack said, barely audible. He was standing in the arch between the living and dining rooms, hands at his side. His teeth were clenched. His eyes were glassy and his pupils looked dilated. Matt felt Fern, at his side, take a small step backward.

"Jack, did you kill Emily?" Matt asked.

"That again?" Jack smiled. He pointed at Matt. "You think I killed Em!" His pointed finger stabbed the air again. "You do, don't you? I don't want you to come into my room ever again! I don't like you, Tex."

"Calm down, Jack," said his mother, and she went to his side. He stood stiffly beside her and continued to smile at Matt.

"You need to leave my son alone," she said to Matt. "In fact, you all need to leave my house right now. We've had enough of you."

"I'm afraid we can't do that, Marjorie," said Matt. He turned to Jay, motioned for the evidence bag, and approached Jack.

"Are these your shoes, son?" he said, holding up the bag in front of Jack's face.

Jack's face became expressionless. "No, they're not. Shark!" He was passive and almost lethargic.

"I think they are," Matt contradicted. "And they've got blood on them. We believe it's Emily's blood, and it sprayed on your shoes when you stabbed her in that tunnel and left her to the sea."

"Those are Joey's shoes," said Jack. "Go talk to him."

"Why did you just say 'shark', Jack?" asked Matt.

"Didn't. Dunno. Didn't."

Fred rose from the sofa and came rushing up to his son.

"Jack, baby, these look like your shoes. Tell daddy if they are, please," Fred pleaded, and put his arm around Jack's shoulders.

"Why should I tell you anything, old man?" Jack asked, his voice still low. He slowly turned to look at his father. "Shark". He began rocking back and forth on his heels. "Am I dead? Are you dead? Is this real?"

Fred staggered and backed away. Fern moved to prop up Fred, and seated him back on the sofa. Then she turned toward Jack.

"Jack, I know you loved your sister, didn't you?" she said in a serene, safe voice.

"Loved Em. Hated Em. Bite! Shark!"

"Why do you say you hated her?" Fern continued, and Matt let her.

"Always touching things. Touched my jacket. Touched my book."

"Emily didn't mean any harm—she just wanted to see your things and be like you."

"Too much touching. We don't touch. Eat! Had to be taught a lesson. Bite!"

"So, did you teach Emily a lesson?" Fern continued to draw him out.

"Deserved to die!"

"You or Emily?"

Marjorie stepped in and, inches from his face, said loudly to her son, "Don't say anything more, Jack. Be quiet!"

Jack, eyes wide, turned his head slowly in his mother's direction. "Who are you?" he said to her.

"That's your mother, Jack," Fern quickly inserted. "Your parents love you and want you to be safe."

"Sit down, Marjorie," said Matt, his voice assertive. She did as she was told.

"Who deserved to die, Jack, you or Emily?" Fern asked again. "You can tell me. I'm your friend."

Jack looked directly at Fern, but said nothing. His eyes rolled up in his head for a minute, and then returned to a glassy stare.

"Jack, can you hear me?" Fern asked urgently, getting right up in his face.

Matt moved quickly to her side, taking her arm, and moving her back a couple of steps.

"Shhh," Jack said quietly. "Can't hear."

"Can you hear the voices, Jack?" asked Matt.

"Voices. Voices. Shark in tree!"

"What are the voices saying?"

Jack suddenly moved away from Fern and Matt toward the foyer. Ed moved quicker, and blocked his path.

"Can I have some food?" Jack asked the wall next to him, his face three inches from it. "I'm going now. Time to go."

The storm, now blowing hard outside, rattled the house, and the sky suddenly darkened. Heavy rain slammed against the living room window. Jack turned away from the wall and stared out the window. His eyes opened wide. His body started to shake all over, and he shivered violently.

"How do you feel, Jack?" Matt asked, taking a step toward the youngster.

Jack smiled and looked down at the floor. "Powerful," he whispered.

Gently, Matt waved off Fern and said to Jack: "Do you remember what you did Friday night, Jack?"

"I killed my sister while I was floating."

"Floating on what, Jack?"

"Floating on death."

"Why did you kill Emily, Jack?"

"So we both could live. I died when my sister was born. Drink blood in order to live! Eat shit! Eat dirt! Take over the world!"

"Your sister had bite marks on her, Jack. Did you bite her?"

Jack swung his head around quickly, looking at Matt again. "Yes. I bite."

"Did you try to eat Emily, Jack?" He heard Marjorie moan behind him, and Fred let out a yelp, but Matt ignored them and didn't take his eyes off Jack.

"I tried to, but the dead were watching. They are always watching. I see them all the time! They don't like me. I am them!"

"Did you get the knife from your kitchen?"

"Maybe," Jack smiled, and violently rocked back and forth on his heels, looking at his hands.

"Did you crawl out Emily's window, Jack?"

"I told her the truth!"

"I'm sure you did, son. Was it foggy and cold on the beach?"

"I am God! Steps all the way down to the beach. Can I have a cup of blood?"

"Not right now, Jack. Can you see the tunnel?"

"I'm walking on the water. What? Are you here?"

"Try to focus, Jack. Do you remember the tunnel on the beach?"

"Tunnel."

"Yes, that's right, Jack. We found Emily in the tunnel."

"Is she dead?"

"Yes, you stabbed her with the knife, remember?"

"Oh. Yes. Blood! Dying! Shark! Deserved to die!"

"That's right. Emily is dead."

"Shark in that tree! Eating shit! Brain tumor! Knife in its eye!"

"Can you come with me now, Jack?" Matt said, moving toward the hallucinating boy. "We need to go for a drive, OK?"

"OK. Are we going to play golf? Can I bring my friend? Pizza! Eat!"

Matt took one arm and Sonders took the other, and they escorted a docile Jack out to the car and placed him in the back seat. Ed sat on one side of him, and Sheriff Johnson sat on the other. Ed placed one arm around the boy's shoulders.

Inside the house, Fern attended to Marjorie, who had crumpled to the floor and was on her hands and knees, finally wailing. Jay got Fred to the sofa and quickly brought both parents a glass of water. Susan and Gary were bawling uncontrollably and holding on to each other for dear life.

Matt came running back into the living room. "Please stay here with the family for now," Matt instructed Fern and Jay. "We'll take Jack to the Buck Bay Hospital for an examination," he said to Fred.

Fred said, rising: "I'm coming with you. I need to take care of my son."

Matt eyed Fred and said, "OK, let's go."

Jack was disoriented and rambled incoherently on the drive to the hospital. His movements were agitated, and he seemed to be having trouble talking. Attempts by his father and by Ed Sonders to bring him back to reality went unheeded. Jack was in his own world, and it was a terrible, terrifying place.

EPILOGUE

Jack was examined by Dr. Joseph Mallory, an emergency room physician at the hospital, and by Dr. Candace Bernstein, a psychiatrist from Buck Bay. Together, they determined that Jack was suffering from mental illness, and was in the throes of an acute schizophrenic episode.

Dr. Lawrence Bush, the dentist who had been called in by Bernice on Saturday night to look at the bite marks on Emily, came to take photographs and plaster casts of Jack's teeth.

After Matt processed Jack's statement—as best he could—Jack was taken to the Chinook County Jail where he was booked for the murder of Emily Anne Bushnell. Jack remained compliant and obedient, with a flat expression on his face throughout the booking process. He did not speak.

The following morning, Friday, at 9:00 a.m., a commitment hearing before Circuit Court Judge Cynthia Hedges was held. The defendant, his father, his defense attorney, and DA David Dalrymple were accompanied by six witnesses. At 9:12 a.m., the defendant was found to be suffering from acute mental disease, and was committed indefinitely to the Oregon State Hospital.

* * *

After the hearing, the county crime team reconvened at City Hall.

Although there was a sense of tremendous relief around the table, and pride for a job well done, there was certainly no joyous celebration.

"Welcome to Port Stirling, Chief Horning," Sonders said in an attempt to lighten up the atmosphere in the room.

"Yeah. Thanks a heap," Matt said. "Am I up for some vacation time yet?"

Subdued laughter.

"Every single person in this room played an important role in this investigation. I want to say 'thanks'. And, while I sincerely hope we won't have to meet with this urgency again soon, I've been mulling around the idea that maybe we should have regular meetings, say once a month, just to keep in touch and to stay alert. What do y'all think?"

"Only if you promise to quit saying 'y'all'," said Patty.

"Shoot, I'm trying!" laughed Matt.

"It's a good idea," said Sheriff Johnson. "This group came together better than past efforts. Personally, I'd like to see us continue."

"The rest of you?" Matt asked.

"How about the first Tuesday of every month, 4:00 p.m" said Sonders. "Where shall we meet?"

"Well, we *should* meet at the county's offices," said DA Dalrymple. "But, you know what, it's worked out pretty good meeting here. I vote to continue on."

"Second that," said Sheriff Johnson. "This shitty room with no windows makes us focus."

Raucous laughter at that because they all knew there was truth in it.

"OK then, next meeting on Tuesday, February 2, at 4:00 p.m.," Matt said, consulting his calendar. "Be there or be square."

Matt stood in the door as everyone filed out, shaking hands one-by-one. Jay and Fern were last, hanging back to let the rest of the team leave the building. Jay started to shake Matt's hand, and then changed his mind and enveloped his new boss in a crushing bear hug.

"You're hired," Matt said to Jay, and clapped him on the back.

As Fern approached, Matt stiffly shook her hand, while giving her a light kiss on the cheek. "You *are* tougher than you look," he said, smiling.

"Told you so," she smiled back at him.

"Is there any chance you'd like to do the same job here for less money instead of at the county?"

"Now, why would I do a crazy thing like that?"

"Because we're a team."

"There is that," Fern allowed. "But I'd need more money to make a move, not less."

"Well, then you'd have to add some education, say an 'Introduction to Criminal Justice' course, for instance," Matt said. "Is that something you would consider? Can we talk about it?"

"I looked at Buck Bay Community College's website last night," Fern said. "They offer that exact course. It's classroom-based, supplemented by practical exercises and scenarios. I figure after this week that I could probably teach the course, but I suppose I would need a certificate before you would hire me, yes?"

* * *

Ted Frolick pushed his grocery cart around the corner to the meat and seafood counter of the market. Patty Perkins took her one pound of Coho salmon from the clerk, and turned around, headed to checkout. "Ms. Perkins, how nice to see you again," said Ted, tipping the brim of his weathered cap. There was a courtliness about him. "I hear our nasty business has been resolved. What an abominable thing for the family."

"Hello, Ted," Patty said, friendly. "Yes, it's always a huge relief to put away the perpetrator, but this case doesn't make anyone happy. I'm sorry we hassled you," she said.

"No hard feelings. You and Chief Horning were doing your job, and you did it well, may I say."

"I appreciate that. You were a big help." She looked down at the wrapped salmon in her hands. "I suppose the Bushnells have a long road in front of them."

"You seem quite sad, Patty."

"It's rough. You hate to see families destroyed. I've always liked Fred, and my heart goes out to him," she said.

"I think we need to cheer you up," said Ted heartily. "I've been meaning to get over to Twisty River and treat myself to a nice cocktail and dinner at The Grill. Man can only eat deli food so often," he said, holding up his packaged dinner. "Would you like to join me Friday night? I think you mentioned you lived in Twisty River."

"I do, and I would enjoy that."

Patty was astonished to realize that she meant it.

* * *

Later, in a small ceremony for city staff at Port Stirling City Hall, City Manager Bill Abbott presented Matt Horning with a shiny gold plaque for his door that read "Matthew Horning, Chief of Police". Matt had insisted that, in addition to his department and all city employees, that Russell Throckmorton from the dump be invited, too.

As Jay Finley thanked Russell for finding Jack's bloody Nikes, and hugged him so hard he picked him up off the ground, Throckmorton said modestly, "I just know how to look through garbage."

* * *

Jack Bushnell is currently an inmate at the Oregon State Hospital in Salem, where he is under the jurisdiction of the Psychiatric Security Review Board. Jack was evaluated extensively by the state's leading psychologist, Beth Dixon, who found that he was mentally competent to stand trial, but that he had been afflicted with a mental condition, and experienced an acute schizophrenic episode when he killed his sister.

Her conclusion was that Jack really believed Emily was suffering from a brain tumor, and that he was relieving her of a painful death.

Jack pleaded not guilty by reason of insanity, and was sentenced to 20 years of confinement and treatment in the State Hospital, with periodic competency evaluations to be conducted.

Jack sat on a chair in his solitary cell with his hands on his knees, staring at the corner wall. He stood up, and turned his chair around to face outward, toward his cell door. He sat back down and folded his arms across his chest.

Brain tumor, my ass, he smiled.

ACKNOWLEDGEMENTS

Although I've always written throughout my career, writing a mystery novel was a complete mystery to me when I began. Anyone who tells you that you can write your first novel all by yourself is lying, as it actually requires a great deal of help from a team.

Thank you to Selina McLemore for calmly and intelligently explaining to me why my first draft of my first-ever novel was crap. And for showing me the way to a decent second draft, and to, finally, a not-half-bad fifth draft. If it's still not perfect, it's not Selina's fault, as her feedback and advice were perfect. She's also really good at picking titles!

Thank you to J.E. Vader for explaining to me how my later drafts still needed work, but why it would be worth it.

Thank you to the literary agents who rejected this debut novelist, but who offered up good advice that I took to heart. There were several along the journey who made it a better book, but Moses Cardona stands out for his honesty, specificity, and his kindness.

Thank you to Scott Westerman who taught me what I didn't know I didn't know about police work.

Thank you to Jessica Reed for her excellent cover design, who gave me exactly what I wanted, even though I didn't know exactly what I wanted.

Thank you to Sharon and Dick for loaning me their quiet beach house to get started again, and for conjuring up the perfect winter storm to help me write the scary scenes.

Thank you to my excellent beta readers, who asked good questions and found some flaws.

Thank you to Coos County Medical Examiner Kris Karcher who promptly and responsibly answered my questions about what happens when a body is discovered on the beach. Thank you to Bill Richardson who explained what happens with Coos County's garbage once it's picked up. The government and public service employees who helped me are not like those portrayed in *Shallow Waters,* and any errors in fact are solely mine.

And, finally, thanks to Steve, who provided me with the freedom and inspiration to keep going.

Thank you for reading Shallow Waters. Book 2 in the Port Stirling Mystery series, The Night Beach, will be released in late 2019.

Please go to www.kayjenningsauthor.com to sign up for my newsletter and to see where I will be appearing, so you don't miss anything.

And, if you are so inclined, please write a brief review of Shallow Waters at www.amazon.com/author/kayjennings. Even an "I liked it!" would help.

About the Author

Kay Jennings is a native Oregonian, born near the south coast, and currently living in Portland with her husband, Steve, a technology entrepreneur. She owns Paris Communications, a marketing, PR, and publishing company, and enjoyed a career in corporate communications in such varied industries as tourism, healthcare, and sports. Shallow Waters is her first novel.

65192883R00204